Blueprint for Raising a Child

by Mike Phillips

LOGOS INTERNATIONAL
Plainfield, NJ

Unless otherwise noted as KJV (King James Version) or NEB (The New English Bible), all Scripture quotations are in the author's paraphrase.

Blueprint For Raising a Child

Printed in the United States of America
International Standard Book Number: 0-88270-280-7
Library of Congress Catalog Card Number: 78-64344
Logos International, Plainfield, New Jersey, 07060

To

my wife, Judy
and

to

Ellen Connett,
whose untiring willingness
to share the wisdom God has
given her has been a
great help to many.

There are only two lasting bequests we can give our children; one is roots, the other wings.

Table of Contents

Acknowledgments

It is customary at this point for a writer to mention everyone he has read and quoted and those who discussed the manuscript with him and all who helped with the typing. Instead, I would like to take this opportunity to confess both to my wife and children my frequent inability to carry out the principles of this book in our home. Thank God that His work is not dependent on my sufficiency, only on my willingness. My daily prayer is that God will make up the difference between your needs and what I, with my limitations, am able to give to you. I love you so much.

I do not write about how to train children because I feel that I am an expert father or husband. Writing this book has actually brought me face-to-face with my daily shortcomings in both areas.

My wife, Judy, has been such a help to me, and I would like to publicly acknowledge her as a woman of God who has made a great commitment to her children, often in the midst of severely trying personal concerns. This commitment has meant daily personal sacrifices and love, and I marvel at her ability to give so much of herself to her children and me. Though she would be the first to insist she is often merely groping along uncertainly, she embodies many of the principles in this book. If I could show you her relationships with each of the children, inadequacies and all, I think I would not need to write on this subject at all. The day will surely come when, as the writer of the last chapter of Proverbs stated, "Her sons will rise up and call her blessed" (Prov. 31:28). I want to add to their praise by affirming, "Many women have done well, but you surpass them all" (Prov. 31:29).

Introduction

Most of what I have read, as well as all of what I have previously written, concerning the raising of children has had one noticeable shortcoming—it fails to deal with the totality of the process. When I wrote *A Christian Family in Action,* my viewpoint was naturally colored by my immediate situation—trying to cope with the daily necessities of handling very active twin toddlers. Therefore, my preoccupation with devising a system of rigorous and workable discipline showed through very clearly. But with the exception of several comments on parental priorities and a child's need for self-esteem, that was pretty much where I left the discussion.

I have read other books—some geared toward the psychological needs of children, others that discuss the need to lead your child into a relationship with the Lord, those which are geared toward the things you can do to stimulate your child's mental growth, ones that stress the emotional needs of children, those that affirm the importance of discipline, and still others that emphasize physical needs and development. Most teaching seems to zero in on some specific aspect of the child-rearing process.

Many of these books are excellent. I often wonder where my

wife and I would be if it were not for the impact of the excellent teaching we have received through books. More and more I am coming to realize how unoriginal I really am and that my ideas, methods, priorities, and values have been shaped by the Lord's use of the writings of many individuals.

As our boys have grown older and our family has increased in size, I have found myself looking at the totality of the experience of raising a child. I have seen that the simplistic approach of trying to view the entire process in light of one or two of its facets just won't get the job done. I have therefore begun a search for the framework that will allow me to perceive my parental role as a unified whole.

Naturally, the entirety of such an enormous responsibility cannot be completely grasped by a single individual. However, that does not negate the effort nor the findings. It simply means we must keep each discovery in its proper perspective. This book then is not absolute truth, yet it is workable and approximate truth.* These concepts and principles, while not a full revelation by any means, are nevertheless valuable in that they are practical.

The principles of this book will not provide you with a ready list of easy-to-apply answers that will miraculously work the same way in every situation and for every child. Though these are indeed "workable" ideas, implementing them will often be severely trying. This book is largely theoretical. You will have to discover the specific ways to apply them in your own family. And that will be no easy task. Every child, every circumstance, every day will be entirely different. You will often find yourself standing back saying, "What do I do?"

My wife and I have gone many times to a woman in our church who possesses great wisdom concerning children and their needs. She is on the church staff solely as a family

* NOTE: This principle is taught by Jim Durkin, author of three books: *Training Your Soul*, *Believe, Confess, and Act*, and *Purpose and Vision*, published by Radiance Media, 39 5th Street, Eureka, CA. 95501.

counselor. Shortly after our first book on the family was released, we ran into some extremely difficult times with our children. We frequently found ourselves crying out to this woman, "*Help*! What do we do now?" I had just written a book on family relationships and children and yet considered myself totally helpless to find answers for the specific situations which were arising in my own home.

It is imperative to understand that though we may have the principles at our immediate disposal, putting them into practice daily is a full-time and thoroughly demanding task. *No one* has ever raised a family without struggles. You and I are no exceptions.

One further danger in a book of this sort is the tendency to overemphasize a particular chapter, idea, theory, or principle. We all naturally stress the importance of those ideas which are most meaningful to us. But in so doing we often disregard how that particular idea blends into the whole, how it fits together with the other parts.

I warn you right now: you will miss the most vital message of this book if you elevate one idea above the rest. All the complex and varied parental roles, responsibilities and opportunities blend together to create a child who is vitally *alive*. By taking just one thing and disregarding the others, you deprive your child of much life that could be his.

In looking for a structure into which many of my random ideas about my relationships with my children would fit, the analogy of a house being built has constantly returned to me. I view the raising of my children as being similar to the construction of a house. In a sense, that is exactly what I am doing, one board and one brick at a time. At this point I am barely past the foundation. It is a long and slow procedure—a continuous process.

The foundation is the first element in any successful building project. Once it is secure, the walls can be erected. The roof then secures the walls into place and covers the whole building.

But the foundation, walls, and roof do not make a completed house. Floor plans vary tremendously. Some houses are huge, others tiny. Doors and windows are an integral part of any home. Furnishings, paint, books, a fireplace, and the yard are other features. When a builder sets out to build a house, he must take each of these details into account. They all have an effect on the final outcome.

Similiarly, there is total interplay between the various aspects of our job as parents. To neglect any part will result in our child's being unable to reach his full potential. Once again, therefore, I stress that though these chapters and ideas are presented one at a time, they are vitally intertwined. There is not the same kind of progression of thought that is usually demonstrated in books. Instead, every idea and principle builds on and emanates from every other idea.

Once a house is built, it comes "alive" through the years as it is lived in, cared for, and loved. It must not only be loved, it must be carefully maintained. In time gutters will leak, dry rot will creep in, weeds in yards will grow, and paint will weather and peel. None of these things in themselves are serious, but if they are not taken into account and properly dealt with, they can slowly begin to undermine the entire structure. Planning, constructing, maintaining, living in and caring for a home are complex undertakings with many facets—all of which blend together in the life of the home and its occupants.

As you read on I encourage you to think of these ideas not as simply an arbitrary list of principles to apply, but as a *total experience* with your child.

PART I

DRAWING THE BLUEPRINTS:

The Method

1

BRINGING VISIONS TO REALITY

The Basis for Our Accomplishments

When my son is one moment looking into my eyes and laughing, the next moment crying, the next reaching for my hand to take me outside to see some new discovery, and the next asleep in my arms, I find myself pensively asking the question, "What is the essence of parenthood?"

There is obviously no concise and simple answer.

My child is like an enormous sponge. Every moment he is soaking up everything around him at a positively incredible rate. My role, then, must be to provide healthy and valuable influences for him to absorb. For what he takes in will actually become part of him.

He is also like a lump of pliable clay waiting to be formed. From this standpoint my function is that of a potter—shaping, molding, kneading, standing back to look, then continuing on. Without constant attention, the clay will quickly become hard and brittle, assuming its own shape, perhaps nothing like what I had chosen for it to look like.

I am also in the position of a skilled builder erecting a house. I lay the foundation, raise the walls, put on the roof, and add years of finishing touches inside, which make the home all it is meant to be—liveable, warm, comfortable. My child is a home and I am the contractor. I am building one step at a time.

I am also like a sculptor standing before a raw and uncut piece of marble visualizing the beautiful statue I intend to create. I chip away here and there, shaping and chiseling extremely slowly, making sure each stroke of my knife removes only excess rock and exposes the beauty of what I have envisaged.

My child is all these things and I occupy all these roles at once in my relationship with him.

In each of these examples there is a common factor. The artist, the builder, the designer all work with a plan clearly in front of them. A sculptor with no design before him makes every cut haphazardly. In the end he has a pile of shavings, but no statue. A builder without an exacting set of blueprints winds up putting together a house that is in shambles. A sponge will soak up whatever liquid surrounds it. It will absorb mud if thrown into a ditch just as quickly as it will soak up the pure, clean water of a mountain stream. But the effect on the sponge is vastly different.

What do we want to create? What do we want to build into the lives of our children? These are the questions we must face. Without specific answers we are building with no design and our children will assume whatever shape they happen to take. They will soak up influences over which we have no control. The end result will be unpredictable.

With a plan, however, it does not have to be so. A plan, even if it is simply a picture in our minds, is something we can work toward confidently with the assurance that we will see at leas good deal of it accomplished.

The Three-Step Process
Visualize—Plan—Act

There is a principle running through nearly every phase of life that can be summarized as follows: an idea (a dream, vision, faith-picture) can be turned into reality by believing in its reality and then acting on that belief. This is a process all things go through. And the procedure involves several distinct steps.

First there is the stage where the idea or goal is conceived in the imagination. It is visualized. Whatever you call it, at this point it exists in the imagination alone. It is not yet solid or genuinely real.

The second step in the process of turning that picture into reality is to determine precisely what steps must be taken in order for it to become a solid and real entity. If I am visualizing a chair, for example, this means more than simply saying, "Second stage—make the chair." This is the time for detailed and specific planning. What kind of chair? How big? What kind of wood, stain or paint? What shape? The craftsman must sit down and carefully figure out each step needed to create the chair. It might involve twenty or thirty different steps to make a simple chair. He not only has to determine what these individual steps are, he also has to designate the order in which they must be carried out.

The final stage is to put each step into practice. When you have completed the last task on the list, the chair is completed, the job over, the goal accomplished.

You have brought your picture into reality.

There is a famous story which has been quoted in many books that illustrates the value of this simple threefold process. Charles Schwab, president of Bethlehem Steel many years ago, went to a management consultant by the name of Ivy Lee. His request: "Show me a way to accomplish more with my time. If it works, I'll pay you anything within reason."

Lee did not return to his office to draw up a detailed plan for the reorganization of the company. He did not suggest books to read or recommend long counseling sessions with top experts. He simply handed Schwab a piece of paper and said, "Write down everything you have to do tomorrow."

Schwab complied.

Then Lee said, "Now number these items in the order of their importance."

He did so.

Lee continued, "Now first thing tomorrow morning, start work on item number one. Stick with it until it is completed. Then move on to item number two and go no further until you have finished it. Proceed to number three, and so on. It doesn't matter how far on the list you get on a certain day. You will have taken care of the most important items; you can then include the others on your list for the following day.

"The secret is to carry out this plan daily. Evaluate the specific things that must be done and the relative importance and order of each. In other words, establish priorities, write down your plan of action, and then stick to it—right down the list. Do this every day and with every job you encounter.

"After you have tried this for several weeks and have convinced yourself of the value of the system, let your men try it. Test it for as long as you like and with as many different types of jobs as you like. When you are satisfied send me a check for whatever you think it is worth."

In several weeks Charles Schwab sent Ivy Lee a check i $25,000. He later maintained that this was the most valuable lesson he had ever learned in his long and highly profitable business career.

A $25,000 idea and it is ours—free for the taking!

This process, however applied, is at the root of all things made and created in the universe. God created the world first by conceiving it in His infinite mind and then commanding it into being (action): "Let there be light!" (Gen. 1:3). Of course God did not have to go through the detailed steps of numbering each phase of the creation process and so on. But the same procedure was nevertheless followed—visualizing the end result, then bringing it into existence.

A designer manufactures a new product (whether it be a chair, a car, a coat, or a new hair style) by following this procedure exactly. He initially envisions something in his mind; he draws it on paper; he decides the specific steps which must be taken in order to bring his drawing into reality. Then—one step at a time—he carries out each particular task his plan calls for. From a mental picture, a solid thing eventually emerges.

This process is not only true in the physical world with things we can see and touch and feel, but also in the realm of growth, accomplishments, relationships, and spiritual progress. If you have a picture of something in your mind; if you have faith in the eventual reality of that picture; and if you believe strongly enough in it, setting your sights continuously on its reality and its fulfillment—you can make it come about as surely as if you were making a simple object. The process is the same. You must plan out your strategy. You must determine exactly what steps must be taken for the goal to be reached. This is a complex stage. It requires thought and planning about every aspect of the goal.

Example after example could be cited about a child who had a dream—to go to college, to perfect an invention, to make the Olympic team, to be elected president, to find a medical breakthrough, to write a novel, to explore an unknown frontier—and who realized that dream because of following through on a plan, never giving up on it. The remarkable inventions of Thomas Edison were born that way—in his mind. He brought his dreams and ideas into reality because he believed in them and acted on them, following his plans one step at a time. Jimmy Carter's phenomenal drive to the presidency is another perfect example. He saw the result in his mind, he believed in what he saw, he devised a detailed plan, and then he followed his plan one step at a time. He set a goal, he acted on it, and he accomplished the result.

The Key—Imaginative Goal-Setting and Planning

There is great power toward accomplishment in focusing in on your objective and then locking yourself into it. This vision of the end result sustains you throughout the entire process of completing the specific details of your predetermined plan.

Though the actual work toward accomplishment is done in the last stage of the three—carrying out the steps of the plan—the real key to accomplishing great things is found in the first two steps.

Why don't more of us experience the results of Charles Schwab, Thomas Edison, or Jimmy Carter? And in the spiritual realm, why are more of us not experiencing the incredible fruitfulness of the apostle Paul, John Wesley, Dwight Moody, or Billy Graham?

The answer lies in the first two steps. Most of us have not nurtured our ability to visualize and plan. Most people live their entire lives on step three—coping from day to day with specifics, without ever standing back to look at the pattern in which these specifics should fit together toward lasting accomplishment. It takes deep insight and discernment to know how to visualize and which mental pictures to make high priorities. Most of us are not encouraged to use our imaginations adequately so they are not developed to the extent they could be. There is incredible power in visualizing. Without it we will not be able to set goals or reach them. Goal-setting is simply channeling our imaginations into positive and definite visualization.

Goal-setting, however, is only the first step. The second is equally important—arriving at a plan for accomplishing what we have seen, the goal. This is the phase where hard mental work is involved. We have to weigh priorities, establish intermediate objectives, and determine the exact steps we must take in order to reach the goal. This step is crucial. No amount of time and effort and thought and prayer is too great to put here. For once this second stage is completed and we have a detailed plan before us, the goal is as good as reached. All that remains is the third and final step, carrying out the plan one step at a time. When the last task is completed, the goal has been achieved.

The first two stages of the process are the most important.

God has made this a principle that works in all aspects of life. It is the key to the fulfillment of dreams and visions—setting the goal (visualizing), determining the plan, and then acting (with your conviction firmly before you) by carrying out the plan. And at every point it is essential that you believe and never doubt the reality of what you see. Keeping your objective clearly in focus is vital.

When this order and process is adhered to, things will happen. It is a principle that is true. It will work equally well for

Christians and non-Christians. It can be used for godly ends or destructive ends. But when it is applied, it works.

How It Works

Let me give you an example from my own experience. I have applied this principle dozens of times in this way.

In our store we are constantly in need of new shelves. So when I am facing the building of a new bookshelf, the first thing I do is to try to see in my mind what I want it to look like. I turn it over and around many times in my mind's eye trying to visualize it as clearly as I possibly can. I imagine myself walking around the shelf; I imagine it full of books; I try to see every tiny detail of that shelf. I get to know it in my mind.

After I am satisfied with my conception of it (stage one), I sit down and try to sketch it. I work on the drawing and take as long as necessary to make what I am drawing on paper align with what I have seen in my thinking. I know this is important because this drawing will provide the basis for the entire planning process (stage two). The drawing is the finalization of step one. It is cementing onto paper what my visualizing has yielded. And once the drawing is completed and I am satisfied that it looks like my mental picture, I am then ready to begin the specific planning process.

So I sit down with my drawing and a blank piece of paper and write down everything I am going to need to build the shelf. My drawing is specific. It tells me the height and length and width of each section of the shelf. I calculate how many 1 x 12's and 1 x 6's I will need. I figure out the cost, what sort of stain I will use. I list the types and amounts of nails, sandpaper, finishing varnish, etc. I try to plan on every possible item I will need to purchase. Then I determine the steps I must take to actually build the shelf once I have the materials—which cuts to make, which edges will require sanding, when to stain the boards, the order in which I will assemble them, and how many coats of stain and varnish to apply. If I were to write down every step of the plans I follow in constructing a simple shelf, there would probably be over forty. I make my planning as detailed as possible, trying to take everything into advance consideration.

Once I have my plan worked out and the order of each step numbered, I am ready to begin. Planning is over and it is time for stage three—action, building the shelf. I begin with the first item on my list and go to the lumber yard to buy what I will need. I then come home, unload the wood, and begin to follow the steps my plan calls for. I make the necessary cuts, sand the boards, stain the wood, and begin assembling the various parts. In a day or two I am looking at a completed shelf. The picture in my mind has become reality.

That is, of course, a fairly simple example. But the same process applies to almost anything. It applies to our spiritual lives as well. Let's say I attend a meeting and get excited about walking closer to the Lord. The Lord puts a picture in my mind of what sort of person I could become—growing, fruitful, mature, trusting in God for everything. If I want that picture to come about, I must follow the rest of the process. I must focus in on that goal of a closer walk with God and plan specifically what I must do in order to see it come about. Then I must follow through on my plan, never doubting that God is indeed bringing me closer to Him through every step. I must act to make the picture real. Praying to be a more effective Christian won't make it happen unless I am willing to follow through on the rest of the process—I must *do* what the vision requires. I must *do* what my plan for a closer walk with God entails—pray, seek His guidance, minister to others, obey His word. I must plan ways to do these things and then follow through.

Or let's say I am having some difficulties in my marriage. Perhaps my wife and I are not talking with each other sufficiently in a meaningful way. So our deep communication is missing. I happen to pick up a book on marriage, hoping that it may give me some insight into my own situation.

The author tells me, "At the end of the day when you come home, express an interest in your wife's day. Be genuinely interested in the small things she has gone through since you left in the morning. Ask her about them; listen to her. You will soon be communicating."

I read these words and I think to myself, "That sounds great! I'd like to communicate with my wife like that."

Already a vision has sprung to life in my mind. I am visualizing something—that my wife and I are communicating and that I am becoming more effective as a husband. A faith picture is coming to life in my imagination.

Now comes the second stage: if I choose to actually bring that picture of communication into reality I can do it. I must arrive at a plan. In this case, however, it is not as detailed as making a shelf. My plan is simply to follow the advice of the book exactly as the author recommended—go home, open the door, and express a genuine interest in my wife's day. The more detailed I make my plan, the better its chances of success. I may think of certain questions to ask her, I may decide to call her before I leave work to let her know what time I'll arrive. Above all, I will determine to display a sincere interest and will listen carefully to everything she has to share with me without launching into a monologue about my own day.

Then the third and final stage comes when I get out of the car that night. The goal has been set, the plan determined. Now is the time to carry it out. I walk through the door and *do* exactly what my plan called for. If I carry it out day after day, putting my wife's needs and interests and activities high on my priority list, our communication will grow. The picture will have become a reality.

I apply this same principle in the management of my business. All successful enterprises are run in this manner. A vital part of any business is planning. Managers and executives must sit down and think through their goals and objectives. "Where are we headed? What do we want to accomplish?" Then they must plan precisely how to go about putting their goals and objectives (pictures) into practice. "What must we do to achieve these ends?" This involves a specific plan of action.

Once that has been done, they can walk out of the planning room. Their work is virtually over. The hard part is behind them. They simply instruct their subordinates to carry out the plan step by step. Before long what was once just a set of ideas around a meeting table has become reality.

You are undoubtedly beginning to wonder at this point what all this has to do with raising children and being a parent.

The reason for so much space being devoted to developing the principle of this three-step process is that I am convinced most parents operate toward their children in the realm of step three. In other words, they simply take each day, each event, and each new development in their child's life as it chances to come. Rarely is goal-setting and long-range planning an integral part of the parent-child relationship. They are carrying out many of the specific functions that should be included as part of step three, but in random order with no clearly visualized goal ever before them.

No goal has been set; therefore, none is reached. Children grow more or less at random when an unplanned, goalless procedure is followed.

The basis for accomplishment (whether it be making a physical object, realizing spiritual growth, or attaining certain results in the life of our child) lies in the bringing into reality the visions God gives us. Therefore, if we desire to achieve certain things as parents, it is critical to understand and begin to function using the tenets of visualizing goals and planning how to bring them about.

This principle then lies at the heart of your capacity to make real and workable everything else we will discuss in this book. This is the core. Unless you think the words which follow are nothing but stale dogmas, you must devise a method to implement them into your own life on the basis of visualizing a goal and planning how to achieve it. Visions and ideas *can* be made real.

2

VISUALIZING THE END RESULT

What Are We Building in the Life of Our Child?

To successfully raise and train children requires first of all that parents have a plan they are following and a specific goal they intend to reach. The groundwork must be laid. Foresighted planning is an essential element in any accomplishment.

Many Christians, however, are not daily engaged in setting imaginative goals and arriving at strategies for seeing them through. Naturally we all hope our children will turn out "okay" and that they will walk with the Lord. We have some rather indistinct thoughts about the future and how we would like to see our children mature and grow. And we have some vague notions regarding the principles set forth in the Bible for the procedure of raising a child. Certainly we pray for our children and ask for God's help to be effective parents.

But the realizations we have about our own control over this process are hazy. We haven't applied ourselves to the process of creatively visualizing specific goals, then planning how to achieve them. We have no strategy. We are unaware for the most part that the largest factor in the eventual maturing of our hope for our children lies in our own hands and is contingent upon our following this three-step procedure. Without diligent visualizing, planning, and following through, we will have little hope of keeping our child from being swept away by the world. If we desire to see our children manifest certain qualities, then we've got to do certain things to insure that those qualities blossom. The maturing of characteristics in our children is predictable according to the extent to which we follow these procedures.

Imagine a contractor trying to build a house with the same lack of planning and preparation most parents exhibit. Such a man would never get a house built. A builder is compelled to adhere to sound planning principles. He has to choose a lot, clear it, test the soil for strength, level the site, and select his materials. After these preliminaries have been taken care of, he must then draw up detailed plans for the house he intends to build. Without this overall picture of what he is constructing he would simply be randomly joining one board to another. The house might possibly get built in such a manner, but the result would be unpredictable. There would be no cohesion to unify the structure and hold it together.

No successful builder operates this way. He spends hours and hours visualizing, thinking, planning, drawing, calculating, projecting. He knows that in all aspects of life, planning is a prerequisite to a favorable outcome. He is aware of Jesus' words, "Would any of you think of building a tower without first sitting down and calculating the cost, to see whether he could afford to finish it?" (Luke 14:28, NEB).

Though many embark on child rearing with no detailed plan of action, Christian parents have a high responsibility to do otherwise. God will call our children to be mighty men and women. They will be called upon to live and serve Him in unique times. We cannot take lightly our charge as their parents and merely "hope" they grow up to "serve the Lord." Accidents do not happen here. At present our children are but lumps of unshaped clay. God has given them into our hands for a time to mold them, according to His purpose, into men and women of whom much will be required.

It is not easy for parents to grasp the enormity of this calling—that in many major respects their child's future rests in their hands. As parents, they will largely determine many of the characteristics their child will grow up to manifest. They can mold him into any shape they choose, or they can ignore the future and simply allow him to acquire whatever shape he happens to.

For the parent, however, who desires to mold and shape and influence his child in the directions God intends, the principle of bringing pictures into reality must be diligently followed.

The Necessity of Visualizing

The first step is always visualization. A goal must be established. A builder must first decide what type of structure he intends to build. Everything from lot selection to blueprints hinges upon the outcome of this stage.

Parents who would successfully build godliness into their child must begin here as well. They must visualize the end result. What do they want their child to become? What sort of house do they want to build? What are the characteristics they want their child to exhibit?

As I have pondered this, the enormity of my task occasionally overwhelms me. What can I build into my children to enable them to face the future fully as sons and daughters of God? If I could open them up and deposit into their hearts and minds and spirits certain qualities, what would they be? If I could mold their lives as perfectly as a skilled sculptor fashions a beautiful work of art, what would be the distinguishing marks I would carve into their faces? What would the finished product look like?

Visualizing is no easy task. These are not simple questions. The process of setting a goal in your mind is never a completed thing. It goes on and on, always undergoing revisions and perfections and modifications.

Of course what father or mother, if he or she had the power, wouldn't give a son or daughter every quality to allow them to absorb all the fullness of life itself? But can one even hope to begin such a task? Our tendency at times is to consider these areas "in the Lord's hands," therefore removing our personal responsibility for their fulfillment. We vaguely pray for our children, take them to Sunday school, and try to be the best parents we can under the circumstances.

But if the principles in the last chapter and the advice of Ivy Lee are correct, then we should be able to do far more than that. We should be able to set a positive goal, arrive at a plan for achieving it, and then bring what we have visualized into being.

Visualizing what we desire for our children is the all-important first step. Once we begin to do so, our imaginations come to life!

It is easy for many to start off on the wrong foot because they do not have practice in this. They inadequately visualize where they are headed as parents. In order to overcome this, we must acquire a clear image of what we are trying to create in our children. Imagination in this sense does not mean simply daydreaming. This is a conscious thing; we need to discipline our minds to make a concerted effort toward seeing (in faith) the end result. What is the completed picture of our child's life which we constantly hold before us?

Without this positive mental effort, successful parenthood simply won't happen. Children don't just happen to turn out "okay." Selfishness, rebellion, pride, and stubbornness are innate in us all. Children won't outgrow these negative traits. We must initiate a specific plan for their removal.

The Enormous Potential in Every Child

As we begin to visualize in faith a picture of our grown children, most would certainly agree that this means they would reach the highest level in life God designed them to achieve. We desire to see our children reach their fullest potential in every way and become productive, confident, creative, loving, and wise.

Such results will not happen haphazardly. We provide the skill and leadership that allows them to attain this potential. It is our responsibility to create and maintain the conditions which will most thoroughly allow God to flow in and through them. We are craftsmen whose opportunity it is to skillfully and knowledgeably and purposefully mold our children.

The planning, foresight, and leadership we exhibit in our relationships with our children are part of an eternal chiseling process, molding what our children will become for all eternity. They are being shaped permanently by our hands. Like the artist who knows precisely what he is creating, we must be patient and deliberate, creatively keeping the picture of the finished statue before us at all times. A beautiful masterpiece is slowly being fashioned by each cut and with every chip that falls to the floor.

Within every child is vast potential, lying dormant and waiting to be brought to the surface. Our children are placed under our care and authority to either reach that potential or else fall short of it. To see that they do reach their maximum potential is *the* most important task of our lives. The investments we make early in their lives pay tremendous dividends later, though at the time they often appear insignificant.

A child during his first few years is so small and easily influenced. The whole of his potential is latent, unseen, hidden below the surface. In the short term of our busy and complicated lives, it is often difficult to realize the true importance of that small life. The proper perspective is often hard to locate in the midst of our hurried pace. The urgencies of life just don't want to wait.

But the potential in each child won't wait either. It will rise—some day. And that time comes sooner than we think.

Though the long-term view is often obscured, it is nonetheless vital that parents tune themselves in to it; there can be no greater use of a parent's time and energy than to pour them into our children. There is naturally a price to pay in terms of our personal freedoms, and the returns are delayed many years. But the stakes in the lives of our children are high and the rewards for our faithfulness are great.

One of the first steps that must be taken in order to lock yourself in to this perspective is to imagine your child as God sees him. Form a "faith-picture" of him. Visualize him in faith as God sees him at the pinnacle of his maturity and potential. Does God see the child as he is at two or three or seven, or does He see him as a full-grown, spiritual individual? Naturally, God loves a young child no less than He does an adult. But in God's eyes each one of us is viewed as what we are becoming, not simply as what we happen to be at some intermediate and incomplete stage. God is always viewing us in the knowledge of the full and glorious potential that lies hidden, waiting to explode into life. That must be our view of our child as well. Our child will ultimately grow to fulfill the vision of him we carry in our hearts. If we want him to turn out a certain way, then we must visualize him that way, believe in that vision, and act so as to bring it to fulfillment.

This means far more than daydreaming about what would be "nice." A builder's visualizing must lead to actual sketches which eventually find their way onto the drawing table as the blueprints are drafted. So parents must visualize actively and concretely in order to predetermine what they see God building in the life of their child and what they, therefore, are setting their minds to work toward. This is the time for definitive decision-making based on prayer and deep thought. It is no time for wishful thinking. Goals and objectives must be arrived at in advance. The visions we have and the faith-pictures we form will determine many of the lifetime characteristics of our children. The importance of our thoughts and mental directions is enormous, impossible to measure. They mustn't be vague or indistinct. Being "decent parents" and "loving" our children is not a sufficient goal to yield a workable plan.

A contractor who builds a house first sits down and decides exactly what the house is going to look like. It is his decision at this point. No concrete is set; the foundation is not yet in place. It may be a two-bedroom home that will house a family of three; it may be a seventeen-room mansion that will house a millionaire; it may be a nine-story apartment complex. He can build *anything*. It is simply a matter of creatively visualizing the result in all its potential, then drafting the plans and following them.

Parents must do the same. They must first decide what they want to build and then draw up plans for the actual construction.

The Need for a Plan

Once a builder has imagined and then sketched the house he intends to build, he must draw his blueprints. These are his detailed plans which will guide him as he builds. Every board, every brick, every nail is specified in the plans. His prior visions do him no good without these specific plans. They are necessary for the actual building. They guide him as he nears completion.

The same process must be followed by effective parents. Once they have visualized the end result, they must map out a plan in order to achieve that result. Without this part of the process parents are in much the same position as an amateur builder trying to piece together some project without having taken the time to think it through, sketch it on paper, and plan in detail exactly what each step is going to involve. So he puts one board on top of another taking each cut as it comes.

But when he is through, the result is different than he had hoped for. "That's not anything like I had in mind."

The makeshift parent also finds himself increasingly doubtful about the outcome of his efforts with his children as the years progress. With no goals and no plan to clearly guide, results are always unpredictable. When the child of such a parent at seventeen or eighteen suddenly turns into a person of his own, oftentimes not even recognizable to his parents, they are stunned.

"Where did we go wrong?" they ask.

But the answer is simple. Like the unskilled carpenter, their work was piecemeal, consisting of fragmentary efforts—some good, some bad, but with no plan encompassing the whole. No goal had been decided upon, so none could be reached.

To raise children otherwise requires that some fundamental

groundwork be laid. This involves, in addition to visualizing and goal-setting, careful planning, evaluating, re-evaluating, weighing costs and priorities, and heavy sacrifice. And, of course, all these things must be part of the plans we draw up.

How does a Christian parent arrive at a plan for building into the life of his child those things which his visualizing has yielded and which his faith-picture reveals to him?

That is no easy question. Its answer will be an individual one; each set of parents must come up with specific answers as they sit down to arrive at concrete actions that must be done for the goals to come about. Your plans must be specific and every step must be detailed.

You can come about your specific plan for your specific child through prayer, through studying his individual needs and personality, from experiences of others, and from books (such as this one). Certain things about your plan will be fairly universal and certain aspects will unfold after you become more intimately acquainted with your child as he grows and matures. Your strategy for each child will undergo continual refinement according to his growth.

One of the key ingredients, both in achieving your goal and in keeping your specific plans fresh and vital, is a conscious and daily decision to reaffirm your commitment to the house you are building, which is your child. You cannot renege on your strategy or the building process will come to a standstill and the house won't get built. Like Charles Schwab, you must proceed down the list from top to bottom.

Conception of children can occur by accident, but effective parenthood cannot. Hit-and-miss tactics won't work. If we simply bring a child into the world and then provide him a place to live for fifteen or twenty years, he will eventually be lured away from us by other forces. We will exercise very little control over his ultimate outcome, personhood, and character.

Any dilegent parent can keep this from happening. Though parents are artists, no particular skill is required for success. What is required is strict adherence to the principles in chapter one, following the threefold plan in order to bring our faith-pictures into reality. It is such a simple—though not easy—process and success will come with practice.

But parents are not trained in such foundational principles. Though it takes a minimum of eighteen to twenty years of schooling to enter many professional fields, not a day of preparation, planning, or training is required to become a parent. Because of this, most parents do indeed enter parenthood unprepared and with no plans to guide their daily efforts.

God did not intend it to be so. He fully intended us to have blueprints before us as we raise and train our children. We need blueprints that provide two very important things: the completed picture, and daily guidelines to follow in order to reach that goal.

Now most Christians are generally aware that the Bible contains the guidelines for parental instruction. Why then are so many lacking specific plans to help them through the daily experiences their families encounter? Why are so many parents not in control? Why is there such common confusion concerning the methods of child raising?

There are three answers I think will provide insight into this dilemma. First, the guidelines in the Bible are designed for a very specific purpose, to guide diligent parents toward a very distinct goal. They are not guidelines simply for their own sake; their whole reason for being lies in providing guidance for parents who are in the process of carrying out a plan to reach a specific goal in the life of their child. So Christians who vaguely try to follow some of the parental guidelines of the Bible without having first established a goal and arrived at a plan will see very little fruit for their efforts. The biblical standards are part of a larger picture.

Secondly, I think we have given the biblical guidelines too great a task. We have mistakenly assumed that they are all we need in order to be a successful parent. But the biblical standards go only so far. And the reason is this: the Bible contains guidelines—not blueprints. And the blueprints are what we need in order to actually complete the construction project. The guidclines are simply the rules guiding the drawing of the blueprints. The parental Scriptures are like the building codes. Blueprints must conform to the code. But no builder ever thought of going out to build a house with nothing but a code book to guide him. It would do him little specific good when it actually came time to cut a board and raise a wall. He needs useful blueprints which conform to the code.

The blueprints for your child are the exact and specific instructions for *you* to follow for *your* child. Every single set must be individually drawn because each set is unique. No two have ever been alike. Every parent-child relationship is unlike any other.

This distinction between guidelines and blueprints can easily be seen in the classic scriptural injunction to parents, "Train up a child in a way he should go, and when he is old, he will not depart from it" (Prov. 22:6).

It sounds beautiful. But what good will that Scripture do for a young mother facing a four-year-old tantrum? She needs something more practical, more relevant to her daily situation.

That proverb is a guideline from which more specific and useful plans must emerge.

The third misconception we harbor concerning the guidelines we often don't know how to apply is this: there is no Child Training Office where we can go to obtain a copy of the specific blueprints we need for our specific child.

We have to draw our own.

Each parent must sit down thoughtfully and prayerfully and analyze the faith-picture of his child he has in his imagination. Then he must carefully draw out in great detail his specific set of blueprints for that child as guided by the Scriptures and his own unique visualization of his child. This is a long and demanding task. And it cannot be static; his plans must be ever renewed, always fresh and alive.

3

MAPPING OUT A STRATEGY

Devising a Blueprint-Like Plan

Deliberate Reflection to See My Child as God Sees Him

Now that the extreme importance of applied meditation on what our children are becoming in the long-range, eternal future has been emphasized, it is time to dig in and focus our thoughts specifically on each one of them. We must form our own vision for our child individually. You are the builder and you must draft your own plans. A picture must be clearly focused in the eye of your imagination.

What do you see?

When I try to visualize a specific future image of my child I catch a quick glimpse of all sorts of things at once. I see him laughing, enjoying life free from guilt, frustration, despair. I observe joy on his face and in his heart. He is standing tall with a thoughtful look in his eyes, ready and capable of tackling whatever stands in his way. I perceive a deep confidence and self-assurance as he is in the midst of some knotty assignment. He knows himself well—both his strengths and his limitations—and his effectiveness is a measure of that realistic and confident self-image.

I see him reaching out. His life is others-centered. He is profoundly and unselfishly motivated to minister to everyone around him, no matter who it may be, from his own children to someone he scarcely knows. His desire is to be like Jesus in every aspect of his life. I see him on his knees; I see him in the early and quiet morning hours poring over his Bible seeking added strength and guidance for the day ahead.

I discern a light in his eye that reminds me of his look at two years when he first fell in love with the mailman—a look of wonder, curiosity, expectation, joy, and anticipation. It is a look alive with wonder for everything that life has to offer. It is this look which lingers in my thoughts. It reveals his continuing curiosity and appreciation for all that is around him. It is this look that is at the root of his creativity and talent and love of life.

Mingled with the joy that obviously fills him and the anticipation which motivates him is also a look which tells me my son also knows pain. He has felt sorrow deeply and God has used it to carve out a deeper cavity for compassion in the depths of his soul. He has walked through the valley of doubts and soul-searching questions and has come out on the other side with a renewed faith and trust in God and a keener awareness of others.

As these various expressions fade, he looks upward. His face is alive with thankfulness. His heart is bowed before the Lord in humble appreciation for allowing him to be so joyfully a part of God's life and creation.

Naturally, I could go on and on. Visions of this sort build upon one another and seem to have no end. And my thoughts for each of my children all turn out so differently. This is how it must be.

If I had to boil down my bird's-eye look into their futures, I would begin with some words. Wisdom is the first to spring to mind, but in my human idealism it is quickly followed by a host of others: faith in God, confidence, love, security, courage, peace, tenderness, stamina, knowledge, self-control, trust, submissiveness, understanding, leadership, joy, patience, compassion, fruitfulness, kindness, perseverance, modesty, gentleness, obedience, sensitivity, worshipfulness, open mindedness, goodness, a praising heart, humility, a serving spirit, calmness, cheerfulness, and thankfulness.

With all these magnificent qualities occupying my thoughts, I find myself sitting with my son's hand in mine, looking into his peaceful, sleeping face. "How can I go about making these lofty ideals come alive in this young life?" I wonder. He is so small, so innocent, so fresh, so humble, so pure. At this point there is barely a cleared building site. Fifteen or twenty years from now there will be an erected and completed building that will stand for all eternity. I am the builder. God has placed his life in my unskilled hands. I know from the moment of his birth there has been a movement afoot to lure him away from me and from the God whose laws I would build into his life. At some points it has seemed deceptively like a far-away battle involving other parents but not really touching me and my son too closely. Yet I know this is part of the enemy's strategy, to lull me to sleep so that he can infiltrate my camp with all manner of seductive and subtle arguments. But in my more lucid moments I know beyond all doubt that a devastating war is on and is slowly encompassing me. The enemy's strikes are furious and he will do anything in his power to gain mastery over my son.

It is a real war and the spirit of my child is at stake. I cannot take my task lightly. What does one do to insure that one's child is not lost in battle? What procedure can I follow in order that the finished house of my child does indeed resemble the picture I now have in my mind, rather than turn out altogether different? How can I build into him these qualities so that their impact will be lasting and will sustain him through the war that is being waged over him?

It is time for a specific strategy—for detailed blueprints that will set me on course. Naturally my child is not altogether like a house. There will come a time when the final product will depend on the will of my child himself. Even if parents do everything right in the training of their children, there is no assurance the children will emerge exactly as the parents had hoped. God has created each person individually unique with a mind and spirit and will of his own. In the long run, parents do not ultimately control the life-altering choices their sons and daughters make. Nevertheless, I realize that at present God has placed within my hands the capability of instilling values and providing an atmosphere of growth which will increase the chances my child will pursue a life with the will of God at its source. The efforts I make and the training I provide, though incomplete in many ways, will still add to the likelihood of my children making right choices on their own.

Though an idealistic goal, it is nonetheless vital.

Therefore, I resolve to have detailed blueprints before me. These I determine to follow as best I can in all my human limitations, allowing for the minor mid-course corrections of God's guidance and my increasing maturity as I go along.

A Closer Look at the House

Whenever I consider my role in my child's life I return to the analogy between raising a child and constructing a home. I think the parallel will be helpful as a framework to organize our thoughts.

As I sit down to think through my plans, my thoughts go to my close friend who is a builder. Listening as he explains to me certain things about the houses he builds has taught me a great deal about life—and especially about my children. As I walk around inside a lovely home he has recently completed, I am first struck by all the things he has done to make the house unique—the fireplace, the carpet, the rooms and window arrangements, the breakfast bar, the entryway. It will indeed be beautiful and exciting to live in! He is a craftsman, not merely a carpenter. And it shows in every detail.

Most of these features were added as the house neared completion. When he stood, months earlier, in the middle of a vacant lot, he began with phases of the construction I cannot even see as I tour the finished product. The foundation, the studs, the insulation, the heating system, the subflooring, the concrete, and the plumbing are all hidden from view even though they provide the solidarity for the entire building.

What has he had to go through in order to build this house?

Even before any dirt is moved, any concrete is poured, any wood is cut, a contractor must establish priorities and procedures, methods of operation, self-disciplining work habits and conditions. This is the framework in which he will work daily. And it is these rigorous work conditions, faithfully followed day after day, which will enable him to move toward completion of his house as he follows his blueprints.

As a parent I know I must do the same. I must think through and establish the priorities that will form the basis for my working conditions and habits. Does my job, my leisure time, my church life, my money, or my son take precedence? I must decide these issues well in advance. A builder works according to a predetermined schedule that has built into it his objectives, working patterns, and habits. He must determine which things to tackle first, what is to demand his attention on a certain day, and which items are of minor importance. A parent with no working conditions and priorities clearly in focus is like a builder who works awhile on the roof, awhile on the walls, awhile on the foundation, and awhile planting a lawn—certainly an ineffective way to build a solid home. To complete a task worthily requires the establishment of a framework of working conditions.

Once this framework is set, a builder is ready to begin the actual construction. The foundation comes first. And in visualizing the spiritual house that will provide the covering for the spirit of my child, I realize the foundation has to be discipline and the early training I provide as I teach him to obey. There is something about discipline that is hard and cold, like the cement that undergirds a house. It is a word sometimes considered ugly, and it is often avoided, misused and abused. Nevertheless, discipline and training are the foundation.

All sorts of things are inherent in effective discipline and these things insure a secure foundation. Far more than the word "punishment" (for which it is often mistaken) discipline implies the following: authority, respect, obedience, love, consistency, parental responsibility, and affection. Without *all* these factors at work, the foundation is not all it should be. If I improperly discipline (for whatever reason and however done) I will build a weak and shaky foundation for the house I will later try to construct.

It is obvious what a weak foundation will do. The buildings in the Italian city of Venice are slowly sinking into the sea because they are built on wet, boggy ground—their foundations do not extend down to bedrock. The leaning tower in Pisa was built with a weak foundation as well. It could only be saved by digging down to re-foundation it with tons and tons of concrete. No matter how beautiful the building, the foundation determines its inherent strength and therefore how long it will last.

Once the foundation has been laid, the building can begin to slowly take form. As it does, the foundation itself becomes less and less visible. Once it has provided the base on which to build, it ceases to be a major concern. After the first several years of a child's life, if the disciplinary foundation has been solidly and consistently laid, it consumes less and less of a parent's thought and energy as he moves on to other aspects of the building project. If foundational training has been effectively built into a young child's life, it will nurture the seeds and budding growth of the characteristics we have visualized in faith for our children and provide them a firm base on which to mature.

If, on the other hand, a foundation is improperly laid, an ineffective parent will continue to vainly attempt to discipline and train his child long past the time when normal foundational work should have ceased. A builder who expends all his energies on the foundation will never get to the rest of the house. In some families this unworkable procedure lasts through adolescence and even right up until the time a young man or woman is ready to leave home. But a foundation must be built early if it is to accomplish its purpose. Beyond the first six or eight years of a child's life only minor foundational work can be done. The concrete sets up quickly. The patterns of life become established. Once the building begins to go up, the foundation (however built and of whatever material it is made) is behind us.

As the building begins to rise, the skilled builder pays closer and closer attention to his blueprints. He must follow them precisely. Unless he does, the completed home will not meet the exact specifications for the picture he originally drew and which his plans mirror. He never loses sight of where he is headed. The full bird's-eye view of the house is ever in the craftsman's mind. It is this vision that sustains him.

Constantly before me must be the vision of my child. The faith-picture, revealing in the Lord all that my child is, must be reality to me. This is one of the most significant factors in the outcome of my efforts, for the power of accomplishment is set into motion by locking in mentally on the goal. The building I am presently constructing is the building I "see" in my imagination. From a run-down shack to a magnificent cathedral, my efforts will follow where my vision leads. Therefore I must consciously keep that vision firmly fixed in my mind as I progress.

After the foundation is firmly established, the house is framed. The walls go up. To begin with there are only studs, a bare skeleton. But as time passes, siding, sheet rock, paneling, and insulation are added to the frame. When they are completed, the walls provide the strength, warmth, security, and privacy of the house. In a sense they *are* the house. They are the first thing to go up, yet the last to be completed. From the first studs to the final interior painting, the many details inherent in the walls are the most exacting procedure of the entire building schedule. But the time spent is well rewarded; the walls supply strength to the entire structure as they rest firm on the foundation.

As we frame up the house which is our child, the walls are the self-esteem we build within him. A child's respect for himself and for God's love inside him is the key to his self-love. And this self-love, according to the Bible, will become his basis for loving others. It provides the bedrock for a confident and complete adult who is able to enjoy life, serve God, and live with himself. The way my child perceives himself will determine to a great extent the strength of his overall person, in many varied aspects. As his parent the key to a healthy self-concept rests almost entirely in my hands. I build or destroy him a little bit every day according to how I respond both to what he does and who he is.

Once the walls are up, the various rooms of the house begin to take shape and come into view. The floor plan previously designed by the builder becomes visible as it hasn't yet been. The unique arrangement of rooms which only a short time ago existed solely in the designer's imagination, is slowly turning into a real house. How many rooms are there? What are they like? Is there a library? A den? An outside deck? A private place for prayer and quiet? All these questions are answered by the floor plan.

The floor plan of a designer's drawing may be compared with the many ways in which we teach our child as he grows. Some parents limit their teaching to the barest essentials, thereby limiting the rooms of their child's mind which they encourage him to explore. Other parents teach their children about a huge variety of things and in so doing expand the reaches of their mental, physical, and emotional capabilities and interests. Whether we build a simple five-room house or a multi-room dwelling depends on the ways in which we teach and lead our child through the first exciting years of his life. We can make his mind and heart as big as we want to through our instruction, example, and time spent with him. We have been placed in the position of being able to teach him—lead him into knowledge, wisdom, and learning to grow up trusting in God. Through our teaching we can expand the capacity and roominess of his house, his mind and spirit. It can be as big for his creative and hungry mind as we choose to make it.

Once the walls are up the roof goes on. It must be strong and dry, for it will keep out rain and snow and cold and storm for years. It protects everything inside the house. The roof which covers the life of a child is the example and leadership provided by the life of his parents. Your example is seen by your child almost daily for fifteen to twenty years and will provide a covering that adds the finalizing touch of security and safety to everything else maturing inside him. There are two aspects of this part of our relationship to our child: daily demonstration of the workability of the principles we are trying to ingrain in him, and the leadership we provide for his life.

A parent is a child's great example. A child's eyes never stop looking to see what his parent is doing, how he is reacting. A parent's demonstration of life to his children protects them in later years from disillusionment and doubt when they begin to question some of the principles of life they were taught as young children. It is therefore important for children to observe their parents in all sorts of different situations. Our living example cements the principles we teach into place. Ultimately, our words will not be enough. The model of our own lives—habits, actions, attitudes, responses, consistency—will be the determining factor. If we stand the test, then their lives will be protected and permanent misgivings about the principles we have taught will not gain a foothold.

An integral part of the model our life provides is in the area of leadership. The most significant way we are able to open up their hearts to receive all that is before them is to take them by the hand and lead them through, pointing out everything as we go along. They need guidance in many areas for years. Telling them facts alone is not sufficient. We must experience life with them, beside them, on the ground with them. As a parent, you are your child's leader, guide, model, instructor, counselor, and advisor all rolled into one.

An essential aspect of a builder's planning is designing and building into his house doors which lead in and out and windows which allow light inside and permit the inhabitants to see outside. A home with no doors or windows would be cold and dark, hardly inhabitable. The doors and windows we build into our children's lives allow them to see outside themselves and participate in all the beauty that surrounds them. The outward-looking windows also look toward the future and things in life they will face. All through the years we must have an eye toward the future, and make provision for it. This involves showing our children what we see on the horizon of their lives—adolescence, college, financial problems, marriage, adulthood, a job, parenthood—and how we can help them prepare for it. Through windows you open your child out of himself into the world, the future, and all that is about him. Windows have a way of increasing the size of one's heart.

And there should always be one very special window which looks directly into your own house as well, with an adjoining door. Whenever they are ready for it, bring your children all the way inside your own home and show them around. One of their greatest ambitions in life is to get inside you to find out what makes you tick. Don't let this need go unanswered. It is the only way for them to view their own house with the larger perspective it needs.

Even after the structure of a house is complete, it will need all sorts of additional things for it to become liveable—a heating system, furniture, carpet, pictures, books, lamps, fires, and music. No matter what the size and layout, it is these final touches that will make a home warm and pleasant. A child's house is made joyful and fulfilling through the years of its construction by the love and affection we have poured out upon him. Unlike a real house where the final additions do indeed come last, our love must begin at birth and continue unabated. It will take many forms; it will be sensitive to needs that will change. But the love—and its expression—must never dwindle. It must spring forth from a genuine heart. Our teaching, discipline, guidance, covering, and great vision for our child's life will all be sterile and accomplish nothing unless we literally cover him with our love and affection.

When love is showered upon a child it strikes a deep root. He comes to life!

Our child's "house" becomes a vibrant, pulsating, joyful expression of all he is in the midst of becoming.

All facets of the building of a house work together. If any part is built incompletely, unwisely, or hastily, the entire building will suffer. Discipline is not the only foundational area. Every phase of the procedure holds up all the others. And wise maintenance throughout the years insures that the structure will last.

Parenthood is an awesome responsibility. We have the power to build any sort of home to house the spirit of our child. The shaping of that spirit is in our hands.

To begin the task requires that we prayerfully consider what is before us. Not that we know all there is to know. No parent ever comes to that point, or even close to it. But it is important that we grasp the enormity of what we're doing and the total interplay of all aspects of the job.

It is necessary to follow the process of visualizing, drawing plans, and then carrying out the plans.

Now that we've considered a rather generalized overall picture and have some rough blueprints in hand, we can move on to examine the building project more closely. But remember, each parent must determine the specifics of his task for himself. This is why it is impossible for me to be utterly specific at times. These are only guidelines to enable you to draw up your own individual plans. Certainly that means work for all of us. But there is no other way for these principles to really become workable.

With that in mind, let's analyze the building process more closely to determine precisely what we can do to successfully complete each individual aspect of the job.

PART II

RAISING THE HOUSE:

The Principles

4

ESTABLISHING PROCEDURES AND PRIORITIES

Creating and Maintaining Conditions for Growth and Love in the Home

In any business, for a certain task to be completed, definite working ground rules must be stipulated and maintained. This is particularly important for people in charge of their own daily schedules who do not have someone above them constantly spelling out exactly what is expected. A self-employed contractor must not only decide what working conditions he is going to maintain, he must also stick to his priorities in order for his job to be finished. He must decide what time to begin work each day, how long to take for lunch, which things to concentrate on and which to reserve for later, how many people to hire, and how much he expects to accomplish in a given period of time. Establishing procedures and priorities is the necessary first step toward his being able to maintain the working conditions that will see him through to the end of his job.

Children—High Priority or Sideline?

Parents are in much the same boat—there is no one telling us exactly what to do, keeping us in line. The effective parent, like the builder, must recognize this aspect of his responsibility and consciously institute some basic priorities into his family structure—procedures and working conditions that will enable him to work efficiently toward his goal.

Most parents do not realize this and therefore do not do it. Some order their lives by wrong priorities and their children are the ones who pay the price. Many become parents without having thought through the implications in advance. They may have given some attention to finances or to the time and energy that will be demanded for a while. Ordinarily, however, there has not been a significant level of thought given to consider what they hope to accomplish through parenthood—what they want to build into their child, what they hope him to become, what long-range vision they have for his life.

For too many parents, often including Christian ones, children are a side benefit to complement one's life, ministry, marriage, and the accomplishment of other goals. When this is the case there is not the intensity of vision poured into the child's life day-by-day. A parent's thoughts center about the immediate rather than the long-range nature of their molding influence over him. A child grows and matures, therefore, without a careful plan guiding the process. Each day comes and goes and he grows a little older. But his parents have no overall objective guiding their actions.

Although this is usually the way parenting is carried out, it is not effective nor is it proper in light of the Scriptures. A glance through Proverbs or a look at Moses' commands to Israelite parents will show that God meant parenthood to be a well thought out priority (Deut. 4:9, 6:7; Prov. 22:6, 23:12-13). And it is indeed possible to build the house of your child's spirit so that your vision of him is attained. To do so requires two things.

It requires first of all that you do indeed have a clear objective in your mind. Your goal is not clouded and is ever before you. A builder must often tack up his blueprints in front of him even as he is working. His mental eyes are always focused on the finished product. Every nail, every brick, every cut, points toward that end result. He is "locked-in" on his faith-picture. Parents too must tack up their blueprints.

Secondly, it is imperative that you decide exactly what things will contribute toward reaching that goal. Priorities must be clearly defined. In order for your child to mature as you would have him, you will discover that certain things are absolutely vital. Those you must set as high priorities and see that they are carried out no matter what. Other things, however, will be seen as good but not essential to the carrying out of your plan. They must therefore always yield to the high priority items whenever there is a potential conflict. You must, in other words, carefully analyze your life, seeking to become aware of those activities that contribute toward the growth and maturing of your child and those that do not. And in that process will always be the question, "What is it that I most want to accomplish in the life of my child? Where am I headed as a parent?"

The first and most trying of such priority decisions is usually the question, "Where does my relationship with my child fit in with my other concerns in life?" For men, especially, a child is often not as high on the list as one's vocation, one's ministry, one's career advancement, one's Bible study, one's leisure time, or other outside activities. But all these substitutes are of lower priority. A man's children must be one of his highest priorities. They should come visibly before a career and ministry and church life. It may be different for Christian men and women who are not parents or whose children are grown, but the most important calling and highest priority in life for Christian parents is to love and nurture their children. Whatever time and energy is left over from being a total parent to your child—that's the time to be used for other commitments and callings God has given you. Many Christians have this order of priorities backwards and their children ultimately suffer.

"But shouldn't one's relationship with God come before everything else?"

Technically speaking, yes, of course. But to use that to justify placing "religious" activities (church life and involvement, Bible study, prayer, witnessing) on a higher level than our children in the scale of time allotment and values is to miss the true meaning of our relationship with God. For when we are faithfully loving and serving both God and our families the two are inseparably bound together. Only in the most rare cases does God ever require a choice between the two. If we feel such a choice is called for, more than likely we are on the brink of actually losing both.

To make your children one of the supreme priorities in life makes necessary some very difficult commitments. While it is relatively simple to paint a grandiose mental picture of our relationship with our child, when it comes down to the nitty-gritty of daily living, many other more immediately attractive options are always ready to assert themselves. To successfully reaffirm the importance of our child's life and squash the rearing heads of lesser priorities demands first of all that each parent has made a conscious decision to accept the charge God has given to him. No one ever becomes a good parent by accident. You must make that decision—a binding one—to make the raising of your child preeminent among your activities. And that is no easy decision to make, for it will involve every area of life. It means letting go of some things that have previously been key interests in your life.

As difficult as it is for Christians to see, this "letting go" sometimes involves seemingly very worthy spiritual things. Before I was married I spent a great deal of time reading, studying my Bible, researching through various reference works, and discussing with other Christians many aspects of the Christian life. Getting married immediately cut down the amount of time I had to spend with others because my wife and I had responsibility to spend that time with each other. But even then we still both did a lot of reading; one year we read some 150 books.

When our children came along, however, that changed drastically. During our boys' preschool years we would be lucky to read a book once every two months. My once well-used *Strong's Exhaustive Concordance* gradually collected three years' dust alongside my other semi-retired books on the shelf. Certainly there is a part of me that misses the time I used to have to devote to such study, but I have chosen this alignment of priorities and will never go back on it. For the man who has not made such a conscious decision there will always be an underlying tension from the pull of various competitors for his time.

A family shrinks one's available day. If you thought before you didn't have enough hours in a day, a commitment to your family is going to compound the problem. As your children grow they will need more and more of your premium, quality time. And you must give it to them. Your priority decision demands it. Being faithful here means increasingly less time for outside things.

But this is only the beginning. Making the decision and giving your children large amounts of time are only the first two demands you will face. From that point on, self-sacrifice, wearing a hundred different faces, will confront you daily. A parent's relationship with his child is much like a man's long-shot investment in a small, unknown company. The immediate return is hardly visible. It is years before the rewarding results are ever realized. Like a young company in its struggling years, a child is so easy to underestimate and overlook. There are so many things to get done *now*—advancement, schooling, job success, church work, and ministry. It is almost ironic that the years when a child needs his parents the most are the very years when other demands are heaviest as well. It is easy to rationalize what seems a pressing need to put our relationships with our children "on hold"—just for a while. We think it can easily wait. Their needs, when intruding upon our involved schedule, appear to be so small, so impetuous, so rash, so easy to overlook.

But a child does not have time to wait. Daily he is growing, maturing, mastering new skills, gaining new attitudes about life and his relationship with us. Our child is learning to cope with life with or without us. If we are consistently unresponsive, busy, unapproachable, he will eventually turn away. We may think his needs and emotions can wait. But we are mistaken. Children will not wait forever. If at present we'd rather they didn't bother us we will certainly be granted our wish. Before many years they won't even want us around.

For the parent, however, who learns to put his other appointments and concerns on hold in order to give himself totally to his child, the payoff will come in a big way. The "young company" in which we have invested the years of our lives turns out to be a multi-million dollar corporation. And ours has been the unparalleled opportunity to invest in it right from the beginning. There couldn't have been a wiser use of our time and energy. There couldn't have been a wiser ordering of our priorities than to have invested wholeheartedly in the life of our child in the small moments and activities of each day. How foolish to have such an opportunity and to let it pass by.

There is a high price attached to such an investment to be sure. Priority selection always implies you will have to say *no* to forty things to be able to give an unqualified *yes* to the one most important thing. A commitment to our child demands that sort of sacrifice. And it is a price that must be paid during the most productive years of our lives, during our child's most malleable years. It cannot be put off till later. With children there is no later. The investment must be made now or there is none to make.

But though the price is high, so is the return. We can see our vision of our child gradually blossom and mature as he grows. Ordering our lives in such a way that we have the time to invest in him is the first step of our part in the process.

Tough Decisions and Daily Perception of the True Order

For a man who is highly success-oriented it is an exceedingly difficult task to sacrifice some of his ambition in order to devote more attention to his children. Don't think this sort of mentality is not found in Christian men. It is. God built into man an urge, a drive, a compulsion to succeed and produce and achieve. It need not be a monetary thing at all. What can match the excitement of a Christian for the work God has given him to do? A man's goal may be to become a school administrator, to be a successful businessman, to start a Christian radio station, or to reach the world for Christ. And such visions consume the men who hold them with the same totality as the drive to be a millionaire does a worldly executive. Though it can, of course, be perverted, this basic drive is God-given. The vision which keeps a man up nights is the same vision which compelled Paul to travel over half the world to tell people about Jesus.

Usually by the time a man finds himself with a family and facing the immense needs of his children, he is just reaching the point in his career and ministry where some major decisions are being called for. These decisions affect the course of his entire future. A tremendous commitment is usually required of men at this point in their lives. It becomes easy to start living in two worlds. A man can become so involved with his job that his family life begins to take second position. Often such a man is caught in what he hopes is a "temporary" squeeze where something has to give. The child's needs will have to wait "just awhile" until this little hump in the road is passed. Then there will be more time.

This is where the nitty-gritty of priority selection becomes tough. All men face these questions, from the executive to the schoolteacher to the seminary student to the laborer. Children just do not fit very well into a demanding outside schedule and a "to do" list. The man who has placed a higher value on his career advancement or ministry simply will not have the time and energy left to do an effective job as a father. It is not an easy matter to be recognized as highly successful in some field and a successful parent at the same time.

It is not impossible. But to do so requires concentrated and tenacious scrutiny of goals, objectives, and the ordering of one's energy. It requires frequently saying *no*. It may require sacrifice of the degree of achievement that had once been sought in a particular field. Anything of supreme worth demands this level of sacrificial decision-making. I have several friends who are in serious training hoping to make the Olympic Games national team. The self-sacrifice they choose is enormous.

Parenthood is easily just as strenuous. You cannot be an effective parent who reaches the goal shown on the blueprints without letting go of some other very important things in your life. It just isn't possible. There isn't enough day, or enough of you, to go around.

The process can be painful, especially to begin with. But the right choices yield great satisfaction and fulfillment. You are constantly molding your child by such choices. When the beautiful expression of your love which is your child matures and comes to life spiritually, your priorities will be seen to have been well ordered. Your children and your own life will have been fulfilled according to God's standards.

> It is said of Boswell, the famous biographer of Samuel Johnson, that he often referred to a special day in his childhood when his father took him fishing. The day was fixed in his adult mind, and he often reflected upon many of the things his father had taught him in the course of their fishing experience together. After having heard of that particular excursion so often, it occurred to someone much later to check the journal that Boswell's father kept and determine what had been said about the fishing trip from the parental perspective. Turning to that date, the reader found only one sentence entered: "Gone fishing today with my son; a day wasted."[1]

In evaluating this significant historical footnote, one cannot criticize Boswell's father too readily. Certainly, according to his son, the time spent that day was quality time and highly significant. But it is interesting that Boswell's father was so totally unaware of the process in which his son was being

[1] Taken from *The Effective Father*, by Gordon MacDonald, Copyright 1976 by Tyndale House Publishers, Inc., Wheaton, Ill. p. 79. Used by Permission.

shaped and molded for life. We may assume on the basis of the time they spent together that he did make some sacrifices for his son, but it is also clear that his priorities were out of order. What was waste in his eyes was in reality one of the most important days of his entire life in terms of its lasting impact.

Unless our eyes are constantly focused to perceive the true order of our priorities, we too will fall into this mistaken judgment concerning the things we spend our time on. The things that so urgently press in on us are in reality far less important than our child's need for special treatment during his early formative years. The other things can wait; our child's emotional development cannot.

A man's goals relative to his career and ministry and a woman's priorities relative to whatever aspirations she has independent of her home and children, therefore, must be clearly defined. Husband and wife must face the question squarely, "Which comes first?" Failure to look the question straight in the eye and demand an answer will ultimately result in frustration. Pat answers provide no help here. The daily decisions required are real and often complex. A host of outside factors will continually demand attention.

Soon after our first two children were born, I encountered several business decisions that occupied my thoughts and energy almost totally. Our store was at a crucial stage. We were considering several aspects of serious expansion which would involve years of commitment, new personnel, and many thousands of dollars. Planning and thinking through these changes, considering what direction our business was to move in future years, was draining. It took a lot from me emotionally.

I know I was supposed to be involved in these things at the time even though our children were young. It was the task God had given me to do. My choices were not between one good thing and one bad; one spiritual and one carnal. No, it was two things of great importance and worth which occupied my thoughts. I found coming home in the evening and trying to shift gears to be extremely difficult.

Even though I had tried to make a thorough decision regarding the priority of my children in my life, it remained difficult to carry out that decision in light of everything else I faced. I found it to be a decision I had to make and reaffirm daily.

I often found myself falling into the trap of thinking, "If I just give the store my all for the next five years, *then* when the boys are at an age when they need me more, I'll be able to spend more time with them; *then* we'll be in sound enough financial shape so that I won't have to spend fifty-plus hours a week at the store; *then* I'll be able to give them more of myself."

It is a deceitful line of thinking, yet it often seduces me. It traps many fathers. But twenty years later, the man who gives in to such a subtle suggestion, probably successful and perhaps wealthy, one day realizes that his children are grown and that their lives have passed him by. He wakes up to the fact that he has spent the most important years of his child's life chasing after the wrong things. His priorities were backwards.

"Where did the years go?" he asks himself.

But it is too late. They are gone forever. Tomorrow never comes for the man who continually says, "Tomorrow I'll do better." Tomorrow the little baby won't need to be held, the toddler won't be scampering into your lap, the five-year-old won't be asking you to read him a story, the ten-year-old won't be asking you to play ball, the teen-ager won't be asking your counsel about school and the dance and making the team. By the time "tomorrow" comes, the young man who only "yesterday" was your little baby will have made many of his major decisions in life and gone his way.

When I first read the following lyrics I was so convicted by them that I quoted them in my first book. They still convict me:

My child arrived just the other day;
He came to the world in the usual way.
But there were planes to catch and bills to pay;
He learned to walk while I was away.
And he was talkin' 'fore I knew it, and as he grew
He'd say, "I'm gonna be like you, Dad,
You know I'm gonna be like you."

And the cat's in the cradle and the silver spoon,
Little boy blue and the man in the moon.
"When you comin' home, Dad?"
"I don't know when, but we'll get together then;
You know we'll have a good time then."

My son turned ten just the other day;
He said, "Thanks for the ball, Dad, come on, let's play.
Can you teach me to throw?" I said, "Not today
I got a lot to do." He said, "That's okay."
And he walked away, but his smile never dimmed,
And said, "I'm gonna be like him, yeah,
You know I'm gonna be like him."

Well he came home from college just the other day;
So much a man I just had to say,
"Son, I'm proud of you; can you sit for a while?"
He shook his head and said with a smile,
"What I'd really like, Dad, is to borrow the car keys;
See you later; Can I have them please?"

I've long since retired, My son's moved away;
I called him up just the other day.
I said, "I'd like to see you if you don't mind."
He said, "I'd love to, Dad, if I can find the time.
You see my new job's a hassle and the kids have the
flu,
But it's sure nice talking to you, Dad;
It's sure been nice talking to you."

And as I hung up the phone it occurred to me—
He'd grown up just like me.
My boy was just like me.

And the cat's in the cradle and the silver spoon,
Little boy blue and the man in the moon.
"When you comin' home, son?"
"I don't know when, but we'll get together then, Dad,
We're gonna have a good time . . . then."[2]

Even though it often seems "the break I need is just around the corner," I must nevertheless daily squelch the pressures that would turn me from my top priority. The "*Then* I'll be free . . ." thought pattern is an illusive dream. It will never happen. If you don't give yourself now, you never will.

Tiny things that crop up throughout the day form the pattern. Adhering to your predetermined priority decision to place your children first often means setting aside things that you can do later for the sake of your child right now. You must constantly gear yourself to recognize the true differences in value between one of your own interests versus a few moments spent on

[2] Copyright 1974 by Story Songs, Ltd. All rights reserved. Used by permission of Warner Brothers Music.

something with your son or daughter. Don't lose sight of what is really going on like Boswell's father did. You are chiseling away at what will one day be a beautiful statue. And your most significant progress is made in the small "insignificant" moments of each day.

Careers and outside involvements threaten to pull fathers away from their children; and, as Dr. James Dobson points out, it is fatigue and time pressure which can most severely undermine a mother's attitude and cause her to turn her eyes from her children. Urgent pressures will devastate a relationship unless there is a conscious decision made daily to keep them in their proper perspective.

> Dad is holding down three jobs and he huffs and puffs to keep up with it all. Mom never has a free minute, either. Tomorrow night, for example, she is having eight guests for dinner and she only has this one evening to clean the house, go to the market, arrange the flowers for the centerpiece, and put the hem in the dress she will wear. Her "to do" list is three pages long and she already has a splitting headache from it all. She opens a can of "Spaghetti-O's" for the kids' supper and hopes the troops will stay out of her hair. About seven p.m. little Larry tracks down his perspiring mother and says, "Look what I just drawed, Mom." She glances down and says, "Uh huh," obviously thinking about something else.
>
> Ten minutes later, Larry asks her to get him some juice. She complies but resents his intrusion. She is behind schedule and her tension is mounting. Five

minutes later he interrupts again, this time wanting her to reach a toy that sits on the top shelf of the closet. She stands looking at him for a moment and then hurries down the hall to meet his demand, mumbling as she goes. But as she passes his bedroom door, she notices that he has spread his toys all over the floor and made a mess with the glue. Mom explodes. She screams and threatens and shakes little Larry till his teeth rattle.

Does this drama sound familiar? It should, for "routine panic" is becoming an American way of life. . . . There was a time when a man didn't fret if he missed a stagecoach; he'd just catch it next month. Now if a fellow misses a section of a revolving door he's thrown into despair! But guess who is the inevitable loser from this breathless life style? It's the little guy who is leaning against the wall with his hands in the pocket of his blue jeans. He misses his father during the long day and tags around after him at night, saying, "Play ball, Dad!" But Dad is pooped. Besides, he has a briefcase full of work to be done. Mom had promised to take him to the park this afternoon but then she had to go to the Women's Auxiliary meeting at the last minute. The lad gets the message—his folks are busy again. So he drifts into the family room and watches two hours of pointless cartoons and reruns on television.

Children just don't fit into a "to do" list very well. It takes time to introduce them to good books—it takes time to fly kites and play punch ball and put

> together jigsaw puzzles. It takes time to listen once more to the skinned-knee episode and talk about the bird with the broken wing. These are the building blocks of self-esteem held together with the mortar of love.[3]

Prerequisites for Growth

Once you have made some serious decisions regarding your family priorities it comes time to determine how to best structure your family's life style and schedule so that your efforts to follow these priorities are most effective. What conditions can you create in your home that will energize your children with all the creativity and excitement about life that God placed within them? What can you do to stimulate their growth so that it attains the full potential that lies dormant deep in their spirits?

As a diligent parent you must act as both an executive who sits down at a planning table and thinks through what directions a certain company is going to move, and the subordinate who later carries out the executive's plan. You have to fill yourself with thoughts and visions and plans and strategies, and carry them out as well. This is an especially difficult task for a mother whose entire day it seems is taken up with just keeping even with all the daily chores. Therefore, a husband and wife must work together, especially in the area of planning and strategy development for their family.

Even if your priorities are all straight, you will not necessarily attain your goal unless you have a detailed plan. A husband and wife must continually be seeking out the conditions for their home which will insure an atmosphere of progress toward the common goal. Conditions will always be changing as well;

[3] *Hide or Seek* by Dr. James Dobson. Fleming H. Revell Co., Old Tappan, N.J. pp. 53-55. Used by permission.

constant reevaluation, thought, prayer, and discussion is vital. Conditions must be sought out; they must then be brought about in the family; and they must be maintained. Parents must be always on the alert for any outside interference which threatens to jeopardize these conditions for a stable and healthy family structure.

This seeking out, creating, and maintaining of family conditions that will maximize growth and potential development is one of a parent's most critical responsibilities. It should be going on uninterrupted throughout the day. "How does this condition, that situation, or that relationship affect my child?" If a certain effect is negative, "What can I do to alter conditions so that he will be able to function more contentedly?"

Love

The primary condition that must exist in every home and which must be maintained at all costs is one marked with affection, love, and affirmation toward every child. This must be the dominant atmosphere. This is the one thing that will enable a child to live at peace with himself in later years. Everything you do must spring from a heart that is genuinely in love with your child and demonstrates that love at every opportunity in a thousand different ways.

That doesn't mean buying things for him. Children need physical attention—kisses, hugs, holding, cuddling, stroking, handholding. Of course a teen-ager won't want it in the same way a six-year-old will. But the need remains regardless of age. You must find ways to properly express it according to their needs. Keep in mind, too, that love is not primarily an emotion, it is an action. If your feelings don't always prompt you with affection for your child, that has nothing to do with it. Your way is still clear. You must do it.

Positiveness

Accompanying these physical manifestations, children need a positive atmosphere around them. They need praise and constant affirmation. The normal routine of your home should be so filled with the living principles of God and be so positive, so encouraging, so uplifting, so pleasant, so satisfying, and so rewarding that all the outside influences a child receives are pallid in comparison. Your all-time best insurance against later rebellion is a home life your child enjoys and will not think of rebelling against.

Control of Environment

Perhaps one of the most difficult commitments for a parent to make (and so few therefore make it) is the decision to assume full responsibility for control of his child's ever-expanding environment. It is natural for parents to try to control the conditions in the home as much as possible but to let the neighborhood, the school, the church, the playground, and other homes teach a child whatever they will. It is not customary for a parent to try to exercise control over these "outside" influences. However, the older a child grows, the more of his time is spent out and away, with neither parent nor family rules and boundaries governing actions and attitudes and the influences that surround him. Naturally parents cannot traipse around after their twelve-year-old wherever he goes. That would place an unbearable strain on the relationship overnight.

The sort of control that is needed here might best be called an "inconspicuous influence" rather than "control." For control in parent-child relationships often implies total dominance—authoritative, almost dictatorial subjection.

Assuming responsibility for your child's environment does not imply the control of a puppeteer over his puppet via the strings. It much more closely resembles the subtle, underlying preeminence of a highly skilled teacher whose students are scattered throughout the room all working individually on a multitude of different projects. There may be a good deal of noise at times, the children are so engrossed in their work they hardly even remember their teacher is present. To the untrained eye it might even appear to be chaotic.

But not so. Though there is great freedom, this teacher is in control of the entire scene—the environment. She has specifically chosen each student's particular project to perfectly match both his capability and his need to be stretched into the new. She knows just what his total need is. Her influence is guiding them all every moment.

When a parent stops to consider what a major portion of his child's decisions and actions are made in the absence of either parent, it becomes easy to see why children often move in directions they would not have expected. The parent with a strict plan for the godly maturing of his child cannot afford to have him casually taught by people he doesn't even know—other children, parents, teachers, accidental acquaintances, and even pastors and Sunday school teachers. Much can be picked up by children carelessly in this way, things the thoughtful parent should scrutinize first.

Critics would quickly argue, "But by trying to control everything he does, everything he sees, everything he hears you'll just tie him to your apron strings. He's got to get out, mingle in the world, learn things for himself." Assuming control of a child's environment is not a popular stance for a Christian parent to take in this day of relativistic thinking when everyone supposedly must "find out what's right for himself," including children. Such thinking will hound you, right in the ranks of your own friends, family, and church.

And admittedly there is a danger that you will make your child overly dependent on you. Therefore you must exercise this parental responsibility with *great* care and thoughtfulness. Assuming control for your child means doing what is for his best. And that is often releasing him to be on his own. Assuming control of your child's environment does not mean dominating him; it means controlling the process of his gaining his independence rather than simply letting him acquire it accidentally.

In short, I intend to screen what my children absorb, and at what age, and how fast. I want to be the one whose influence determines the rate at which their ever-widening and expanding environment extends beyond the family boundaries. Much of this task will be in giving independence a little at a time, in being aware of his need to learn to relate with friends and peers apart from the family, in giving him the confidence to take his stand in society. I want to be a part of my child's life—from popularity and peer pressure to clothes and schools and toys and money. Only through total involvement can I possibly be in the position of the skilled teacher whose alert eye is constantly roving the classroom looking for any sign of trouble.

Communication

To accomplish the goal of communication will never be easy. It will make parenting very demanding. A total mental awareness is necessary. It takes an involved and concerned parent, one who communicates with his child about everything that goes on during the day. In the final analysis, honest and complete communication is really the only way to maintain control over your child's environment once he gains more mobility. Your child will pick up many things from outside the home; that cannot be avoided. And many of these things will in themselves be negative. But if the lines of communication are always open and if your son or daughter feels a freedom to share openly and candidly what he has seen or experienced, without fear of any adverse action on your part, then such experiences can be converted into positive learning situations where the family principles are reinforced.

Attentiveness

It takes a keenly focused eye for a parent to know when to take an authoritarian stance or to stand back and allow his child to experiment with freedom. A parent must be sensitive to each family member's own inner needs and continually look ahead for opportunities to meet those needs. Neither a father nor a mother can be effective in their respective roles by simply waking every morning to face another day as it comes. There must be a method of seeking out and then creating opportunities rather than trying to cope with them haphazardly.

Family experiences and parental responses must be carefully weighed and chosen so that a healthy fusion builds and matures your children. This implies foresighted attention to everything your family does and says; every response, every situation is significant. Every family experience (from an outing to a simple everyday breakfast) should make some contribution to this process of growth and must be viewed in that light. There will be times when you will create experiences—trips, games, discussions, activities, special occasions, a weekend of camping—where learning will take place because the family is tightly bound together. Every moment is an opportunity to build and develop a child's unquenchable spirit. Continued exposure to various experiences, coupled with our own responses during them, shape and motivate our children.

Sensitivity

Sensitivity is a key trait in every dynamic parent. This implies a totality of awareness of what is going on inside your child and an effort to share it with him—easing the burdens and participating in the joys. Sensitivity means listening. But listening is often more than what we do with our ears. Good listening requires a consciousness of spirit finely tuned toward the emotions of our child. Like a shortwave radio operator, we need to make constant readjustments as we sensitize our ear to notice slight changes inside our child.

Listening

Our spiritual ear must ever be attending to the small things. Good listening takes rigorous discipline on the part of the parent. And practice! The facility to hear one's family (both the things they say and the things they don't say) must be developed—through practice, by spending time alone with each child regularly, through prayer and constant evaluation. Parents must listen for questions, moods, frustrations, doubts, and joys. They must know when to jump in with both feet (and how to do so) and when to tread more gently. Their responses during the critical times in their child's life will greatly add to his inner emotional security.

Time With Each Child

The older children grow, the more private time they will need with each parent, time to discuss and question everything that is on their minds. They need both parental perspectives; both father and mother must be capable of providing quality time in huge chunks. Unless parents have previously made this a priority, such time will be extremely hard to find. Time is never free; it must be carved out of existing activities.

Stability

Quality time spent between parent and child, coupled with the effective listening and wise spiritual attentiveness of a parent, is one of the most stabilizing of all childhood influences. There are many times in the up-and-down life of a child when an extra dose of security is needed. Such intimate times with a parent does wonders to solidify his world once again and reassure him. Children must always sense an equilibrium undergirding their lives. Parents provide this, and must be constantly aware of this aspect of their role.

One of the most significant needs of a child's spirit is to sense that his parents are in control. He needs to know there is a hand steadying what to him is often a wobbly world. To begin with, this end is met simply because parents are *there*. They are big, they are strong, they know things. It must seem they are always awake, they provide food and clothes, they answer questions—they are utterly in charge. To a very young child parents are like God—all-knowing, all-powerful.

But it does not take long for a child to begin to grow and acquire knowledge and insights of his own. Once this process begins it will continue rapidly for many years. Parents will have to prove in an increasing number of ways to the deep spirit of their child that they are still "in charge" when the boat is rocking if they intend to keep their child secure and at peace with his surroundings. As a child's life increases in complexity, he becomes ever more aware when his parents occasionally lose their grip on circumstances.

Evaluation

One of the key ways a parent must learn to maintain a firm hold in rough family water is to practice constant evaluation of the current situation and where it is headed. Parents must be aware of the meaning of the present; they must also attempt to anticipate future situations. Strange as it may seem, children also gain tremendous security from watching their parents handle their mistakes. Children do not want perfect parents, but parents who can demonstrate to them how to humbly face mistakes and problems and then lead them through and past them. They learn for themselves by seeing it happen. Their spirits find solidarity in knowing, not that their parents are perfect, but that they can admit mistakes and know how to turn them into positive experiences.

An important condition for family growth, then, is being able to stand back and evaluate what is happening. All fathers and mothers make horrendous blunders with their children. God made children tough. They can endure a lot with no permanent scars. It is one of the wonders of life. Parents must accept this and then learn to reassess their behavior or the behavior of their child. Apologies will be called for, as well as prayer together and discussion: forgiveness must be an integral part of every family relationship. To see his parents on their knees or deep in thought is reassuring to a child. He must see that though his parents do not have every answer to every problem or situation, they turn to God for the answers. A parent who makes occasional mistakes but who is able to conquer them does not devastate a child; it shows him his first picture of God's grace at work.

Spiritual Convictions

Such spiritual convictions must be solid in our home for us to be capable of living out the priorities we establish. By vaguely trying to order our families according to God's Word without down-to-earth specifics about what we actually allow in our families, we will not show our children the reality of God's laws in daily life. Forgiveness must work between us in the nitty-gritty of relationships; grace must be seen as what allows us to stand tall and go on after having blown it; our love must demonstrate God's love to our children and must not be conditional; the thankfulness that flows to God from our hearts must be in all circumstances, not just pleasing ones. Our children are always watching. If we carefully work into the growth of our family beliefs and convictions based on God's Word which we consistently demonstrate and from which we will not compromise, then our children will find security in a definable and predictable order. And they will grow to respect those convictions and to begin living them on their own.

These priorities we must think through; and these prerequisites for optimum family growth form the basis for the conditions we must maintain to carry out the job before us. With this beginning, it is time to tackle the actual building of the house of our child. It is time to don our overalls, sharpen our saws, dust off our hammers, and go to work. With these working procedures before us, we are ready to begin to build.

5

LAYING THE FOUNDATION—PART 1

*The Discipline Of Boundaries**

When a builder stands gazing at a vacant plot of ground on which he intends to build a house, he has but one thing in mind as his starting point. Though he may be excited about the completed structure and may have that wonderful picture firmly in his mind, he knows before anything else happens he must build forms and pour concrete—he must lay a solid foundation on which to build. This foundation provides maximum strength to support the sheer weight of the building, and it also provides the initial outline of the outer walls of the house-to-be. The foundation gives a first look (however incomplete) at the outline of the final home.

There are two components of a strong and effective foundation in a child's life—discipline and training. They are separate only in the same way that the gravel and cement are separate components in the concrete mixture that undergirds a building. Once the concrete is mixed, poured, and dried they become totally one. You can no longer even talk about them

* NOTE: Much of the material in this chapter, as well as some from Chapters 4 and 7, first appeared in my book *A Christian Family in Action*, published and copyrighted in 1977 by Bethany Fellowship, Inc., Minneapolis, Minn. (in chapters 5, 10, 11, and 12 of that book) and is here used by permission.

separately. The strength of the foundation comes from the combination of the gravel and cement when mixed with water just as the discipline and training you provide in your child's life, when mixed with the water of love, becomes his foundation.

It is therefore almost misleading to try to discuss discipline and training separately, for they can never be separated in practical reality. Nevertheless, to do so here will be beneficial in giving us a better understanding of how they both function. For though the gravel and cement are inseparable, they still perform different jobs in the concrete. Discipline and training also, though inseparable, address different needs in a child's nature and we need to understand these needs thoroughly in order to lay a solid foundation.

In this chapter, therefore, we will investigate the foundation provided by discipline and in the next the corresponding training necessary. In families of today's society we are witnessing the results of parents trying to build magnificent homes for their children without proper foundations. Just as no builder would try to build a home without all the necessary ingredients in his foundational materials, it is impossible to build love, self-esteem, interest, imagination, motivation, and potential without both discipline and training.

In the majority of today's homes, discipline as a vital element in a parent's relationship with his child is highly underestimated. It is like trying to mix concrete with an improper cement-to-gravel ratio. Yet strong discipline itself does not necessarily insure a strong foundation. For years children were raised according to very strict measures, most of which would be considered unthinkable today: speaking only when spoken to, receiving ruthless whippings for the slightest disobedience, given heavier workloads than a child could reasonably bear, etc. The results of such over-discipline were as unfortunate as the results of today's often too lenient methods.

In order for a foundation in the life of a child to be strong and supportive, it must be laid carefully and lovingly with an eye constantly looking ahead toward the rest of the process. Discipline must be viewed in the total context of the "house" to be built. It is not an answer to anything in itself, but is a base on which to build all sorts of other things. Parents who discipline for discipline's sake are accomplishing nothing. A foundation on an empty lot is worthless if there is no house built on top of it.

A foundation must be strong, well-planned, and solid enough to hold several stories and many rooms. The solid foundation of discipline is necessary for a child to reach the full potential God has for him. Recall Jesus' parable: to build a firm foundation it is necessary to dig down beyond the sand and loose soil to solid bedrock. There is the point where a foundation must begin—on the solid rock of God's Word and instruction and example. What has God taught us regarding discipline?

The Bible tells us that God disciplines those He loves, that discipline is inherent in love, that parents who do not discipline their chilren do not really love them, and that there is no better way to raise a godless child than to withhold discipline from him (Prov. 3:12; Heb. 12:6; Rev. 3:19; Prov. 13:24, 29:15).

Undoubtedly strong words for some twentieth-century ears! Yet their repeated use in God's Word certainly behooves us to investigate more thoroughly what their implications might be in our families today.

Discipline and Training— The Positive and Negative Guidance a Child Needs

Discipline is a word with heavily negative connotations.

Training, on the other hand, seems to have a more positive thrust. Yet they are words which spring from the same source and in that sense can almost be thought of synonomously. Inherent in training is preparation for our children to live in the world as God has commanded we live. God's discipline is the same; it is training for us to live as His children in the ways He has instructed.

In every aspect of life, training is a necessary condition for success. Nothing "left to itself" will grow and mature to its fullest potential. A garden without care will quickly revert to an overrun field. An orchard without pruning will become a collection of fruitless trees. Proper and skilled guidance and care—training—is necessary for potential to be realized in any sphere. An athlete is trained by a coach, a garden by a gardener, a horse by a trainer and jockey, and a train is "guided" by tracks.

God tells us that humans are no different. In fact, the Bible states that if "left to himself" man will become totally depraved. It describes the human heart with these words: "The heart is deceitful above all things, and desperately wicked. . . ." (Jer. 17:9 KJV). In all of God's creation, man has the greatest potential—for good or evil. Therefore, man stands in the greatest need of training and guidance for that godly potential to be realized.

Guidance implies leadership. There must be a guide. And God has established the family to be the institution to supply the necessary guidance, direction, and training for children. He has sovereignly chosen the father, and to a lesser degree the mother, to sustain that leadership and to maintain the vital order in family relationships.

In this role both the father and mother search out ways in which each member of their family can grow to be what God made him to be. Their leadership is designed to bring each of their children (as well as themselves) to the farthest limit of their maturity and potential.

That growth must begin at a very basic level. Newborn children must simply be taught the rules—what to do, what not to do, how to eat and maintain a sleeping schedule, how to move and crawl and investigate. Most of this is, of course, instinctive. Yet parents nevertheless "oversee" the procedure, making certain the child is safe and his needs are met.

Before long, some actual teaching begins. They learn to walk and say a few words. By the time they are two we are talking with them daily. Elemental conversations are taking place as we show them things, investigate with them. By three and four they are full of questions; by six they are in school and are branching out, growing up.

To begin with it seemed all our training was correctional: saying "no" to everything. But soon teaching and talking was blended in. By the time a child is ten, the process has nearly reversed—we are correcting very little and teaching a great deal.

Discipline and training, therefore, provide us with a twofold look at the way we guide our children, easing them into the mainstream of life. There is the negative aspect in which we must correct, reprove, and punish. And there is the positive aspect in which we lead and teach and share.

Both are essential in a strong foundation.

Gordon MacDonald has said of this dual nature in the guidance of our children: "The head of the home—like the Shepherd in Psalm 23—carries a kind of rod and staff: the staff for rescue and pointing direction, the rod for discipline and enforcement. When both are capably used, there is stability in relationships and steady progress in growth. When both are unused or misused, there is drift and deterioration among the shepherd's sheep and the father's family."[1]

Foresighted Punishment—Redemptive and Correctional

One of the sources of the present misunderstanding about discipline has arisen because it is so often exclusively associated with punishment. But this exclusion has led us astray, for punishment is but one aspect of discipline. To get at a more complete definition we must also consider training, its counterpart, and the total context of the leadership in our child's life that we are trying to achieve.

Children must be taught rules and guidelines of life. This is not a negative thing, but a very practical one. The Bible says that humans all have the inherent tendency to stray. Sticking to the rules is something we'd prefer not to do. Obedience is not natural to us. We instinctively will try to find every loophole, every excuse we can, not to obey. Children are this way from the moment they are born.

Therefore the first job for every parent is to introduce his child to the boundaries that exist in life. There are certain rules to follow, certain consequences which result from ignoring them, certain things are right and others wrong. Children must be taught these things.

So discipline is first of all preparatory. Its aim is to teach a child to live and function in a world that has been ordered a certain way and which must, in certain broad areas, be conformed to.

As children grow older and become gradually accustomed to the basic foundational boundaries that exist in life, their parents can guide and lead them in more sophisticated ways. To begin with, however, a disciplinary foundation must be laid through

[1] Taken from *The Effective Father*, by Gordon MacDonald, Copyright 1976 by Tyndale House Publishers, Inc., Wheaton, Ill. p. 23. Used by permission.

dedicated and prayerful use of correctional tools. The foundation is built largely with the rod, but as children grow the staff becomes the predominant instrument for their training.

In a child's early years correctional punishment is the key to effective disciplinary training. Punishment can be of two kinds: judicial and redemptive. Judicial punishment is a judgment or response to an action. Many parents discipline by punishing the wrongs of their children. There is an action followed by a punishment. And that is the end of it.

Redemptive punishment, on the other hand, is foresighted. The punishment is not simply a response nor an end in itself. The foresighted parent is always looking ahead. His punishment is geared toward a lesson which will be valuable later on. It is corrective, positive, and redemptive in nature.

God's love for His people is never more clearly seen than in His continued use of this redemptive, corrective punishment. Though in the moment of pain this form of discipline might seem just as intense, the heart behind it is one of tenderness and love. God wants to perfect and purify His people and bring them to full maturity. To accomplish this end He must often discipline, correct, and punish us, not merely as a judgment against us but in order to teach us the ways that will ultimately bring us the greatest joy and fulfillment in life.

This is the punishment employed by parents who would effectively provide their children with a strong foundation of obedience. Their punishment is meant to teach their children valuable lessons, particularly in obedience. A child spanked for getting too close to a fire is not judged for some moral wrongdoing, but to teach him a boundary that will protect him in the future. It is a carefully planned, loving response looking ahead to a useful and important preparation for life.

This is the essence of discipline in a child's first several years—using this correctional form of punishment to train him, to provide him the guidance he needs to learn about life. God's ways, like those of a wise parent, are always purposeful. So must be the discipline of our children. Quick and thoughtless responses to childish mistakes are inadequate.

It is easy for parents to make the mistake of punishing their children without having the corrective and redemptive long-range viewpoint clearly in mind. In the heat of emotion they can lash out in anger when they have been inconvenienced or when one of their favorite things has been destroyed or damaged. But such thoughtless punishment (even if it seems justified) has no place in child training. Discipline must *always* be carried out by a parent in full control of himself, never impulsively or in anger. Inconsistent punishment can begin deep resentments inside the heart of a child.

I know that my effectiveness as a father is in direct proportion to the extent that I am unselfish, calm, consistent, and loving in my discipline.

Learning to Live within Boundaries

Understanding the two kinds of punishment is but the beginning of disciplinary training. The positive implementation of discipline into a child's life requires guidelines concerning when such correction is needed; thus the need for clearly recognizable boundaries which outline the limits of acceptable behavior. In a sense, all training revolves around the boundaries a child is surrounded by; they are the essence of a positive program of discipline. A child needs them to feel comfortable and secure, and to learn how far he can and cannot go in certain directions.

God created the world with built-in boundaries. They are for our safety and for our good. To ignore them means certain harm. Before we can teach our child about God's boundaries concerning the greater questions of life, he must become accustomed to the whole prospect of limitations in the smaller scale of his world. We must, therefore, teach him to obey, to curb his own will, to live within the structure of the family as all men must live within the structure of God's order.

As parents then it is our job to establish boundaries for our young children and then do two things. First, give children all the love, affection, encouragement, and praise possible within the confines of those limits, losing no opportunity to build confidence and security into them through our positive approach to everything they do.

Second, it is necessary to strictly enforce the boundaries we set. When they are challenged (by disobeying or by defying our authority) we must see that punishment is promptly given for the action. Spanking therefore becomes necessary in limit enforcement. This is correctional and compassionate punishment in action. Such punishment teaches a valuable lesson about the boundaries in life. It is a lesson that cannot be learned any other way.

Without this twofold approach to the limits you set for your child (building love and security within the limits, disciplining disobedience to the limits) it is impossible to build into a child love and confidence and obedience that will last a lifetime. Without this approach, consistently applied, it will be very difficult for a parent to teach his child about the character of God. For God certainly employs rigid boundaries in everything He does.

The Bible is the story of two kinds of people—those who accepted God's boundaries and lived according to them, and those who rejected God's laws and went their own way. The first people inherited the blessings of God; the latter, the curses. The principle of obeying (or disobeying) established standards, rules, laws, limits, and boundaries pervades all of Scripture.

This makes properly understood discipline emancipating for parents. The basis for discipline is the setting of limits for children. Each set of parents will arrive at their own specific limits for their children. For various parents the limits will be different.

There will, however, be certain universal qualities about all effective limits. In order to work, boundaries must be set in advance and must be clearly understood by the child. A limit must also be specific, not vague. Parents must train themselves to be very clear and to convey exactly what they expect of their child. The younger the child, the more precise must be the language.

It is also important to be keenly aware of a child's awareness, comprehension, and skills. To direct him to do something he cannot accomplish is pointless. Sometimes a child may not grasp the entire message. He must understand and be capable of obeying or the boundaries will not accomplish their purpose.

Most important of all, the limits a parent sets must have the best interests (long-range, foresighted purpose) of his child at their core. Asking children to do things merely for our own convenience is selfish. We are teaching them through our instruction and our limit-setting and enforcement—about ourselves, about life, and about God. Therefore, we must be thoughtful and serious about our responsibility.

Whereas most of the specific limits of parents will be different, certain ones will be universal. The most important is open rebellion or defiance. When a child willfully defies his parent's authority he must be disciplined immediately. Cold, calculating disobedience (stepping across the line while looking you right in the eye) must be met the same way—with painful punishment. Respect for authority and obedience are two absolute guidelines set down by God himself which we must consistently back up. These two limits are of utmost importance.

It is crucial not to set so many limits that you are unable to enforce them properly. It is better to exercise tight control over a half dozen limits than to have thirty you are indecisive on. The only worse thing than having no limits in a family is to have boundaries and rules that are not enforced. Therefore, it is necessary to draw our initial "lines" around our child wide enough so that he has plenty of space to run and play freely without fear of accidentally crossing some line he had forgotten about. The boundaries will not accomplish their purpose if they are so close they inhibit a child. They must be wide, with plenty of room in all directions. But the boundaries signaling the limit to what is allowed, though few in number, must remain solid and visible.

It becomes easy for Christian parents to be deceived at this point. "By being so strict and uncompromising, won't I be somehow failing to love my child?"

Granted, it is not always easy to spank a child you dearly love for something that seems small (which crossing some limits does appear to be). But by giving in to the temptation to "let it go this time," a parent slowly allows himself to become a gentle, sympathetic, understanding, loving father or mother who is totally controlled by his child. Gradually the limits on a child's behavior grow fewer and fewer. There are no constant rules governing his actions. Such giving in and allowing the child to determine his own behavior teaches him the very undesirable lesson that he is his own master. He grows up not understanding authority in the least.

This often comes about from an inadequate understanding of God's character and God's dealing with man. The relationship of a parent with his child is a model of his own relationship with God. And certainly God does not allow us full control. He does not give us all we desire, nor does He allow us to go our own way unhindered. He knows the effect of this would devastate us.

The same is true with children. We do them permanent harm by catering to their every whim and fancy. Just as God sets boundaries concerning how we are to live (boundaries which have definite and predictable consequences if ignored) we must set limits for our children.

God has made us so that our only ultimate joy and satisfaction in life comes by living according to His laws. When we step outside the commandments of God we call a temporary halt to the fulfillment and blessings of life He has for us. It is the same for a child. God made him to thrive in the love and security of a family. A child is most content and happy when he knows exactly what the boundaries are. He wants the lines securely drawn. He does not want to be left on his own, to be totally "free."

When the Boundaries Are Challenged

Why then does a child test the limits time and again? Why does he constantly seem to disobey?

A child may test the limits you have established for two reasons. He may simply be trying to determine to his own satisfaction that they are still there. Or his testing may be the result of insecurity; he may be unsure of exactly what is expected of him and is, therefore, pushing out toward the boundaries, trying to distinguish the point where they cease being flexible and become solid and consistent. He wants to know precisely where they are; he needs to know exactly how far he can legitimately go. If his parents consistently stand firm when he challenges a boundary at a certain point, he knows beyond any doubt what to expect. If they waffle on every decision, insecurity will result from unsure conditions. He will try desperately to find out where his parents will stand firm. *He needs to know.*

If "yes" means maybe, and "no" occasionally means nothing, and commands are not followed through, a child will disobey his parents. He will keep disobeying until he finds exactly where they mean business. This is not caused primarily at first by his inborn rebellion but simply by the insecurity arising out of uncertain conditions. A child needs solid handles in life to hang on to when everything seems out of kilter. His parents' words are one such handle; he has to know what they mean. His seemingly hostile behavior is oftentimes nothing more than an attempt to make his parents define their terms through action. When his parent says "no" and the child disobeys, if nothing happens, he has learned something about his parent's definition of the word "no." So he will try it again and again, if necessary. He is merely seeking a definition. (Such disobedience is not to be confused with defiance, an altogether different case.)

Often the parent finally exclaims in an angry outburst, "I can't understand that boy, he never does a thing I say!" This is a parent with a confused understanding of what is really going on. The needful plea of son or daughter may be going unheeded. Through disobedience he may in reality be trying to say, "I need your love. I need to know where my limits are. I am insecure when I don't know. Those boundaries give me something to hold on to."

When a child does cross a line, it is almost a satisfying thing to be punished. For with the punishment comes the knowledge that the boundary has been found, it is still there. There is security in knowing it has held fast. A child consistently disciplined for disobedience to a clearly defined set of standards is submitted to an authority he knows he can trust. He knows his parents are strong. He knows the meaning of their words. He knows they won't waver, for he has tested them and they have stood the test. There is freedom and love in such obedient submission.

But even such a secure child whose boundaries are rigid and clear and enforced will occasionally disobey just to make certain they are still there. Remember, obedience is for the most part unnatural to us. The most angelic of children have a streak inside them that urges them to cross the line. Part of this is due to the original sin within us all; part of it is the entirely normal need to occasionally check to make sure everything is as it should be—the boundaries are still there and will still be enforced. And if they remain intact and if disobedience continues to be forcefully punished, the child will grow and mature as a happy and obedient and contented child. He is in his proper place in God's family and he knows it. He knows his father and mother are in charge. Later he will find submission to God all the more natural because he has learned to live under the loving and trustworthy authority of his parents.

As a child grows, his need to test the limits becomes less frequent. If parents have laid a solid disciplinary foundation and then remain consistent with their enforcement of the limits as their child matures, testing and resultant punishment should have almost disappeared by the time a child is eight or ten.

Children reared in such a consistent atmosphere will occasionally feel a deep subconscious pang of guilt when *not* disciplined for something they feel they have done wrong. This may not necessarily mean a parent has been inconsistent, he may simply not have felt the incident warranted discipline. Nevertheless, if the child feels in his heart he has crossed the line without having suffered the consequences he will often begin to rebel in more open ways and may finally erupt openly enough to know he will be punished. This is of course a deeply subconscious thing the child is unaware of. He is simply trying to be justly disciplined for what *he* felt deserved it. This is guilt in a primarily healthy sense and is the forerunner of true repentance. It will only show itself in a child who, as a result of the consistency of his parents, is beginning to know right from wrong and can sense the difference.

The Results of Flexible Boundaries

In contrast to the child who is securely surrounded by firm and well-defined limits is the child whose parents have either established no boundaries or else whose boundaries are constantly changing and unpredictable. This occurs as frequently in Christian homes as it does anywhere else; the principle applies regardless. With unpredictable boundaries there can be no consistent training. As a child grows under these conditions he will become increasingly disobedient in a desperate attempt to find a solid, inflexible line he can confidently trust as the limit for his actions. Finding none, he continues to push further and further, appearing more unruly all the time. Such a pattern begins not long after a child leaves the cradle and is in full swing by the time he is three.

Though specific situations and boundaries will change daily, a child's need for a firm parent who recognizes his role as a leader and limit-setter begins at birth. A toddler in charge of his mother is an unfortunate sight to behold as she chases him from one thing to another. She already has much ground to regain if she hopes to train and teach him in the ways of God.

One of the worst consequences of such a pattern is that a child who is forced to live in the instability of drawing his own lines gradually loses his respect for his parents. Disobedience that begins as a simple desire to know where the boundaries are does not end there. The maturing of a child's selfish will is growing daily stronger and is soon a major factor in the process. By the time a child is eight or nine his self-will is in control. What was once the godly attribute of genuinely wanting to submit himself to the authority of recognizable boundaries is all but gone. He now *wants* to be in control and woe to anyone who stands in his way.

There are two deadly effects of leaderless parents in the lives of children. One, they grow up not knowing how to obey and feeling the insecurity of having had no limits to govern them. And two, they lose their respect for others in the process and their own selfishness is vaunted all out of reason. Their disobedience, which began in insecurity—the need to find and live by the limits—after some years hardens into total self-centeredness in all aspects of life. Finally a teen-ager, and then adult, is submitted to no one and cares for no one but himself. The child who has thus controlled his parents loses respect for them because he knows better than anyone that their leadership is spineless. They did not stand up to him, even when he was young. He realizes how easily he twisted and manipulated them. So how can he possibly respect them? They have no backbone.

Such a child is likely to openly demonstrate this disrespect more and more the older he becomes. He slowly begins to reject his parents and everything they stand for. Since the basis for a child's response to authority is born out of his relationship with his parents, a child growing up with no consistent boundaries to guide him learns to disparage everything around him. He mocks authority. It is hardly a wonder he cannot form an adequate picture of God. There has been no loving yet unbending and consistent authority in his background. Such a thing is foreign to him.

With inconsistent application of a parent's authority, words become empty and meaningless because they are not backed up.

In contrast there is an authority (the parent's words) that can be enforced. The boundary, clearly established through years of practice, is simple: "When I tell you to do something, you do it." Of course, there are all sorts of implications to this, such as, "I will not make unreasonable or embarrassing demands on you; I love and respect you as a person; everything I do in one way or another is meant for your ultimate best; I will not make artificial or selfish demands of you."

A consistent parent earns the trust and respect of his child by considerate and loving use of authority. The bottom line, however, always remains solid—"When I tell you something, you heed my words. If you choose to disobey, you will be disciplined. I will enforce what I say. It is for your own good I do so. I love you too much to allow you to disobey and get away with it. I know to tolerate that would do you an injustice in later years as you relate to the world and to God. I *must* teach you to obey. Better you learn from me who loves you, than the hard way on your own. So believe me, if you choose to disobey, you will regret it. My love compels me to back up my words."

Children Must Be Taught Obedience

At the root of such actions by a loving parent is the conviction that a parent is indeed the rightful and appointed one to set boundaries, establish rules, and enforce the limits. Permissive theorists say just the opposite: a child should be free and restrictions must be minimal. They contend that a child should be on an equal footing with his parents who have no right to arbitrarily determine what he can and cannot do.

But such a theory is hardly biblical. From the beginning of time God has worked in the lives of men through authority. Obedience to the established authority has always been required. There are many instances in the Scriptures where disobedience to God's instituted order was severely punished even when the person in authority was wrong or was not walking with God. Obedience was required anyway.

Noah's youngest son was cursed for disrespecting his father who was drunk. Noah was obviously wrong, but he was still God's instituted authority in the home. Ham failed to see the dignity of this authority.

Miriam and Aaron incurred the anger of God for speaking against Moses. God's words to them did not justify Moses' marrying the Ethiopian; for all we know Moses was indeed wrong to marry her. But Miriam and Aaron had spoken against the authority of God and for this they were punished.

David was a man who knew this. His father-in-law, King Saul, was a man who late in life grew more wicked and further from God daily. But David knew the principle of authority. He knew Saul was in the position of the Lord's anointed king and would therefore do him no harm (though he had many occasions to do so) nor speak a word against him. David even killed to defend the integrity of Saul's position because he was so determined to submit himself to it.

In the family it is the father and mother whom God has ordained to be in authority over their children. From the child's perspective, especially in his early years, it does not really matter whether his parents are necessarily right every time. They won't be. They are to be obeyed regardless. The Bible says very bluntly, "Children, obey your parents" (Eph. 6:1). Period. This does not give parents license to abuse the awesome power God has given them. For Paul also exhorts parents, "Fathers, do not irritate your children and provoke them to resentment, but rear them tenderly in the training and admonition of the Lord" (Eph. 6:4). But it does point out the need to teach children obedience, as a thing in itself. We are *required* to teach children to obey and to love them as we do.

God will, of course, judge parents on their consistent use of authority. Keep in mind that these principles of discipline are but one aspect out of many facets of child-raising. We are working on the foundation at present, but we still have an entire house to build. Inconsistent use of the authority God has given us will result in failure in many of the other areas for which we are equally responsible—making a weak foundation. Recognizing, therefore, that we must teach our children to obey, we must proceed with caution, care, and a sense of humility and awe of the great responsibility God has placed in our hands.

As a child grows older, the need for utter and absolute obedience will gradually lessen through the trust he has earned through faithful obedience. We will more and more be able to talk things out with him, listening to alternate points of view, allowing him to share a role in the overall disciplinary and training process. His freedom and responsibility in the family is also growing because of the firm and unwavering foundation of obedience which has been taught in the early years.

This is a model of our relationship with God. He must teach us to obey utterly, asking no questions regarding obedience itself. Then after we have proved ourselves with years of obedience in small matters, He is able to lead us into areas of greater responsibility and freedom in His will. He allows us wider latitude in making decisions and greater positions of decision-making in His work and among His people; He knows our hearts are utterly submitted to His purpose and we would not intentionally do anything that conflicted with His will.

So it must be in the raising of our children. The foundation of total obedient submission must be taught; the rebellious will must be tamed. They then learn and grow and mature as God would have them. Unless their wills are brought into subjugation, they will never mature properly because their wills will forever be trying to go their own way.

A parent who consistently loves his child with this firm attitude and with this godly model ever before him doesn't have to get mad at his child. The rules—absolute obedience to the parent's words—have been laid down well in advance. The child knows exactly what to expect from disobedience: his parents' follow-through. He respects and loves them, knowing they are wiser, stronger, tougher, and more experienced than he is.

Consistent Boundaries—A Parent's Responsibility

When a child does cross the line of disobedience, the stage is set for one of the most significant learning experiences of his lifetime. When he confronts his parents nose-to-nose and says, "I won't!" it is not the time to sit down with him and tell him why he "ought to be a good little boy and do what mommy says." Nor should he be sent to his room without his dinner to pout away the evening. When a young child defies his parent openly, he is really asking, "Who's in charge here, you or me?"

And you must tell him!

You must answer that question conclusively each time it is posed or your child will continue to ask it in increasingly insolent ways. Willful disobedience must be met with physical punishment or it will not sufficiently answer the child's challenge. When spanking is lovingly and consistently carried out at such times, very few future occasions will demand it (once the ground rules of obedience have been laid). Naturally, when a child is two or three, spelling out the boundaries for the first time and enforcing them often requires considerably more than just a few spankings! The child has to learn the boundaries and be able to comfortably function within them. Once the spanking is over, the child can be taken into your arms and you can explain to him why the discipline was necessary. This is the time to shower him with affection for he is emotionally wide open to your love. He needs to see that your love for him is the basis for your discipline.

A child whose parents exercise well-thought-out and reasonable discipline is a contented child. No child really wants to be in charge, despite what his actions would often seem to indicate. God did not give a child the capacity for it. He created him to be "under" wise, loving, consistent, strong leaders who train him up to obey authority so that he can later obey God for the remainder of his life.

When parents back down from that responsibility and do not insist that their children obey, an internal frustration develops in the heart of the child. Though his actions may begin to look disobedient and out of control, inside he is crying out for discipline, rules, guidelines. His spirit knows that a good part of the love he needs is guidance and direction and stable boundaries to show him how to live and obey.

It is a myth that children want to be free, to do whatever they choose, whenever they choose. On their own, children quickly seek out order and routine and rules. Chaos is unnerving to them. A child feels secure when well-defined limits exist about him; there is safety. Children have an inborn sense of order. A newborn child needs to feel tightly wrapped—in arms, in blankets, in pillows. He is insecure if he is left loose with his arms flailing about. School children have been observed to be less secure when no fence surrounds their playing area. The fence provides a sense of security.

Our home is located in town on a corner lot. We recently put in a redwood grape-stake fence to border the lawn toward both the streets. It is a low fence made of only two stakes running lengthwise, one a foot from the ground and another about two feet high attached to upright posts every eight feet. It is an easy matter to crawl under or through, or jump over it. Even though it offers no real protection from the traffic, we noticed a marked change in the play habits of our children on our front lawn. Immediately there seemed to be greater freedom to run and tumble and roll on that section of lawn. Far from inhibiting (as some progressive theorists would say such a thing would do), the boundary of that fence introduced new freedom into the lives of our children.

Not only are limits a source of security for children, the same is true of their need for order, neatness, and predictability. These all point to their innate requirement for security, for the stability which firm boundaries provide. When my wife was teaching first grade she often stood back to behold her class in action at the end of the day. As they were bustling about the room tracking down their books, games, building blocks, construct-o-straws, crayons, and other paraphernalia, their awareness of order and routine was clearly visible.

"That goes on the top shelf, Chris."

"No, James, that book goes on the right, not on the left."

"Kelly, Clinton, where did you put the paints we were using?"

"Here, Rodney, I know where that goes. I'll put it away."

"No, the blocks go in *this* box."

"David, which cupboard did you say the Richard Scarry books were in?"

"Over there to the left, with Dr. Seuss."

"Jimmy, didn't you have the play dough? Where'd you put it?"

They were very exacting, almost ruthless, in their scrutiny of the room before going home. Everything had to be in its proper place. They took pride in its appearance. It was *their* room and it was in order. "And the most amazing thing of all," concluded Judy, when telling me about it for the first time, "is that it's nothing I taught them. It's just natural to them."

Both mental and physical order are necessary in the life of a young child; the physical, to learn obedience; the mental, to learn to use the memory, logic, and imagination.

Often, therefore, it is the little things—family patterns and a home's atmosphere—that lay the groundwork for a child's later response to the boundaries his parents set. Order is often a subjective quality, but children are intuitively aware of it and must sense their limits and restrictions as fitting into a larger system of routine and harmony.

It is unfortunate that often Christian parents consider "train up a child in the way he should go" to mean Sunday school, family devotions, prayer meetings, church attendance, Bible school, religious discussion, and summer church camp. Unless these activities are part of a loving program of discipline—setting boundaries, clearly spelling them out, and then enforcing them—a child will grow up knowing a lot about God while inside he finds himself unable to respect either his parents or the church.

If a child is taught that God must be obeyed but his experience at home tells him that rules are not enforced, it becomes nearly impossible for him to come to an adequate conception of obedience to God. We all need models to help us clarify spiritual principles. That is one reason Jesus came, to act as our model so we could see how life with God is to work. For a child, the model is his parents. If their relationship with him does not demonstrate the very thing they tell him to exhibit toward God, confusion is all that can result. He is told one thing, yet trained differently. Though the exact reasons for it may never surface, the child is in conflict and will feel the tension.

Because his view of parental authority and his respect for it forms the very cornerstone for his later outlook on all authority, the underdisciplined or erratically disciplined child acquires the mistaken attitude that he need ultimately submit to no authority. His father, the church, his teachers, the law, society in general, those he works with, and finally God himself—he thinks he can manipulate and control them all. Permissive parents teach disobedience and rebellion rather than submission and obedience.

Christians instill such rebellion and disrespect just as readily as anyone else whenever God's principles are ignored or overlooked. It is true that actions speak louder than words. Spiritual "words" change nothing. A child must be taught—trained—to obey.

Two Miracle Tools

There are two tools that, when properly and consistently

applied, work wonders in the process of teaching a child obedience. The first is spanking. Numerous Scriptures confirm that God intended spanking to be used in the training of our children. (Proverbs 20:30, 22:15, 23:13-14, and Hebrews 12:6-7 are but a few.) This use of pain is a marvelous teacher; it is one of the things a young child understands best.

It is true that a spanking often seems a harsh measure for the "little" acts of disobedience. But unless one begins at that point, there will be no way to avoid the major clashes later on. The parent whose words carry no accompanying enforcement "rod" gives his child an unbalanced picture of life, which will one day erupt in the open hostility and rebellion of a teen-ager. Adolescence is a composite of twelve to fifteen years of prior training. Anything left unsettled during that time will come to the surface then. A parent who either loses the early confrontations with his child or else pretends not to notice when he is challenged will find later clashes harder to win and conflicts more difficult to resolve.

A spanking is quick and concise. It is over in seconds. There need be no hurt feelings, pouting, hostility, bitterness. Once done, it is over. Like a cut, it heals. It does not grow and fester. The spanking puts an end to the long-term and undying forms of punishment which work more ill in a relationship than they solve.

Once a child reaches three or four and is familiar with most of the boundaries in his still rather limited life, a spanking should be reserved for those moments of defiance—those times a child challenges the boundaries by stepping disobediently across them. By this point it should ordinarily not be used for everyday wrongdoing unless actual disobedience is involved. (The ways to deal with misbehavior other than defiance and disobedience are different.)

A spanking must always be carried out by a parent in complete control, never impulsively or in anger. The guidelines for its use must be consistent and the child must understand those rules as well. His own ability to cope with rules will in large measure come from watching his parents conform to theirs.

Spankings must also be just, never arbitrary. Ordinarily one should not spank a child for an attitude (except that of defiance); it will only make him angrier still without accomplishing any purpose. Parents must have pre-established guidelines for their use of spanking. One of the most important is that it always be done in love. Though it is painful, love must always come across to a child in one way or another.

Punishment, therefore, is inherent in discipline. But punishment (like the spanking) is a tool and as such can be abused and misused. To use this tool wisely, parents must perceive the enormity of their responsibility. Corrective punishment must be implemented to build and redirect wrong actions and attitudes. If incorrectly used it will do nothing but tear down and devastate the spirit of a child. A parent must be highly sensitive to his child's spirit and will. While preserving and building up his spirit, he must work to break his stubborn self-will which is at the heart of rebellion. Only so can his energies be channeled to serve God with all his might in later years.

This is no easy task. The line between the two is often invisible. To tread the tightrope is a delicate business, especially when you realize that the spirit of your child is at stake. Nevertheless, such is a parent's calling.

Children won't simply "grow out of" rebellion. It must be purged from them. If they are not punished and disciplined properly early in life, their rebellion and selfishness will simply grow and grow, taking on more and more subtle forms that will ultimately undermine the whole family relationship.

We must be thoughtfully aware of this as we discipline our children. It is necessary to search for those forms of correctional discipline which fit each child (with his own unique tender areas and his own form of rebelliousness) and each situation individually. We want to achieve the desired effect—to break his self-will while building his spirit. We can do no more or no less. Our responses, therefore, must be controlled and must have the child's long-range good always in mind. Punishment is not meant to humiliate but to control the destructive will. Punishment which does not bring about a change in attitude is worse than nothing at all. Ineffective or token punishment which lets a child off the hook can develop an unhealthy lack of respect for firm and natural boundaries he is certain to encounter in later years.

This points up the need for sensitivity on the part of each parent toward each child. While one particularly strong-willed child may need a severe spanking, another child may come to full repentance with a simple reprimand or mild spanking. We frequently notice vast differences between the responses of our boys to various types of discipline, not only differences between each other, but diffferences from one day to the next. Great individual sensitivity is called for. Punishment is not meant to judge or humiliate but to achieve results. It should, therefore, be done in private, should have a distinctive beginning and end, and then should lead into forgiveness and a restored relationship. The entire process must be complete so that when it is over, it is truly over. *Discipline emanates from a heart of love.*

The second tool at the disposal of parents to instruct their children is the simple word no. It is a word which must never be used lightly. You cannot carelessly fling it around. It should be used only when you have the full attention of your mind on the actions of your child. Whenever you say no to your child, you must mean it and be prepared to back it up. When you say no and are disobeyed, you must be prepared to spank your child. He must see that the boundary is solid. No means *no*!

Inconsistent use of this word is every bit as damaging as an arbitrary spanking. It teaches inconsistent limits and meaningless words. It teaches a child that his parent is wavering, indecisive, and thoughtless.

The word no must be treated as a tool. Use it carefully and thoughtfully. Do not overuse it. Say no only when you are conscious that a lesson is being given and when you are prepared to take action or your words are ignored. Such use will bring great rewards later.

Balance is a critical key in all effective discipline. Too much spanking and too little spanking both have the same destructive effects on a child. If you still entertain any notion that you can be a part-time effective parent, that fallacy will have to go. Discipline requires the full focus of your attention and energy.

Steps Toward Meaningful Discipline

Just as there are certain disciplinary tools to be used, there are certain conditions that must exist and steps that must be taken to insure that discipline achieves its most beneficial results. Bill Gothard, founder of Basic Youth Conflicts seminars across the country, has been given extraordinary insight into workable parent-child relationships. The following principles are developed from his suggestions for carrying out the various disciplinary techniques most effectively.

See that a Child Accepts Personal Responsibility for Disobedience

In order for a child to truly repent of an act of disobedience or an attitude of rebellion, the offense must be clear in his mind. Discipline will accomplish nothing if he does not feel he has done wrong. A parent can ask the child, "What did you do?" This helps the child to clarify the problem. There must be no accusation involved. The child will usually have the tendency to either deny what he feels he is being blamed for or else blame others. It is important not to ask him why he did something or "Did you do it?" This will only blur the issue. You must simply re-emphasize the original question until he says what he has done. God tells us to confess our sins even though He certainly knows of them far more clearly than we do. Whenever a child either refuses to comply or cannot, move on through the rest of the steps.

Get Alone with the Child

Whenever a child is disciplined in the presence of others it will be very difficult for him to focus on his actions and his need to repent. He will be embarrassed and conscious of what everyone around is thinking. Rather than producing a repentant attitude, this will make the child look for ways to justify himself in the sight of others, especially if any of his friends are around. He will subconsciously try to gain their support against his parent. The discipline will be ineffective because the child will be unable to admit to himself that he was wrong and in need of correction.

Embarrassing a child in this way erects a barrier for future communication between parent and child because in the child's eyes his parent has betrayed a trust by downgrading him in front of others.

Reflect in Silence on What Has Happened

A short period of silence gives the child the opportunity to think about what he has done and to come to the point where he is aware that discipline is necessary. This may not always happen, but silence provides the opportunity if it is to come. It also allows any parental anger to soothe itself while the parent quietly prays that God would give him wisdom to choose the most appropriate means of discipline. The parent should also pray that the child will come to repentance, that his self-will be broken.

During this quiet time together a parent's expressiveness must communicate genuine grief for the offense and love for his child, not anger. The depth of a relationship between parent and child will make this grief self-convicting to a child who seriously cares what his parents think and feel regarding him. It gives him the opportunity before anything else is said or done to come to repentance within himself, which is always the best way.

Associate Love with Discipline

Though it usually appears to be just the opposite, in God's design love and discipline spring from the same source. This is something a parent must communicate to his child, that his love compels him to discipline rebellion. It must be made clear from an early age that this is a reflection of God's own character. God loves us and, because of that love, must discipline us when we disobey Him. In the same way, parents prove they love their children by disciplining them when necessary. This love must always be a parent's motivation for correction, never personal irritation, pride, or anger. The principles of Hebrews 12:5-7 should be regularly communicated to a child in the midst of necessary discipline: " 'My son, do not think lightly of the Lord's discipline, nor lose heart when he corrects you; for the Lord disciplines those whom he loves; he lays the rod on every son whom he acknowledges.' You must endure it as discipline: God is treating you as sons. Can anyone be a son, who is not disciplined by his father?" (NEB)

Establish That God, Not You, Is the Final Authority

If your child mistakenly thinks that authority originates with you, he will then feel safe if he can deceive you. Your child must realize that you are in a chain of command which originates with God. When you as a parent make mistakes (which you will certainly do) and when your child does things you are unaware of, he must know that in God's eyes the need for repentance still remains.

Use an Object When Spanking

Whenever possible something neutral (which the Bible calls a "rod") should be used to spank (a wooden spoon, a brush, a stick, etc.) rather than the hand. If the hand of a parent is used, the child will subconsciously associate it with pain and punishment. A neutral object prevents any fear from entering a child when his parent later uses the same hands to hold him and express love to him. The use of a rod also further ingrains the feeling that the need for discipline is almost something "outside" either the parent or child and is required on the basis of God's laws rather than the parent's arbitrary judgments and emotions. Often the very process of getting the rod can begin the process of repentance and the putting away of the rod signals the finality of the discipline. It is not uncommon for a well-disciplined child to ask for the rod when he wants to repent and to let you know when he is ready for it to be put away.

Spank to the Proper Point

A parent must be very sensitive to his child's will and spirit when spanking is necessary. He must spank until the child's stubborn self-will breaks and then stop. Overdiscipline can work all sorts of ill in the heart of a child. You must work on his will without injuring his spirit. Though you need to give sufficient discipline, you must use the least amount possible to achieve repentance.

After a Spanking—Give Reassurance, Comfort, and Love

When a spanking is over a child needs to see and feel and hear assurances of love so that it is a reality to him that discipline and love are indeed "one." This is the time for hugs, tender words, wiped-away tears and, finally, smiles. To send a child to his room after a spanking is a double punishment with no reconciliation. The parent who has carried out the discipline should also be the one to follow through with the time of comforting. If possible, this time of togetherness can lead into some shared activity. The effect of discipline occurs during the spanking. Once over it should be put far away. An activity afterwards can completely restore the relationship in a joyful way.

Discuss Any Further Action Necessary

Full correction for misbehavior and rebellious attitudes not only involves a child's repentance through his parent's disciplinary action, but also his acceptance of the responsibility for his actions. When others have been hurt or when property has been damaged, a parent should discuss with the child the need either for restitution or asking forgiveness. The child must learn to face the consequences for his disobedience and make situations right as soon as possible.

Humbly Evaluate Your Own Behavior

Parents make mistakes. You will not always discipline fairly. You will find times when you have acted emotionally and have accused your child falsely or have spanked him in anger. When you realize you have embarrassed your child or have disciplined him wrongly or have failed to love him in any way, you must go to him and ask for forgiveness. This should not be done immediately after a discipline session, but later when all emotions have calmed.

Children have an acute sense of fair play. When a parent is too proud to admit mistakes and apologize, future successful discipline becomes more and more difficult. But when a child knows his parents try to be fair at all times (even in the midst of their mistakes) he will submit to their discipline knowing he will not be wronged.

Advice From The Past

In his book *The Vicar's Daughter,* nineteenth-century Scotch novelist George MacDonald set down what he felt to be several basic principles of discipline and child raising in general. His suggestions are wise, and very practical. Here is what he says:

> First for a few negative principles:
>
> 1. Never give in to disobedience; and never threaten what you are not prepared to carry out.
>
> 2. Never lose your temper. I do not say never be angry. Anger is sometimes indispensable, especially where there has been anything mean, dishonest, or cruel. But anger is every different from loss of

temper.

3. Of all things, never sneer at them; and be careful, even, how you rally them.

4. Do not try to work on their feelings. Feelings are far too delicate things to be used for tools. It is like taking the mainspring out of your watch, and notching it for a saw. It may be a wonderful saw, but how fares your watch? Especially avoid doing so in connection with religious things, for so you will assuredly deaden them to all that is finest. Let your feelings, not your efforts on theirs, affect them with a sympathy the more powerful that it is not forced upon them; and, in order to do this avoid being too "English" in the hiding of your feelings. A man's own family has a right to share in his good feelings.

5. Never show that you doubt, except you are able to convict. To doubt an honest child is to do what you can to make a liar of him; and to believe a liar, if he is not altogether shameless, is to shame him.

6. Instill no religious doctrine apart from its duty. If it have no duty as its necessary embodiment, the doctrine may well be regarded as doubtful.

7. Do not be hard on mere quarrelling, which, like a storm in nature, is often helpful in clearing the moral atmosphere. Stop it by a judgement between the parties. But be severe as to the kind of quarrelling, and the temper shown in it. Especially give no quarter to any unfairness arising from greed or spite. Use your strongest language with regard to that.

Now for a few positive rules:

1. Always let them come to you, and always hear

what they have to say. If they bring a complaint, always examine it, and dispense pure justice, and nothing but justice.

2. Cultivate a love of giving fair-play. Everyone, of course, likes to receive fair-play; but no one ought to be left to imagine, therefore, that he loves fair-play.

3. Teach from the very first, from the infancy capable of sucking a sugar plum, to share with neighbors. Never refuse the offering a child brings you, except you have a good reason—and give it. And never pretend to partake; that involves hideous possibilities in its effect on the child.

The necessity of giving a reason for refusing a kindness has no relation to what is supposed by some to be the necessity of giving a reason with every command. There is no such necessity. Of course there ought to be a reason in every command. It may be desirable, sometimes, to explain it. But not always.

4. Allow a great deal of noise—as much as is fairly endurable; but the moment they seem to be getting beyond their own control, stop the noise at once. Also put a stop at once to all fretting and grumbling.

5. Favor the development of each in the direction of his own bent. Help him to develop himself, but do not push development. To do so is most dangerous.

6. Mind the moral nature, and it will take care of the intellectual. In other words, the best thing for the intellect is the cultivation of the conscience, not in casuistry by studying it, but in conduct. It may take longer to arrive; but the end will be the highest possible health, vigor, and ration of progress.

7. Discourage emulation, and insist on duty—not often, but strongly.

The Changing Faces of Discipline

If discipline is the entire foundation upon which a child's house is built, that base is given its strength and solidity through the love in which we carry it out. Boundaries, punishment, limits, spankings, and obedience are the fiber of the early training of a child. But the consistency with which we implement these things into our relationships is what determines their value. Alone they can achieve nothing without love to cement them into place. In fact, when love and consistency are missing to any substantial degree, a child will be damaged more than helped.

Children are incredibly delicate. God has placed them in our homes to receive training. The framework of this training is our gentle and understanding love. A child's spirit can easily be broken, his fragile self-image crushed, and any foundation we hope to build destroyed through wrong or inconsistent use of these disciplinary tools.

Discipline must be carried out in the context of the whole "house." A foundation by itself serves no purpose. In everything we have discussed here, the thoughtful and wise parent must also keep in mind the other factors of parenthood we will be discussing. Discipline especially goes hand-in-hand with the instilling of self-esteem. They are different perspectives of the same goal—that a child learn who he is and what is his role in God's creation. Sloppy discipline leads immediately to a distorted concept of self-worth in a child. One of the most precious commodities God has given a child—joy—is lost when a parent does not demonstrate his love and tenderness in all he does. A parent deeply involved in applying the techniques of discipline needs to constantly remind himself of this.

Discipline and training change as a child grows. Respect for authority must continue to be taught. Correction and punishment must still remain part of the family framework when necessary. But as the relationship between parent and child matures, these things take on a more mature nature as well. There begins to be more leeway in the relationship. Training techniques for areas other than discipline (chapter 6) begin to assume greater and greater importance as the need for discipline lessens. (Spanking should probably be drawing to a close between a child's eighth and tenth years.) A child is showing himself increasingly trustworthy, therefore the parent is able to loosen the reins somewhat.

Rules are vital for harmonious family living and always will be. But as a family matures, the boundaries become gradually less rigid. A father's leadership must continue to be decisive. The father who unknowingly forces his family to exist in constant uncertainty because he has not provided solid rules (few in number but faithfully observed) will create an unstable home life for everyone. He will try to make his children behave simply with impromptu rules thrown together as he goes along.

In a Christian home the basis for such rules lies in the laws of God. There are certain standards of behavior which are absolute, not open to our own personal interpretation. Truthfulness, obedience, respect, kindness, unselfishness, faithfulness to God and so on are all inherent principles that God insists on from all people. We must insist on them in our families as well.

But there are a host of things about which certain families may have differing convictions. These will differ from person to person and family to family. Work habits, financial stewardship, the hours we keep, eating habits and the like are a few examples of such things. It is the responsibility of individual parents to build these personal convictions and preferences into their children as family standards. If they are well thought out, just, loving, and unselfish, then children will accept them and may even come to adopt them as their own someday. They will respect their parents for decisions they make if they see that their parents are reasonable and do not make arbitrary evaluations. They come to see in their parents an integrity and level of commitment they respect and admire. They sense wisdom in their parents.

This is not necessarily to say that every one of these family convictions is something the parents dogmatically insist is right in an absolute way. It will be clear that all families operate using a different set of rules. But, "this is the way we do it in this family" is a valid justification for establishing family rules. If children see that these rules are well founded, they will be at peace living under them. This is the greatest safeguard against teen-age rebellion: parents who have demonstrated wisdom in establishing and living their convictions.

Even though these individual rules differ from the absolute guidelines God has instituted, it will still be necessary for parents to discipline children for ignoring these standards the family has agreed upon as grounds for behavior. But such discipline will be just and the children will know it. Such an uncompromising stance on these convictions provide the entire family relationship a solid base on which to build. There will be security in this consistent order and dependability. If the convictions are sound, a child will be the first to defend them—even if it means his occasional punishment for overstepping them.

The Future Training Discipline Provides

There is an aspect of discipline that conditions a child for later life. Many Scriptures confirm that discipline is valuable in instilling such qualities as endurance, fortitude and patience (Rom. 5:3-5, James 1:3-5, Prov. 6:23, 10:17). Pain—both physical and emotional—that is gently and wisely introduced into the life of a child provides useful preparation for the stresses of life he will one day encounter. Through it his capacity to endure and produce and perform is expanded. An athelete's training is based on this same principle. The exertion of a workout is geared to push the body to its utmost limits of endurance. Then, when the day of the race arrives, the body is accustomed to the maximum degree of effort.

Most parents, however, withhold pain and shield their children from outside disturbances as much as possible. We naturally want to keep our child from having to cope with the same frustrations, sufferings, sorrows, and disappointments we experienced as children. There is love in this desire and it is basically a worthwhile goal. But there is a danger as well. Overprotection can result from it; a child then becomes ill-prepared to confidently handle the natural frustrations and setbacks of life.

God does not withhold pain from His children. In fact, the Bible says He uses it to purify, perfect, and prepare us. In every situation we are placed in, God is attempting to make us more like Jesus. He does this largely through the loving use of discipline. Wisdom is usually reserved for the person who has experienced discipline and has learned self-discipline. Discipline, properly exercised and effectively balanced by esteem-producing influences, enlarges the capacity of the human heart to endure, produce, love, and serve.

In addition to the value of discipline to teach obedience and respect for authority, then, it also helps children to learn practically that feelings of pain, setbacks, and all manner of problems are temporary; in fact, they are valuable assets to prepare for the race of life. Wise parents will help their children stand up to and conquer barriers of moods, school problems, fatigue, punishment, and physical handicaps. Like a coach, such a parent increases the capabilities of his child and thereby motivates him and builds confidence.

The Justice of Discipline

A maturing child grows daily more aware of the consistency with which his parents enforce the standards they have laid down. A child of two must obey regardless of whether his parent is always consistent. But a child of ten, if he senses a lack of fair play, may well ask: "Why?" Our instructions to our children, therefore, must originate in love and reasonableness, and continue to be well grounded and thoughtful. In all respects there must be sensitivity to the justice of discipline.

If a child is tired, for instance, that may provide a clue to his misbehavior. It doesn't necessarily justify a wrong, but it is certainly one additional factor we must consider before carrying out any discipline. The thoughtful parent must always have the circumstances behind wrong behavior in mind. We must exercise reason. Children need the flexibility of having occasional bad days. Sometimes it seems to a child that he is worthless, that nothing is going right.

Disobedience is disobedience, regardless. But our responses must always take into view the entire scope of the house we are building. An act of selfishness may sometimes need to be interpreted as a questioning of self-worth rather than an act of rebellion. Our responses must consider that. If the foundation of discipline has been solidly built, then a hug and some tender words to any angry child will not compromise it. And they will usually do far more good toward reinstating a feeling of worth and security than a trip back to the "woodshed."

Thus, the older a child becomes the more we must integrate understanding and flexibility into his training. We are to see that he is provided with conditions that will lead him to maturity and enable him to make decisions on his own. For a two-and-a-half-year-old toddler who is constantly asking, "Who's in charge?" the response must often be physical and painful. For the twelve-year-old-girl experiencing the hormonal changes of adolescence, reassurance and talk may be most helpful.

Older children will be acutely aware of the justice of our training by the ease with which we forgive them. We adults always desire forgiveness for our own mistakes, but often are hesitant to extend that same level of forgiveness to our children. This can be seen by the readiness with which we often punish our children for things done unintentionally, things which can not always be classified as disobedience so much as childish carelessness. In such moments, especially when the carelessness damages something or inconveniences us, we are prone toward angry punishment with little thought to the internal reactions inside our child. By angrily lashing out, we can force a child into the corner of self-defense where he must make excuses simply to defend his pride against the guilt that assaults him. What is needed instead in such moments is to demonstrate understanding and forgiveness. This will cause the child to usually honestly evaluate his own behavior so we don't have to.

Constantly cracking down on a child for everything he does just slightly out of line forces him to raise barriers—excuses, defense mechanism, buck passing, lying, etc. This is especially true when there are extenuating circumstances which we fail to take into account prior to our evaluation and judgment—such as tiredness, depression, questions—or when we punish a child for something he did not do.

How much better at such times that a child finds total forgiveness in the arms of his parents. If he knows he can approach them any time, no matter what he may have done, he will remain open and will not erect barriers to communication. This does not imply that punishment will not occasionally still be necessary. In the tender and forgiving arms of a wise parent, a child will often be the first to recommend that something be done in retribution for his misbehavior. But in order to feel that proper evaluation of self-guilt, a child must first experience the total love of a compassionate parent and know that forgiveness already exists in his parent's heart.

6

LAYING THE FOUNDATION—PART 2

Training Through Shaping Behavior

The second aspect of the foundational process in the life of a child is the training his parents provide that enables him to live and function in the world. Although shaping a child's behavior in this way is closely interwoven with discipline, it is yet distinct and is geared toward an altogether different need inside a child. While discipline is primarily intended to instill obedience, the sort of training we will now turn our attention to is designed to teach acceptable behavior. It is often impossible to separate the two. Yet obedience stems from the attitude of the heart while behavior must often be learned by a child on a purely physical level. There are, therefore, very different tools to be used to educate and train a child to function in a mature way.

When engaged in discipline, a parent is imposing his will upon his child by virtue of his God-given authority in the family structure. But when shaping behavior a parent seeks ways to make his child *want* to learn desirable habits on his own. A parent's goal is that the child become able to regulate and control himself. One day he will be on his own and this early training gives him the skills and maturity and responsibility to behave normally and wisely with the self-control necessary to live a meaningful life.

This training process involves everything—learning to handle a knife and fork, being able to tie shoes, dressing, relating with others, sharing, studying, expressing oneself, developing skills, carrying out responsibility. But children often do not particularly care about learning improved social behavior in these areas. They would be content to remain at a present immature level. However, they cannot be *made* to learn these things (through discipline); they must come to want to learn within themselves. Permanent changes can rarely be imposed upon children without their willingness. Surface compliance can sometimes be achieved, but true self-regulation will not come.

Motivation, then, is the key to this training process. A parent must find techniques that motivate a child to change his own behavior. But though a child cannot be forced to learn, there are ways his motivation can be increased and even changed. Just as there are certain definite tools that work in the area of a child's attitude of rebellion when authority is challenged, there are certain tools that work to mold a child's behavior and habit patterns. And the two types of tools are not ordinarily interchangable. It is necessary to be aware of which particular aspect of your child's learning and training process you are dealing with. *You can rarely motivate your child to change his behavior using the disciplinary tools.*

If the tools to be used for developing attitudes are confused with those used to shape behavior, problems will be compounded. In so saying, of course, we need also to bear in mind that these two aspects of the foundational training process go hand in hand. They mix and flow together in such a way that in practical daily living you often cannot distinguish them. Certainly boundaries play a large role in the shaping of a child's behavior and habit patterns. And if a child is refusing to eat, there is a strong possibility that there is both a behavioral problem that needs working on (using the tools of this chapter) *and* a problem of obedience which needs dealing with (using the tools of the previous chapter). We are dissecting these two things—discipline and training—for much the same reason a boy takes apart a clock: to see how it works and to understand it more thoroughly. But the boy knows the clock cannot work when its pieces are scattered all about the table. When he puts it back together it functions as a unit—together; the individual pieces are no longer even visible. We are in much the same position here. We need to understand these things, so this sort of analysis will help. But in the application, it will rarely be as simple as looking over a list, selecting an appropriate tool, and then applying it by itself and observing remarkable changes taking place. Life with children is more complex than that. Very frequently more than one tool will be used in conjunction with another. And when both discipline and behavioral training are involved in the same situation, tools from both chapters will have to be employed.

Tools for Teaching

When dealing with a child's behavior apart from his attitude toward authority, there are two situations which come up in your educating and training. When a child is eager and willing and motivated to learn, your job is easy. About all you can do wrong is to keep him from learning or else dampen his enthusiasm with your own indifference. When a child, on the other hand, is not so motivated, then you have the task of devising ways (sometimes forced) to induce him toward desirable behavior. Since you as his parent are in control of many of his circumstances and ordinarily he cannot live without you, there are many things you can do to modify his motivation. We'll look at these two types of situations one at a time.

Instruction and Example

Naturally the most obvious way to teach a child to do something is to tell him how to do it and then demonstrate the process. Especially when a child is eager to learn. He will usually be waiting for you to tell him what to do, even begging you for instruction. If you are teaching him to tie his shoes, for instance, he needs to be shown the process step by step as you explain it to him. Probably most of what a child learns to do he learns in this manner. In his younger years he is particularly enthusiastic and willingly watches and listens to you teach him about anything.

Practice

Real personal learning does not come as a task is explained and witnessed, but through a child's trying it for himself. He needs the initial instruction, but then he needs to get the feel of it with his own hands, fingers, feet, and emotions. For instruction to be most effective it must work a child's practice into it. Rarely are the two carried out in a nonreversable order but interwoven simultaneously. As you explain about tying the shoe, you need to let him practice the various steps as you go.

Several factors make this practice all the more effective. Praise and encouragement along the way are vital throughout every step. Nothing will motivate him to learn faster and further than such support. (There are many other positive things that such praise accomplishes, as will be discussed in chapters 7 and 8.) Large tasks must be broken down into small enough pieces that a child can practice them one at a time. The entire process might be overwhelming, but a child can gradually master it by taking small chunks which he can master singly. This is where great patience and flexibility are called for from a parent. This is a point where such behavioral training becomes quite distinctive from disciplinary training. When teaching obedience you must be hard and unbending and you must insist upon obedience. When teaching a new task, however, great leniency and patience are called for, with not so much as a hint of criticism or punishment for failure. Nothing will destroy motivation faster than criticizing a child's first attempts at a task.

Imitation of Parental Model

Much of the behavior a child acquires does not come through direct instruction but from observing and imitating what goes on around him in the family. A child learns to talk, not by being told how to do it, but simply from being immersed in talking itself. His mind absorbs what is all about him, assimilates it, and he then begins practicing it on his own. As he grows older much of his behavior becomes part of him simply because he is so constantly immersed in your particular family. Basic habit patterns a family demonstrates are passed along to a child with no instruction or planning whatsoever.

Tools for Modifying Motivation and Shaping or Altering Behavior

When a child is willing and eager to learn a task, then simple instruction, imitation, and practice will usually give him the skills to perform it. But children are not always motivated to listen, copy, and practice. Many times they would rather have nothing to do with what you want to teach them. A toddler, for instance, would be content to eat with his fingers forever. But you know he must learn to use a fork and spoon. A preschooler would just as soon behave at the dinner table like an animal, but you recognize he needs to learn proper manners. A sixth grader would rather play than study but, aware of his long-range need, you must take it upon yourself to teach him to study and make sure he does. A teen-ager would often rather be out with his friends than working on his family chores or fulfilling his responsibility at a part-time job; it is your duty as his parent to see that he learns responsibility in these areas for his own benefit later in life.

No child (of any age) *wants* to clean his room or take out the trash or pull weeds or do his homework when there are more enjoyable things to do. But you know that by training him to responsibly carry out such small tasks today, you are insuring that in the future he will be able to function in his place in the world with responsibility, integrity, and maturity.

This is precisely where the line becomes so obscure which distinguishes this need of a child to learn responsibility in performing tasks from his parallel need to learn respect for authority. Often there is rebellion at work in a child's heart, as well as his wanting to avoid some new area of learning. But this is not always so—a child who balks at learning to do something new is not necessarily being disobedient; he is behaving like a normal child. Discipline is not called for in such a case, but rather the implementation of other tools which will motivate him to learn the new task. There are a number of techniques that can be employed to increase a child's self-motivation and mold his behavior even though at first he may be an unwilling learner.

Reinforcement

Any time a child does something that is rewarded, he will be motivated to do the same thing again. There can be both positive and negative reinforcement. A child who does well on a school paper and gets a word of praise and a hug from mom will want to succeed again. On the negative side, a child whose tantrum is rewarded when he gets his own way will try kicking and screaming in the future. All sorts of things are learned by reinforcement. A baby quickly learns that his crying brings attention (a reward) and so he continues with it.

The most effective positive rewards are not pieces of candy, privileges, or a bigger allowance, but praise and affirmation and appreciation. Your child wants a relationship of love with you more than anything. He is intensely motivated to gain your support and respect and love. You can use this to motivate him in areas where he is not naturally enthusiastic. If you are trying to get your son to mow the lawn and clean up the clippings, though he may not be internally motivated to do so, your appreciation and praise (and even help with the job) will be a reward he will want to experience again and again.

Though this is a tool which a wise parent can skillfully use to help his child, many times we are completely oblivious to the many things we reward. If a child is not receiving ample love and attention and shared play with one of his parents, he may well become disobedient and obnoxious knowing that such behavior will gain him attention. Even if he is punished for it, there has still been a reward (with the punishment there is attention) and the disobedience will continue. The unknowing parent is reinforcing the negative behavior.

To be effective, rewards must be immediate and should be as closely tied into the job itself as possible. Money will prove a poor reward for doing your homework because the two are not related. But an extra half hour of TV for getting one's homework done early would be an attractive enticement. Timing is important too. Several days later, the emotional energy of having cleaned up the kitchen or the yard will have dissipated. Praise will therefore not have much of a motivational effect. But when given immediately there remains an emotional charge from the job (most tasks are not purely physical but involve the emotions as well) which can be given a great boost by praise and reinforcement. Part of growing older entails being capable of thinking more about the future and older children can increasingly be taught to pace themselves over a long period of time toward a long-range goal. In my family we drank powdered milk for several years (learning personal sacrifice) with the intention of using the money we saved to buy a trampoline. This was an example of long-term reinforcement.

It is important that rewards to reinforce behavior are used to achieve *positive* habits. Rewards should not be given a child for *not* doing something negative, but for *doing* the positive opposite. This may seem like it would work, but actually the negative behavior gets rewarded, even if in reverse. In other words, a child should not be rewarded simply for *not having* a sloppy room (negative emphasis) but for *having* a neat room (positive emphasis). It may seem a minor difference, but rewarding backwards subtly insures the continuation of the negative behavior since it is the basis for the reward.

This is closely related to the danger that comes with confusion over the need to shape positive behavior and the need to instill discipline. Obedience of the heart cannot come about through rewards in the same way that motivation to change behavior can. When a child says, "No, I won't obey you," a parent is dealing with rebellion of the heart which must be purged (using the principles in the last chapter). Trying to use reinforcement to win obedience—"If you'll do what mommy says I'll give you a nice snack of some cookies"—can be deadly. Surface compliance may temporarily be obtained, but the attitude of that child's heart remains in the same rebellious state. And in time it will grow worse because the child is gaining control. The disobedience has been rewarded through the mistaken use of reinforcement and will therefore be repeated.

Extinction

When behavior goes unrewarded it will tend to die out of a child's habit patterns. This is a useful tool when trying to rid a child of some bad habit or negative tendency. Tantrums are an excellent example of a behavior pattern which is unacceptable in society and which therefore must be extinguished. They usually continue or else die out depending on the way they are rewarded.

Several methods are commonly used. If at five P.M., just as dad walks in the door after an exasperating day at work, a four-year-old asks for a cookie and is denied, a tantrum may ensue. Mom is fixing dinner and has a headache. Dad hardly has his coat off and is in no mood to hear screaming for forty-five minutes until dinner. So he willingly gives Junior a cookie to quiet him down. "Just this once," he adds. But Junior is hardly convinced. He has learned that a tantrum brought results. The next time he wants his own way he will probably use the same method. His screaming has been reinforced.

But if dad is the emotional sort and has just had to deal with a frustrating situation before leaving work, his response might be quite different. Junior's tantrum could well be met with an explosion and a spanking. The screaming continues and now *everyone* has a headache. And Junior has some deep hurts to add to his other problems as well. The reason? Because dad has mistakenly used a disciplinary tool for a behavioral situation (using it in anger has not helped either).

Tantrums must be extinguished through negative reinforcement. No matter how difficult it may be for a time, mom and dad can motivate Junior to cease his screaming spells by ignoring them, by refusing to reward them in any way. He will gradually learn there are more effective ways of achieving results than throwing tantrums (if mom and dad are alertly using positive reinforcement, love, and attention at the same time to reward pleasant behavior). Temporarily, a tantrum is difficult to ignore. But the long-range benefits of seeing it slowly extinguished are worth the effort. If negative behavior (such as a tantrum or a bad habit or sloppy manners) is always met with a bribe ("I'll give you this piece of candy if you'll just. . . .") the child will continue to exhibit the behavior.

Extinction can have negative results as well. Often good behavior goes unrewarded without a parent's knowledge and therefore gradually dies out. If a child is good and cooperative and obedient, but receives little attention from his father every night after work, he will seek ways to gain that attention. If instead of being calm and neat and pleasant, he discovers that yelling and screaming and writing on the walls with a felt-tip pen and trying out the scissors on the living room curtains wins his father's attention (though it may be in the form of a spanking), he will continue with such behavior. His good behavior has gone unrewarded and is therefore extinguished, while his reckless new adventures are reinforced.

Reinforcement and extinction are going on all day long, day in and day out, in the life of a child. Most parents have no idea the extent to which they are subtly rewarding their children, both positively and negatively. When used with awareness, these can be very useful tools in motivating a child toward self-regulation.

Reasoning and Communication

The older a child grows, the more a parent will be able to reason and communicate with him in ways that can modify actions. There will still remain many times when reasoning will not be enough. But if there has been a relationship of deep trust built up and if you as a parent treat your son or daughter with respect—as a mature person whose ideas you consider significant—there will be a basis for communication. You will be able to discuss the pros and cons of a situation (arriving at a Friday night curfew for example) and arrive at a mutually acceptable solution without your having to excercise your parental authority and say, "You do it *my* way."

Dialogue can often bring a child into new areas of learning and understanding. To be deeply understood is one of a child's most basic needs. Without someone to share your emotions with you, life can be bleak. When a parent and child are communicating and when the child deeply senses that his parent is "one" with him and is applying no pressure whatsoever, somehow the windows are opened so that he is able to see things much more clearly. This requires sensitive and attentive listening. It means allowing a child to express himself freely, even his negative emotions. Having negative feelings is vastly different from being rebellious. When a child knows he can open up his insides and let his emotions flow without having to fear your punishing him for something he deeply feels, he will grow in a very healthy way. But it is not enough simply to let these emotions come out; you must respect them, feel them with your child. When he hurts, his relief comes in knowing that you hurt too.

A technique for drawing out of your child what he feels is

called conversational feedback. In short, it is a method for working into your replies a restatement of the emotions your child has just expressed. Rather than offering advice regarding everything he says, you feed back to him what he is feeling. And in this process your child is encouraged to think and feel further along the same lines until he comes to a solution or an understanding on his own (with your subtle guidance). Providing instruction is sometimes valuable, when it is the proper tool to be used, but when communicating in the area of deep emotions, potential hurts and frustrations, giving parental advice is probably the worst thing to do. These various tools are different and they are to be used for different circumstances.

Reexpressing your child's emotions does two very important things: it shows him that you have heard, not just his words but what he is actually feeling, and that you care; and it provides a springboard for further communication.

For example, your eight-year-old son comes home obviously mad and disgusted and says, "Boy, am I ever frustrated with Bobby for what he did today. I'm more than frustrated, I'm downright angry!"

You have three choices.

You can piously say, "Son, a Christian isn't supposed to be angry with his friends," in which case your son will promptly clam up. He will quickly learn not to share his feelings with you. He needs understanding—not sermonizing. (This is not to say there is no place for spiritual instruction and counsel. There certainly is. But this is not the time.)

Or you can say, "Why? What happened?" This would be much better because now you are a neutral observer rather than a critical parent.

But by responding, "I can tell you are really upset and frustrated. It must have been really something," you are accomplishing something far greater. You are no longer neutral. You have now involved yourself actively in your son's frustration. You have not just heard what he said, you actually felt it with him. You are not just casually responding as you take a break from the sports page but are placing yourself in the midst of his emotions. Communication will be happening. (This won't work as well by just parroting back the words or using the phrase that no one really likes to hear, "I understand what you mean. . . ." To be most effective such feedback must express the felt emotions in a genuine way.)

Such interested communication usually leads immediately to further explanation. We are all anxious to express ourselves and in an atmosphere where our ideas and feelings are accepted, we are more than willing to let them flow.

"Yes, it was something. I couldn't believe what he said to me. It was really mean! And I'm supposed to be his best friend!"

"He really lashed out at you, huh? His own best friend?"

"It wasn't like him at all."

"No, it sure doesn't sound like what I know of him. It must have really hurt you. There must've really been something on his mind to make him treat you like that."

Dialogue and communication are going on. There is no pressure, no critical glare for attitudes or frustrations. The child sincerely feels mom or dad is part of this thing with him. And out of such deep communication oftentimes a genuine motivation to change one's attitude can emerge. (This cannot be a parent's only motivation for such communication or else disappointment will creep in, and with it pressure, when a child fails to "come around." Sometimes such changes take a long time and results will not be noticed until much later.) Such changes could usually not come by telling a child, "This is what you should feel. . . ." Advice just wouldn't work. A child needs to experience a motivation springing up from within him to alter his behavior or attitude. This can be triggered by an understanding parent who knows how to listen and respond.

"Yeah, I guess there has been something on his mind. He's been acting a little depressed all week."

"That's too bad, having your best friend depressed."

"I've tried to cheer him up a few times, but nothing seems to help."

"That's neat that you've tried to help him."

"I probably didn't do as much as I could have. He is my best friend. I should try to help."

"That's what best friends are for, to ease each other's burdens when the going gets rough."

"Yeah—now I feel a little bad for getting mad at him."

"It's okay. It's impossible not to get mad once in a while. God knows that. He forgives us."

"Maybe I ought to call him and talk. Maybe he'd tell me what's wrong. What do you think, dad?"

"That sounds like a good idea. I think it would be a nice thing to do. It really shows you love Bobby in your heart."

"Yeah, I do. He's a good friend."

"Why don't we pray for him just for a moment together before you call?"

"Okay . . . thanks, dad."

Certainly in some respects this may be a simplistic example. Results won't always be so total, visible, and quick. And you mustn't expect this of your child or he will sense the pressure. Your motive must be to really share with him and to understand his feelings. And when you do, his self-motivation will take over, even if it is in ways you often do not see.

Natural Consequences

When you are trying to rid your child of a certain behavior but have had no success with communication, reinforcement, or extinction, you can often correct the habit by doing nothing—by allowing nature to take its course. Many times a child's behavior has mildly harmful or unpleasant consequences from which we naturally try to shield him. But by sheltering him from the consequences of his actions we greatly reduce his own internal motivation for avoiding the behavior in the future. So he continues to ignore our instructions. A solution is to let him face the natural consequences of his actions rather than protecting him from them.

The father of the prodigal son in Luke 15 was well acquainted with this method of training. He did not try to tell his son, "You need to grow up!" Even though there was a certain amount of stubbornness and rebellion in this young man's heart, his father recognized his need to learn and mature by facing the natural consequences of his actions. So he let him go. And his son later returned home much more "grown up."

You may be trying to teach your child not to put dirt in his mouth while playing outside. But no matter what you say or do, he continues to try it. Training him by using the natural consequences of his actions would simply mean allowing him to eat as much dirt as he liked—enough to make him sick. You would need to say nothing more. His own actions would bring an end to this habit soon enough. Finicky eating can be cured in the same way. Rather than catering to a child's refusal to eat during meals by giving snacks and preferred foods, a parent can simply allow the resultant hunger from not eating take its course. A few missed meals with no snacks offered in sympathy will quickly motivate a child to eat.

Of course there must be moderation in this approach, as

always. It is obviously inappropriate to teach our child to be careful with fire, to swim, or to get over a fear of heights using this method. A child must not be placed in danger. If hazards exist it is time to protect your child and find other tools to use.

Logical Consequences

Logical consequences are very similar to natural consequences except that rather than allowing nature to determine the outcome, you as a parent have a hand in structuring the logical outcome of the behavior. If a child is perpetually late and forgetful, through logical consequences you can teach him to remember to be on time. If he is to get certain chores done by a certain time in order to go out to play, the logical consequences of his not completing them would be that he would miss his playtime. If he dawdles every morning and occasionally misses the school bus, his irresponsibility should not be "rewarded" by driving him to school. He should either have to walk or stay home as if he were sick (no playing or TV). If he cannot remember to take his lunch, it should not be dropped off at the school office for him by dad on his way to work. The logical consequence of his forgetfulness is simple—no lunch that day.

Teaching through both natural and logical consequences will motivate a child very quickly. By having to assume the responsibility for his own actions, he will take it upon himself to alter his behavior so that the consequences are in his own best interest. If he is constantly protected from these consequences, he will never have the opportunity to learn this kind of responsibility.

These are just two tools out of many methods. They must be used with thought and care. Using the logical consequences method must not become an excuse for a disinterested "hands-off" life style of a parent too busy to take the time to really discover what is best for his child. These techniques must be used like all the others in this and the previous chapter—with foresight and thoughtful planning. Because consequences are logical and natural does not mean we are to let them occur haphazardly or at random. They must be carefully worked into our training program. A child must be aware of what we are doing and should know in advance what to expect. We are trying to teach him, not punish or surprise him. Through his awareness he will come to fully realize his own responsibility for the results of his actions. And he must know we are doing it for his ultimate best because we love him. We employ these techniques not to "get back" at the child but because in certain key instances they are indeed the best thing we can do for him.

Isolation

Misbehavior that is others-directed can often be extinguished by isolating him from anyone else, especially those his actions are directed against. A tantrum, for instance, is a key example of behavior that is designed specifically to exasperate a parent to the point that he will give in and meet a child's demand. It is an attempt to overpower a parent into submitting to his wishes. Though it is a battle of wills (which might ordinarily look like a disciplinary situation) its solution requires behavior modification (extinction). If a child is placed in the private seclusion of his own room during a tantrum, it will often quickly die out. Its sole purpose is to gain some end, usually from a parent. Once the intended "victim" is gone and with it the goal for the tantrum, there ceases to be any purpose in screaming.

Isolation is a method that can be used either as a disciplinary *or* a behavior-modifying tool and often works in conjunction with the other techniques as well. Often the logical consequences of behavior that is unbearable to everyone else is that they will all leave—hence isolation.

Giving Responsibility and Seeing That It Is Carried Out

Motivation can often be created inside the heart of a child to perform to new levels when he is given responsibility which he is able to carry out on his own. He must be given tasks that he is capable of succeeding at and a parent must make sure he does succeed. Praise and encouragement will come into this very significantly. Giving a child responsibility is an excellent way of helping him learn good behavior because it triggers internal motivation. A child whose parents trust and respect his abilities enough to turn certain things over to him is a child who will be stimulated to succeed. He will want to please. For such responsibility to have its full effect, the results must be verbally appreciated (reinforced).

There is a reverse side to the coin of responsibility, however. That is the need to learn diligence. Once the motivational "high" of being given responsibility wears off, a child will quite naturally often want to be let out from under it. But at this point he needs to be taught to follow through with his responsibilities. This is hardly an easy task, for diligence is not innate in the heart of a child (or an adult)—it is developed through practice. To effectively instill diligence many of the other tools often need to be used as well, notably natural and logical consequences.

If a boy wants a paper route, for instance, or to have a dog or a new bike, a key part of your using that desire for his benefit is to teach him to faithfully carry out his responsibility. When the time comes (and it certainly will) when your son is hesitant about delivering his papers in the rain or doesn't want to go out after dark to put away his bike or when he tires of feeding his dog twice a day, you cannot give in and allow him to shirk the responsibility he earlier accepted. If he is unwilling to carry through, the consequence must be giving up the paper route or the dog, or letting the bike rust. You cannot bail him out every time.

Of course it goes without saying that there must be great leniency in your attitude as this teaching of responsibility is increased through the years. A child having his first exposure to it will have a hard time without some patience, encouragement, and help. Learning responsibility and diligence must be a progressive thing. It will not come all at once. You cannot expect a child to be more responsible than he can be at his age. But by the time a child is fourteen or fifteen he should have been brought to the point where he is able to accept full responsibility for many of his own actions and duties. Unless parents can instill in their children this sort of stick-to-it-iveness early in their lives through smaller responsibilities, they will have difficult times as adults in areas of self-discipline.

When I was in seventh grade I accepted a gardening job at a neighbor's home for several afternoons a week after school. It was one of my first exposures to a long-term responsibility which I had to carry out whether I liked it or not. There were times I had to work when I would much rather have been involved in some attractive after-school activity with my friends. There were many times I did not go willingly and would have quickly ducked out of my responsibility if I could have. Yet how deeply thankful I now am that my parents recognized my need to learn diligence through that job. I feel my present attitude toward my own business has many of its roots in that early experience.

Self-discipline is a very necessary trait for a successful and balanced life. But it must be learned. And this learning comes through sticking to responsibility. Parents can help their children in this process in two ways. First, by teaching responsibility in the daily affairs of the home—spending money wisely, household chores, tithing, taking care of possessions. Secondly, a parent can help keep a child's motivation level high by being interested in his performance. Not simply through praise and encouragement (as important as they are) but also by occasionally sharing duties or giving him a temporary break for a day or two when you see it is wearing him down emotionally. Responsibility must be heavy enough to require diligence, but not so heavy it becomes a burden.

Deciding Which Tool to Use

As you have already noticed, most of the time two or more of these techniques work together. Rarely does one method used alone completely clear up a problem or alter a habit pattern. But there is usually one particular method that will be most suitable for a certain occasion. Your job—a difficult one—is to find which.

The key is sensitivity to your child—his feelings, his needs, his attitudes, his level of maturity, his capabilities, and his potential. You must initially try to determine whether you are dealing primarily with rebellion or behavior. That will narrow down your options immediately. From that point, you must decide which of the various behavior or disciplinary tools would work most effectively. You will not always know this ahead of time. You may have to experiment to find what will work. This is okay. If you love your child and are genuinely sensitive to his needs, he will not be hurt because of your uncertainties if your motives are pure. Generally speaking, this is the order to follow in trying out various behavioral tools: communication, reinforcement, extinction, natural consequences, logical consequences—proceeding from the least to the most harsh. Many of the others are in continuous operation (imitation, instruction, practice, and so on). When all these methods fail to achieve results, a parent can then begin to assume the child's attitude may be more deeply a part of the problem than suspected and can think about disciplinary tools, even though it may appear to be a behavioral problem on the surface.

There will be times (many of them!) when both rebellion and childish actions (attitudes *and* behavior) are involved at once. You will then have to draw upon all the information in both of these chapters to arrive at a solution. You may have to spank, isolate, and use natural consequences all at once. But remember (and this is very important), you must use each tool for the particular need for which it is designed. Even if you are using all these tools at once, you are spanking to curb the rebellion and you are employing natural consequences to change the behavior. *If you are spanking primarily to change behavior or are trying to talk your child out of his rebellion, your efforts will not achieve their maximum results.* This is a difficult differentiation to make since often in the heat of the moment we simply act, almost by instinct. You must, therefore, have these things well thought out so that when you do act (though you will of course make mistakes) your basis for doing so will be well grounded.

Many, many writers have succumbed to this danger and have mixed these two distinct needs in a child—the need to learn obedience and the need to learn acceptable behavior. They discuss tools such as these we have been looking at but fail to distinguish between the different needs they address. The writer of one of the leading Christian child-rearing manuals says that spanking should be a last resort and that reinforcement and natural consequences should always be used before a parent resorts to spanking. But this can be confusing to the young parent who concludes from this that they are addressing the same need and situation. This same book says that isolation, reinforcement, and natural consequences are far more effective methods of handling the parent-child power struggle than spanking. But again there is confusion. For a power struggle often occurs in the arena of discipline and must be handled as such.

Secular writers are confused at this point as well when they declare that spanking is an ineffective means of getting a child to behave properly and therefore condemn it. They are right; a spanking is a poor means to motivate a child to change his habits. But when dealing with rebellion it is the scriptural tool to be used above all others.

In other words, even though in the practical and daily situations you face there will be *much* overlapping, you need to keep these needs separate in your thinking in order to wield the tools effectively. This will not be easy! In teaching your three-year-old to dress himself and your six-year-old to take care of his books and your eleven-year-old to carry out his household responsibilities, you will be training in the arena of behavior *and* you will be dealing with resistant (sometimes rebellious) attitudes in your children which oppose your teaching. The older your children become, the more intertwined all these factors become. But the various tools still must not be confused. If you use logical consequences to instill responsibility, you can at the same time spank your child for an attitude of rebellion against your authority. But you must have it clear in your mind that you are *not* spanking him because he filled up on snacks after school and now won't eat his dinner, but rather because he disobeyed a command and gave you back talk in the process. In order to motivate him toward more mature eating habits, you need to employ a behavioral tool. You use both oftentimes, but you use them for different reasons.

There will be many times as well when you don't know exactly which area you are dealing with. If you told your daughter to be home by five o'clock and she wanders in at five-thirty, there has surely been disobedience. But are you dealing with open rebellion against your authority or simple childish irresponsibility that must be handled through extinction or consequences? Disobedience is not always rebellion, nor does following instructions to the letter always signal a submissive heart attitude. I can offer you no clear "pat" solution. You must simply know your child well and be sensitive and full of love while you are asking God for wisdom. Every situation will be different.

Having made such a point of this distinction between attitude and behavior and the various tools, I will further blur the issue in your mind by saying that as a child grows older in many ways this distinction begins to fade away. Once a scriptural basis for authority has been laid (the biblical basis is discipline according to the "rod") in the early years, discipline (even with respect to attitude) often must begin to be carried out using some of these behavioral tools. It is obviously unwise to physically spank your thirteen-year-old for a rebellious attitude. But if in that child's early years a strong foundation has been laid, you can now employ tools such as logical consequences in the arena of attitude and achieve results. This would seem at first glance to contradict what has been said before. But your success in being able to do this will be a result of the effectiveness of both your discipline and training earlier. This gradual process of increasing the use of the behavioral tools for disciplining attitudes is a very slow one that comes about over several years.

It is parallel to a child's increasing independence. The more independent he becomes, the more you must see that he is responsible for his own actions *and* attitudes. Both logical and natural consequences can play a very significant role later in a child's life in both training and discipline.

Further Help

This discussion of behavior-altering techniques has been very brief. There are other sources you can go to for many, many examples which will greatly assist you in actually putting these things into practice. In nearly any bookstore you can find dozens of books on child raising. Many of these have useful information to offer. Modern child psychology has given us many, many valuable insights about how to more effectively understand and love our children and mold their behavior.

But there is a danger with these books as well. What you must remember when reading most secular writers today is that they are operating from a base which largely denies the separateness of these types of needs—respect for authority *and* acceptable behavior. The behavioral side is usually the only one dealt with and disciplinary concepts are therefore condemned as ineffective. The modern trends of thought which scoff at the biblical need to respect and submit to God and others in authority are heavily influential in such writing. Therefore, the disciplinary measures supported by the Scriptures are completely disregarded or else recommended only in desperate circumstances. The two arenas of a parent's responsibility are not distinctly seen.

This is not to say these books should be totally rejected, because they can be very useful and of great help for the concerned parent. But you must often overlook a writer's comments at certain points (noticeably with respect to discipline) where he is unaware of this dual aspect of the training and disciplinary process.

There are several books I highly recommend. For a deeper understanding of the disciplinary measures discussed in chapter 5, I recommend *Dare to Discipline* by James Dobson (Tyndale House) and my own *A Christian Family in Action* (Bethany Fellowship). For more practical help on applying the various psychological techniques of modifying behavior that we have been discussing in this chapter, I recommend: *Help! I'm a Parent* by Bruce Narramore (Zondervan), *How to Parent* and *How to Father* both by Fitzhugh Dodson (Signet), *Children: The Challenge* by Rudolf Dreikurs and Vicki Soltz, and *A Parent's Guide to Child Discipline* by Rudolf Dreikurs and Loren Grey (both Hawthorn), and *Between Parent and Child* by Haim Ginott (Macmillan).

7

ERECTING THE WALLS

Instilling Self-Esteem

When the foundation of a house has been laid, the walls can go up. The solidity of the foundation provides support for the walls. The strength, thickness, and construction of the walls in turn furnish structural strength that will bond the entire house together as a unit. Walls are to a house what bones are to a human frame. Without them there can be no structure, no shape, no power, no firmness, and no usefulness. Such is the importance and role of self-esteem in the human make-up.

In the building of a house there is a definite order to the process. The foundation must always precede the raising of the studs which will form the interior of the walls. Our analogy between house and child, therefore, breaks down at this point and we must constantly be aware of this difference. For in the training of a child, both discipline (the foundation) and self-esteem (the walls) go hand in hand. They must be ingrained simultaneously. *Neither comes first or can be elevated to the exclusion of the other without weakening the entire structure.*

They are separate like the individual blades of a pair of scissors, yet they function together or they accomplish nothing.

A Parent's Most Important Task— Revealing to His Child Who He Is and What He Can Do

The nurturing of self-esteem in his child is *the* most important task a parent faces. By "self-esteem" I simply mean the value a child has for himself, the worthiness he feels, his own appraisal of how his parents and God and other people view him. A child with a healthy dose of esteem regards himself highly (in a properly humble sense) and therefore has confidence and peace. Low esteem fills a child with feelings of inadequacy, worthlessness, and inferiority. He feels that others do not like him because he does not like himself.

Without supplying a child with a proper regard for his own personhood, everything else a parent does, no matter how good, is in vain. I admit that I have repeatedly stressed the importance of viewing your relationship with your child from many angles and seeing all these aspects of the process we are discussing as connected and interrelated. Nevertheless, if you had to follow the advice in just one of these chapters to the exclusion of all the others (which I don't recommend), I would say to you that *this* is that chapter. It is important to remember, however, that everything in every chapter is intricately woven into the fabric of all the other chapters. Nevertheless, *this* is probably the single most important chapter in the book. This is not to say that you should elevate these few principles so that you forget the others. However, you must grasp the gravity of what we are dealing with here. This provides the structure of the whole building. Without this you have nothing. So read solemnly, remembering its *extreme* importance. At the same time, however, keep in mind that your success in being able to follow the principles of this chapter is largely dependent on how you follow the principles in all the other chapters.

Children are like lumps of clay, soft and pliable at first but growing steadily harder through the years. During the first years of their lives, we are the ones who largely determine the final shape of their characters. Our words and opinions are the ones that matter most to them. The impact of what we say and do is overwhelming. Every day we stamp into our children attitudes, words, ideas, beliefs, habits, and responses that will one day, when they are older and the shape of the clay has set, be an automatic part of them. What we say and how we react can either build or destroy. The impressions we create in their early years set the stage for an entire trend in life. Our responses to their first attempts at independence, at personhood in their own right, will shape their personalities, their motivations, their dreams, their abilities, and their views—because for several years we are the most important people in the world to them. Everything we say and do has a tremendous inner effect on the shaping and molding process taking place—*everything*! The extent of a parent's investment now in his child will determine the depth and richness of his later growth.

One of the most significant areas where this shaping process first begins and occurs daily for many, many years is in a child's view and concept of himself. His basic goal and drive in life, for up to twenty or twenty-five years, is simply to find out about himself. Drawings of young school children of various ages reveal a preoccupation with different parts of the anatomy at different levels, signifying shifts in self-concept. A very young child's picture of himself is all head; mouths play an important part early too. Then there is the stomach which begins to be seen. Finally, at an older age, children become aware of legs and arms, surroundings, other people. A young child reveals fascinating things about dawning self-awareness. A child is interesting to himself. He enters the world knowing nothing at all about who he is, where he came from, what makes him run, what others think of him, what his capabilities are, what his role is toward others, in his family, toward God, where he is going in life. These are all things a child's deep subconscious processes are trying to figure out, from the moment he is born. When we say a teen-ager is trying to "find himself" those are no hollow words.

A child is therefore keenly aware of what his parents think of him. He grasps for every tiny clue that will shed some light on him as a person. Anything anyone says or feels about him is noticed immediately and tucked away in the corner of his memory for future reference. He cares more for the opinions of his parents than anyone else. So he is constantly on the lookout for anything that will give him additional insight into what he is like.

The thing you must remember about this process is that a young child really doesn't know what to think of himself. It's quite unlike the procedure adults follow when they grope for compliments or listen for what others think. An adult is usually already convinced in his mind one way or another and is simply trying to find confirmation. Not so with a child. A child is genuinely a virgin field whose opinions of himself can go in any direction. And in a child's life, adults (especially parents) represent the all-knowing, all-wise authority about everything. A child utterly trusts and believes what he hears. In that sense he is totally gullible. He will swallow anything. A child of two or three is formulating a lifetime self-image simply on the basis of the things he hears about himself. Every comment adds to the program inside the computer of his brain. Stray comments downgrading a child do not bounce off. They are taken inside, stored, and form the actual program which his brain will slowly develop into a personality. A child actually becomes what we visualize and tell him he is.

And let's face it: a child has several strikes against him immediately as this search for self-identity begins. When you think about it, isn't it rather remarkable that God gave to children such an innate drive that gets them successfully over these hurdles of early life? For during his first several years, a child is in fact vastly inferior in many ways to everyone else he regularly sees around him. He is smaller, naive, uncoordinated, often confused, can't communicate as clearly, and certainly he lacks power and authority. His entire life is being told what to do by someone else. Even if a baby brother or sister comes along who is more helpless, it seems the little one gets more love and attention. There is no way for a child to win. No wonder inferiority is such a problem!

And in many ways, growing older—despite the fact that his physical and mental skills increase remarkably—only makes matters worse. When a child goes to school, the papers he brings home have red marks all over. But are these marks of his learning, of what he did right? No. If he got a 70 or 80 percent, what is marked? Only what he got wrong. A child doesn't remember the unmarked 70 or 80, only the brightly colored 20 or 30. If he turns out for sports, or even tries to participate in normal recess games, his coaches and teachers are quick to point out mistakes and flaws, but rarely are one's best efforts—even if average—rewarded. The emphasis everywhere you turn is on the negative rather than on the accomplishment (unless you happen to be brilliant or a star—which very few children are).

If there is anywhere a child should be able to find a healthy and positive view of himself, it should be in the church. But here it is often just the same. In a popular tract designed specifically for use with children to tell them the "good news," the very first concept stressed is that we are all black with sin. This is often the Christian mentality, to begin with the negative so that a person will realize his need for repentance. For an impressionable young child, who barely knows enough about life to get by, to be told he is a sinner from the moment he enters Sunday school is only to further deepen his sense of lowliness and defeat. *Children need some genuine good news about themselves.*

It is not that a child is on a search for self-esteem. He is simply on a campaign to discover anything he can about himself. By nature, humans thrive on positive feelings about themselves. This is how God made us. He created us so that our capacity to extend outward is based on our inward love of ourselves. Hence, giving a child a healthy and positive image of himself is a necessity if we expect to raise him able to function as God intended. Consider the simple injunction, "Love your neighbor as yourself." Its foundation? A positive self-love.

There exists no other way for a human being to live to his full potential. A man with a poor image of himself—however he came by it—is a man destined to mediocrity, ineffectiveness, depression, failure, and selfishness. If you want to give your child a joy-filled life which reaches the potential God has for him, you must seek to program his brain with a positive picture of himself as he investigates who he is and what he is able to do.

How It Is Done— Approval, Affirmation, Appreciation, Encouragement, and Praise

You must begin with an understanding of what gives a person

a good feeling about himself and what motivates him toward esteem-building accomplishments. Feeling good about who you are is only the first half of self-esteem. The second is possessing capabilities to perform. A person's respect for himself is directly proportional to his ability to carry out various tasks. A person who can *do* things for himself is a person who feels competent and worthwhile. Each small job or ability a child masters gives him enormous pride (of a healthy kind). As he grows and increases in his proficiency in larger and greater tasks, he will become properly independent and self-assured. Confidence is built on what we can do for ourselves, rather than on what we must rely on others to do for us.

Our role, then, is twofold: to give a child a good feeling about who he is and about what he can do.

The remarkable thing, however, is that both these goals are accomplished via the same means. The very thing that increases a child's image of who he is, happens also to be the same thing that will motivate him to learn to accomplish tasks with greater competence. From the very moment of birth humans thrive on approval, encouragement, appreciation, and praise—responses that affirm positive qualities and accomplishments.

Approval by others is a fundamental human need. We were created needing it. We flourish and grow and mature, or else wither and die, according to a large extent on the approval we receive—both for what we are and what we do—from others, from God, and from ourselves.

Many parents do not realize to what a huge extent approval, or a lack of it, is transmitted to their children every moment. The small moments we would often overlook are often the most significant of all. The less we are conscious of this ongoing process, the more likely it is that we are in fact passing along a negative picture to our children. Teaching is done through neglect just as easily as by thought and design. And the results of such accidental teaching are unfortunate. For one day a parent wakes up to the realization that he has actually passed on his own crippling traits, flaws, and weaknesses which his child must live with forever.

To avoid this, parents must realize their task and set out to transmit approval, encouragement, appreciation, and praise. Such affirmation must be on the basis of a child's tremendously significant personhood before God (if there are any doubts about this, memorize Psalm 139 in *The Living Bible* and teach it to him) and God's love. This is in contrast to what society would tell us when it emphasizes physical appearance, athletic prowess, expensive clothes, and popularity. We cannot think such false values are only "out there" in the world. They penetrate every one of our thought patterns and we must daily squash them. Recently my wife made an interesting observation while at Sunday school. As class was about to begin, one sweet little girl, with an "ugly duckling" sort of appearance, was very matter-of-factly told, "Now go pick up your jacket and hang it up. Come on now, we're ready to start." Several minutes later another little girl walked in. She was very cute with a winning smile, the daughter of one of the church's well-known couples. The response of the teacher was dramatically altered this time. The class was stopped completely. "Well, hello, Mary, how nice you look today. Here, let me help you get your coat off and we'll hang it up right over here. Say hello to Mary, everyone." Both were well-behaved girls. But the attention they received was quite different. The false value system of the world often sucks us in and we must beware of it.

When a foundation of affirmation is built upon God's principles, then these more fleeting things (like appearance) that are sometimes important to a child can be recognized and complimented (to a degree) in order to build his confidence. But if we try to build his esteem principally on them, with no firm base, we do him nothing but harm. For the hollowness of those values will eventually pop like a balloon and he will be left with nothing.

We provide a secure foundation for esteem most forcefully through what we say to our children. A child's mind is a fertile field. Everything that is said regarding him in any way will be planted there. Something is certain to grow, and whether that field blooms with weeds and crabgrass or with daisies and marigolds depends on the seeds that are sown. By planting negative and critical words, we can count on a harvest of self-doubts and feelings of worthlessness. If seeds of praise and encouragement are planted, however, the yield will be rich in positive feelings and therefore in capabilities for performance and service to God.

Words can build and motivate or crush a tender human spirit. The first budding shoots of personality are extremely fragile. They can easily be bruised or broken. There is no such thing as an innocent word. A child is all ears, even in what for us is an unguarded moment. Attitudes are being shaped during such times. Even when we may not be talking directly about our child, our words and points-of-view mold the way he views the world. "I wish that guy next door would cut his lawn! His yard's a blot on the neighborhood." A casual comment. Yet our son or daughter picks up our negative attitude, our free tongue which talks about others critically. The homes of many children are filled with such talk (much of it about "little" things, to be sure—yet the chiseling is going on, a child is being formed with such attitudes) about friends, neighbors, the government, the police, relatives, the pastor, some aggravating business associate, and many others. Every word is being tucked away inside the child's computer-like brain.

Most important are the words a child hears about himself. He is quick to notice any tiny shred of information which will reveal what his parents really think of him, even though it may be second or third hand. He desperately wants to know. Though what he hears may destroy him, nevertheless, he seeks it avidly. This is what makes the indirect compliment (or criticism) all the more powerful to either build or tear down. What he happens to overhear his parent say about him to someone else is something he *knows* they really feel deep down inside. There is no better way to compliment a child than to tell someone else what a good job he did and how much you appreciate him, all within his earshot. And conversely, an overheard criticism is so powerful that it is nearly intolerable for a child to bear.

Every word spoken is planted in the garden of a child's sprouting self-image and will one day mature and bear fruit. And sad to say, negative words strike root deeper and are remembered longer and more easily than positive ones.

We must, therefore, cultivate the habit—and certainly like any worthwhile habit it takes work and practice, it rarely comes naturally for anyone—of verbally affirming our children. We approve and affirm them for the persons they are, and we appreciate and praise and thank them for what they do. Our positive opinion of our children must show through to them. No one-way mirrors are allowed here; our feelings of high regard must be transparent.

Children are usually confident about what their mothers think because positive feelings ordinarily flow easily from a mother to her children. Unfortunately, the same is not generally the case with fathers. A father is around his children less and is less communicative. They do not really know how dad feels; he isn't as close to the daily, hour-by-hour, family situation as the rest of them. So his feelings are often almost a secret. They therefore seek hard to discover what he thinks of them. They are on the constant lookout for any subtle sign that will reveal dad's true feelings. They quickly learn to tell the extent to which dad is interested in their lives. Of course he is unaware that this investigation is going on with him at its center. Because of daily absenteeism, men have a specially difficult task in transmitting affirmation to their children.

But this very difficulty also gives a father an unusual advantage at the same time. Because a father's approval is generally more difficult to come by, it is all the more special when it is given. An interested and affirming and encouraging father can therefore make miraculous things happen in the self-esteem of his child. He is such a special person to him that his approval counts much more highly than that of any other person. Likewise, a child who finds his father demanding and impossible to please may spend the rest of his lifetime subconsciously trying to achieve a level that will satisfy. A father's power to influence his child is difficult to fathom. His words, his looks, and the hope of his approval can motivate a child like nothing else. When he responds to his child in praise, the joy it causes is deep and motivates still further.

The appreciated child is happy and well-adjusted. He is secure in his family relationships and he is aware of his worth to his parents. He knows he is important to them and that knowledge satisfies his chief concern in life. A few instances here and there won't generate this security. It must be constantly reaffirmed, not only with positively spoken words, but also with physical tenderness and affection. A family needs touching, hugging, kissing, closeness. For a child these things cement into reality what spoken words merely say.

The atmosphere in a family which allows children to grow to their maximum potential and maturity in God is one in which affirmation and gratitude between family members is clearly visible. Never can a parent relax in his recognition of all there is to discover deep in the heart of his child and in his search for new ways to tell him how greatly he loves him. Nothing can substitute for this aspect of your relationship with him. Nothing else can accomplish the same building and strengthening of his person. A child comes to recognize his greatness as a child of God only on the basis of our daily demonstration of how completely we are convinced of it ourselves.

The childhood years are formative. If approval is not enthusiastically ingrained in a child during his early years, the need can never fully be taken care of later no matter how great later achievements may be. Self-esteem is born in childhood. If lost, it cannot ever be completely recovered. A child not permitted a positive picture of himself as seen through the eyes of his parents will develop a picture of himself that will cripple him for life. The fragile spirit of a young child is where the potential lies for great opportunities or great tragedy.

Seeing Through a Child's Eyes

It is critical for parents to train themselves to view life through their child's eyes as well as their own. Only in so doing will they be able to cultivate and nurture the curiosity and imagination and energy and potential God put inside their child and cause those traits to mature into confidence, security, creativity, and joy. Our responses provide the fuel that will make these traits grow. God placed in every child boundless and energetic resources. If we stimulate, encourage, listen to, and talk with our children on their level, looking at the world in the exciting and fresh ways their eyes perceive it, we will nourish their creative growth. Everything looks so different from where they are standing. However, if we do not take the time to share their world, making no effort to penetrate the world as they see it, we will suppress their childlike exuberance and spontaneity. And, in addition, we will lower the view they have of their own value because of our disinterest. Unencouraged children whose intoxication with life is stifled, grow up unproductive, lethargic, and with little self-confidence.

Getting sufficiently outside oneself to do this is extremely difficult for the adult with a busy and demanding schedule (as all seem to be). I find my constant prayer must be, "Lord, open my eyes to see the needs and feelings of my children."

I am aware that I am teaching my boys all day long, even without realizing it. I quickly convey to them my lack of enthusiasm in their affairs whenever my mind is preoccupied. I am giving them perceptions of themselves by my own picture of them. Do I see my son as lazy or unproductive, or as skilled and helpful and interesting to be with? The answers to those questions largely determine whether my child will come to be aware of the potential contributions he can make as God's child or not. My daily vision of my child is of eternal importance. And that vision is communicated by my genuine interest in his little life—seeing things through his eyes, being able to get down onto his level and live with him there. This means far more than just allotting some time each day to spend with him. It must mean really getting into him, where he ticks.

It could truthfully be said that by "mature" standards children do not possess great wisdom, interact daily with influential people, and have what we would consider remarkable ideas and insights to share with us. Yet God's evaluation usually takes more than "absolute value" into account. He looks at potential, He looks at the growth process into which a particular bit of insight fits. He looks at a person's raw material and can, therefore, see how one tiny bit of wisdom might be to one person a fantastic revelation, but to another just a commonplace piece of knowledge. Once we have eyes to see them, the insights of children are phenomenal!

It is easy to thoughtlessly put children off. "We'll listen to them later," we rationalize, "when they're more grown up." Tune in to your own voice and count the number of times you hear yourself carelessly throwing out the following phrases: "Just a minute. . . .", "Not now, I'm busy. . . .", "I'll look at it later. . . .", "Wait. . . !" Children get several very significant messages from all this. They get the message that their parents are busy and important people. This is really the least important thing we communicate. They also get the message that mom and dad's "other" affairs take precedence over their own. This is a more important message that comes through loud and clear. And it leads to the most important message of all— *I* am not as important to my mother and father as other things.

The result? An undervalued sense of their own personal worth.

But if Jesus is to be our example, he approached the children He encountered quite differently. He told His disciples very clearly that children are important, they are to be listened to, paid attention to. Whenever children came upon the scene of His activities and travels, Jesus took time from His busy schedule (full of important things to do, important people to talk with, important things to say—*the* most important ministry the world has ever seen) to talk with them. We don't know what Jesus asked the children, or what He said to them. But we do know they liked Him and sought Him out. This says something for His sensitivity to their world.

There are all sorts of areas where we face constant opportunities to share our child's world, and in so doing increase the esteem he feels by giving importance to his concerns. But it takes an alert awareness and a continual denial of the values which would draw us away from them. Good attentive listening is most important. It is vital that a child who is discovering new things about the world and himself daily has someone to tell it all to. Being an interested parent takes time and training, often self-discipline.

As a child grows and begins to experience feelings of inadequacy (which all do) he needs more affection and companionship and tenderness. And always a caring ear. He will need unconditional acceptance; our open arms, willingness to listen, and positive responses will provide it.

The Significant Moment—
A Parent's Response to a Child's Effort

When a child first begins to reach cautiously out of himself—tentatively, with weak knees—to express or create or do something he has never done before, the response of a parent may set in motion trends that will last his lifetime. Such are among the most crucial moments in the child's entire life. We *must* respond in praise. No matter what the "product" may be—a silly poem, an off-key solo, an unrecognizable drawing, a flat instrument, or an error-ridden performance. The very act of trying, of extending oneself outward into new regions of accomplishment, is in itself worthy of our highest praise.

Vocal responses are crucial. Criticism is a subtle snare to fall into without realizing. It often masquerades as a compliment. Such a common parental evaluation is, "You can do better than that!" We are even deceived into thinking that we are praising at such times. We somehow feel that such a rejoinder is going to uncover hidden talent in our son or daughter and spur him on to greater heights.

But the boy or girl who has just poured his or her all into an effort, of any kind, is not presently interested in how well his parents think he might do ten years from now, or even tomorrow. He needs to know that *today* he has succeeded unconditionally, that his parents are proud of him. Therefore, when a wide-eyed and bright-faced youngster encounters a you-can-do-better evaluation from his parent before anything else is said, he takes it to mean only one thing— "*Today*, I failed." What a blow to the self-image, to the motivation to accomplish more of the same. Small wonder that many children, by the time they reach junior high, couldn't care less about schoolwork, athletics, accomplishments of any kind. The child unmotivated to succeed beyond straight C's and D's is a child whose motivation in life has been systematically undercut by his parents, one small comment at a time.

Check yourself; it will amaze you. How many times do you say yes and how many times do you say no to your child? It is astounding! *No*, the cornerstone of our vocabulary, also embodies the very essence of the negative response. We obviously cannot remove it from our language, but such a test should at least serve to keep us on our toes about the negativitism which so easily flows from our tongue.

If a child is told no five times a day (a conservative estimate by any standard) by parents and teachers, by the time he is ten his wants will have been blocked almost twenty thousand times! Certainly many of these times it will have been for his good. But this should give us an idea of what a child is up against. It must seem that *everything* is a *no* at times. We must use no as part of our disciplinary program to be sure. But when discipline is not going on, our responses must be overwhelmingly positive. If they aren't, and if we thoughtlessly allow negative reactions (no matter how subtle) to color our child's image of himself, is it any wonder so many children grow up lazy, unproductive, and with inferiority feelings that stretch back to the day they were born?

A psychologist friend has explained this self-response of a child in terms of what she calls the "line of acceptable behavior" which all parents subconsciously erect to mark the difference between what we consider acceptable and unacceptable actions on the part of our children. Every child's behavior varies considerably. And to a large degree, how a child comes to view himself is a result, *not of the actions themselves*, but of our response to them. If we draw our own personal "line of acceptable behavior" at an unrealistically high point, our child will come to think of a majority of his actions as falling below that line and being therefore unacceptable. If we can take a somewhat more relaxed view and draw the line at a lower point, then our child will feel much more accepted and worthwhile because a majority of his actions fall above the line and are therefore acceptable. How a child sees himself is a result of how much of what he does we are willing to accept.

The interesting thing about this concept is that the child's actions can be the same in either case. The only variable is where we personally decide to draw the line between the acceptable and the unacceptable. At the lower point, most of what your child does is acceptable to you. At the unrealistically high point, most of what he does is unacceptable. A child will grow up feeling basically accepted, worthy, and valuable (or thinking that everything he does is wrong and unacceptable) simply on the basis of where we draw the line. The choice is ours.

Our child may be very skilled, polite, creative, and intelligent. Yet if we are consistently perfectionistic toward him (drawing the line of behavior too high so that 80 percent or 90 percent of what he does isn't quite good enough for us) he will grow up with the notion that he can never succeed no matter what he does. For we have been telling him all his life in essence, "Most of what you do is unacceptable to me. It just doesn't quite measure up to my standards." No matter that a good many things still fall well above the line. He is still aware that *most* of what he does isn't good enough. It hardly matters if the parent does not really feel this way toward his son or daughter. If the child *thinks* his behavior is considered unacceptable, the result will be the same. Generally speaking, a perfectionistic parent will place heavy demands upon his child to meet certain arbitrary standards. The self-image of that child will be low, because a child who constantly faces critical, grumbling, negative, dissatisfied comments about what he does translates this into, "As a person I am intrinsically unacceptable and unworthy."

There is a precarious balance between criticism and approval. In every person's life there is a need for honest criticism. When we must critically evaluate something in our child's life, what we say must be well thought out, deliberate, and sensitive. Our words must *always* ring with kindness, respect, and appreciation—even in the midst of negative evaluation. Criticism must never be an automatic response.

Every little compliment, on the other hand, builds an inner confidence and strength and self-respect in a child. Later a man will be capable of accomplishing greater things because he has a secure and healthy self-image. And he will have learned to respect others because he has been respected himself. A positive parent seldom produces a negative child. There is cause and effect working here. The outcome is predictable.

As a child develops he must come to sense himself as an individual who has worth in his own right. This is something his parents foster, by caring, by taking time with him, experiencing things with him, letting him know how special he is as a unique individual made by God's hands. He needs to feel this uniqueness. Only so can he blossom as he is capable.

Much of this uniqueness is allowed to surface through personal expression. The need to release what lays deep inside is a universal human characteristic—communication, the outward flow of what is within. Every child must express himself daily. He has to tell what's on his mind and what he feels. Since his brain and comprehension of ideas and thought patterns are not usually as well developed as this need, it comes out through his hands and feet. He runs, plays, throws, draws, paints, builds, cuts, pastes, dresses up, and explores—all to express himself. He doesn't care whether he has talent or whether his work is beautiful or proper or skilled. It's *him*, that's what counts. It's *his* expression, *his* creation.

This is why hobbies, sports, music, books, crafts, and other interests are so vital in children's lives. Such things allow them an avenue for expression, give them situations where they can be regarded as capable. And in such an environment their abilities will soar. Interests and hobbies and activities develop a total mental and emotional enrichment which will not only teach them but will give them a good feeling about themselves. Creativity and expression are valuable means of release for a child. Parents must see that these activities provide their children with success. From our daily living to the major activities of their childhood, there must be success. Success (measured by *our* eyes and responses, not the world's) is the very cornerstone of confidence and self-esteem.

Small doses of failure teach us to cope with life. There must be a healthy inclusion of it as well. But the foundation of self-esteem is built on confidence. We instill confidence in children by affirming and encouraging them, by making their lives a success. One child may be an athlete, another a musician, and one may tie fishing flies. Whatever his interests and abilities, *he must succeed.*

And that success is measured, not by the outward scale of worldly values, but by our responses alone! This is so difficult to grasp. The only thing a child really cares about is what his parents think. If his parents say "great," and he knows they mean it completely, then all his peers can say "boo" and it will hardly daunt his pride. A child must know that to his parents he's absolutely tops, the *best* in the world. Parents make every effort successful by their response far more than the actual performance level does. Even a minor and incomplete result, which an outside observer could well judge a miserable failure, if treated properly by a wise and loving parent, becomes a gigantic accomplishment which builds confidence and further motivates the child. No matter how little the visible and measurable progress, our enthusiastic and praising response insures that our child will be built up and motivated to continue to learn. Motivation is self-generating. We can start the process in motion through praise and continue to feed it with encouragement. From that point on, a child will become internally self-motivated from his own enthusiasm.

Praise motivates; criticism tears down. There is always something you can praise in a child's behavior. I have no intention of deceiving my children. I simply want to recognize the level at which their efforts are being made and not compare them with skills they cannot possibly achieve. Praise early in life will yield efficiency and top performances later. There will be plenty of time for me to evaluate with a critical eye. If my seventeen-year-old son is trying out for the starting quarterback position, then he will need me to point out every defect in his delivery. But my second grade son, who can hardly hold a football, much less throw it, needs only praise and admiration.

The parent unaware of the incredible influence he is exerting can unthinkingly tear down the regard his child has for himself. Comparing, teasing, sarcasm, always expecting better—these will all serve, not to motivate as we may think, but to undermine what we hope to accomplish in our child. We can aim high, certainly. But we must keep ourselves aware of how great achievements come. It is through internal motivation. And that only exists inside a person who feels good about himself and is excited about what he is doing. Nothing is accomplished toward building motivation by criticism. When an effort is made, there must be excitement at that effort, not always the result. Only so can a child be motivated further.

A Child's Expanding and Growing Need for Esteem

In any recipe for esteem, there is one universal and essential component which must always be present. Without it, building love and security into a child is not just hard, it is impossible. That ingredient is time. Time does not come easily for anyone. All of us have the tendency to think, "*If* only such-and-such, and I therefore had more time, *then* I would spend more with the kids."

But if you don't do it now, you wouldn't then. It is easy to envy someone whose schedule looks less demanding. To look at a school teacher who spends months with his family, camping, traveling, working, and playing it can be a temptation for someone to think, "If I were in that guy's shoes I'd be able to do that too. But I just don't have the time!"

But that school teacher has had to make a choice too, a choice to spend his time with his family. It might not have been easy for him either. We are all in vastly different situations. Some of us have more time away from the job than others. Nevertheless, we *all* have many, many hours available every week if we know where to find them. And our children have a rightful claim upon a good many of them—the premium hours, not the leftover ones. It may take painfully cutting some things out of your week for the sake of making yourself available to be at home. It's no use complaining about all you have to do. God has placed you in a particular situation for your good. And He intends for you to spend lots of quality time with your family in the midst of your demanding schedule. It may mean cutting out the bowling league, it may mean reducing the number of regular activities with nonfamily friends, it may mean cutting out the weekly home Bible study group you are in, it may even come to cutting out a church service or two every week. No price is too great to pay if you do so to love your children as God instructed. Whatever it means and however it comes, you must find time and then take that time to spend with your children. And your time must be interesting and exciting time. If you begrudge your child's intrusion into your life, you are defeating the purpose and might just as well not bother. Your child will know how you really feel. This takes some priority decisions again. But look at it from your child's point of view for a moment. What could be more exciting than to show mom or dad the fort or to play catch with them or have dad help you learn to ride your new bike? *A child wants more than anything to incorporate you into his life.*

With this in mind, a wise parent begins to look more closely at the importance of what consumes his time. He begins to look upon everything he does with his child as something that can teach his youngster and something that will build into the child's growing "legacy of memories." He begins to look for family experiences that are geared to build up, that provide opportunities to share, chances to learn skills while working with a parent. Young boys especially seem to need daily opportunities to prove themselves physically. A wise parent senses this and gives him such opportunities. Remember Boswell's father? Nothing we do is ever wasted. And in all of our time with our children, we must learn to maintain an attitude that says to them, "I am available, interested, concerned. You may always approach me without fear of being shut off. I will respond to you. I am never too busy for you. For you are the most special person in the world to me."

In addition to our making sacrifices to have time available for our children, one of the major tools we can utilize to build the confidence of a child is to thoughtfully turn responsibilities over to him. At first these will, of course, be small things. But it can begin as early as two with asking a toddler to carry a shoe for you. A schoolchild will be starting to help regularly with household chores, a teen-ager with hard work. Our design is not to find someone onto whom we can unburden our own work load. Our motive must ever be to build both the confidence and capabilities of our children. Naturally part of having responsibilities is learning to be diligent in following through on them so this is part of our task as well. But if it becomes a drudgery that threatens to come between a parent and child, perhaps you are trying to teach too much too soon. For there must be success in these experiences; success, rather than nagging, will motivate a child. As a child learns to do more and as his parents trust him in a wider variety of tasks, his competence is increased and with it his sense of confidence and usefulness to the family. This is invaluable as he becomes aware of his increasing contribution in the total family life. And all along we must be appreciating him for what he is learning to accomplish.

But with increasing responsibility comes the potential for irresponsibility as children grow into the shoes we are giving them to wear. Responsibility and diligence do not come all at once. We must expect lapses. We must expect a child to revert at times into total irresponsibility. This is not necessarily something to punish. He is a child, after all. We cannot forget that. We must be careful not to discipline for irresponsibility in the same way we do disobedience. By doing so we can smother his curious and childlike instinct and his desire to once again reach out beyond his abilities. Our attitude must be to encourage him to reach out, but not to punish him when he wants to revert back to the temporary comfort of his immature world. He needs to know it is always there to fall back on. Knowing that, he will be more willing to let go of it and strive ahead.

Seeing through a child's eyes means an awareness of and respect for his characteristics and personhood and needs at every age and stage he progresses through. Because a child's world often does not fit into our daily pattern, to do this requires a constant refocusing of our priorities. Although it is difficult, we simply must shove aside more urgent but less important matters. The lessons of our child's life that will most profoundly affect his development will usually come during the small and seemingly insignificant times we spend with him.

The eventual result of the combination of these three factors we attempt to incorporate into our relationship with him—time, responsibility, and respect—is a growing sense of freedom. As we have given responsibility to him, shared our time with him, and communicated respect to our child, a capability will have begun to rise within him to face life more and more on his own.

He is slowly becoming independent of us.

This, of course, is our goal as we prepare him for adulthood—to give him just the proper degree of freedom and independence, coupled with just the right amount of corresponding responsibility, at just the right time. This process of turning the reins of his life over to him is one of the noteworthy components in the building of his self-esteem. The more responsibility he possesses and the more capably he performs with that liberty, the better he will feel about himself and therefore the more capable he will become. The job of a parent in this process, then, is to provide experiences where his child is able to discover the success of standing on his own feet. We must know when it is time for a child to branch out one step further—the process inches forward and we mustn't hasten it, but let it happen at its own pace.

The maturing child, properly related to his parents and secure in their leadership, branches out a little further all the time, taking slightly greater risks, experiencing greater latitude in his self-development. He begins to work out some of his own problems and to use his own maturity, insight, and judgment to discover his own flaws and weaknesses and determine ways to correct the problems he sees. A parent does not leave his child alone at such times, but is sensitive to the child's need to take at least part of the initiative. The parent must know when to step in and how to help his son or daughter push through barriers, always looking ahead to the time when they will be on their own. Each lesson and demonstration is preparatory, but in the early years, a parent will share a good portion of the load.

All this can happen for one reason alone: a child's wholesome development has his solidly affirmed personhood at its core. This is one of a parent's most solemn, yet most joyful, responsibilities. From the moment of his child's birth, a parent is affecting the way a child views his own person every moment—whether they are aware of the process or not. And when a child reaches the point where he is learning more and more to stand alone, preparing to face the world, he must know that his parents are right there whenever he needs them. Especially when teen-agers, as questioning and groping young adults, encounter bumpy water (which all do), the responses of a loving parent reinforce the foundation of esteem and confidence.

It's easy to forget what growing up is like. Parents must sensitize themselves to the struggles going on inside the spirit of every young person trying to cope with the process. From the ages of six to sixteen a child faces fears and frustrations and doubts, all of which are marked by the recurring question, "Who am I and what am I like?" Parents must help their children discover the answers to this question and lose no opportunity to communicate with them. Only so will a child have any self-regard preserved by the time he reaches twenty.

Growing up is a traumatic process! Self-esteem holds it together.

8

DETERMINING THE FLOOR PLAN

Teaching Your Child

While the strength of a house is not dependent upon the shape of its floor plan, its comfort and uniqueness certainly are. Though a house can be solid and can remain standing for years, unless careful preparation has gone into the arrangement of its rooms, then its occupants will be deprived of some of the joy the house could have otherwise afforded. In the many ways a child is taught by his parents, he is provided a floor plan for the house of his life—an arrangement that can constrict his growth or that can fully open him to all the glory of life God would reveal to him.

Love—the Motivation to Learn

The human brain is more sophisticated than any computer man will ever devise. Scientists have estimated that the brain reaches half its capacity by the time a child is four, three-fourths by the age of eight, and full maturity by about age seventeen.

The cortex is said to be capable of storing millions of separate facts.

But like man-made computers, the brain of a child must be programmed to be used. If a child is given enough of the right input throughout his first few years of life, his brain can be programmed for learning and absorbing all that life has to offer. His horizons can be stretched for the rest of his life.

God put into every human an instinctive hunger to learn. From the moment of birth, babies, then toddlers, then schoolchildren chase after knowledge furiously. It is a basic drive. Nothing you can do is able to keep this from happening. But with help and guidance and healthy motivation, they will even learn faster, will enjoy it more, and will keep learning longer.

God designed the universe as a classroom. And the home is a microcosm of it. For the young child the home *is* the universe—and his parents are the teachers. A child can drift through life learning and absorbing whatever comes his way; or he can be guided through life by parents who provide him with stimulations which allow him to mature and learn more rapidly in a godly direction.

The teaching a parent provides for his child is what will determine the bigness of that child's world. Like a beautifully structured placement of exciting rooms, teaching enriches his life; it lets in sunshine for him to see himself, the world, and life. God has made this world a dazzling show, and it is ours to experience. The wider the diversity of a parent's teaching patterns, the more abundant his child's life will be and the larger will be the home which his spirit will occupy.

Most people associate "teaching" with the transmission of information. But this is only one minor aspect of how a parent teaches his child. As easy as it is to think of reading and arithmetic and writing and history as separate entities that must be "taught," actually a child's capacity to learn even these subjects is totally woven in and through every other area of his life. Learning is not a separate thing for a child. The physical exercises he goes through from morning till night—crawling, organizing blocks, walking, running, riding, playing, throwing, competing, climbing—are actually contributing to the energizing of millions of circuits in his brain. Physical exercise prepares the brain for activity; the body and mind are one unit.

This is important for a parent to grasp, for we must see that learning is often more dependent on less tangible things than our lectures. A child learns more from his own actions than anything else. And he especially learns from watching us. Talking to a child is vital, but it is only one factor. From the moment of birth a baby is learning from us all the time. We are not, however, passing along information to him. To begin with, all we can do is love him. And that love provides the basis for future learning. A well-loved baby is comparable to a giant sponge, ready to absorb everything and anything the world has to offer.

A baby needs stimulation and almost as soon as our love begins to flow toward him, we should be stimulating his learning and imaginative processes. We are already building the foundation for more advanced forms of learning with stroller rides, crib mobiles, peaceful music, and our talk (which yet means nothing to him). It may seem that life at first is nothing but diapers, colic, bottles, crying, and sleep. But he is actually learning faster than he ever will again. Teaching begins immediately. We can't reserve it for later.

Curiosity—the Great Teacher

An additional factor in a child's learning process, which also begins at birth but becomes more outwardly visible as the months progress, is his curiosity. Though a baby is curious about everything, he is capable of little. So he must content himself to simply look and wonder.

But that will change!

By the time he is two, his curiosity will be leading him into hourly "hot water" at the expense of his capability. He has indeed acquired remarkable dexterity in two years, but his physical skills still have not caught up with his curiosity. Curiosity is his most untiring teacher. Even if a child had no parents around at all, his learning rate would be phenomenal because his curiosity never tires.

But as a child matures and his skills gradually begin to grow more solid, his capability and curiosity blend by degrees into a third quality which will become a more direct measure of his learning. That is his creativity.

When a child's creativity begins to blossom, he is approaching a time in life when outside guidance and stimulation are more regularly required. Like soil that has the same things planted in it year after year and eventually becomes depleted, a young child has enormous inherent drive and curiosity that can eventually deplete themselves. Without steady nurturing of his inquisitiveness, his creativity will shrink. But with watering, care, guidance, and teaching by parents who awaken continued growth in new directions, it will grow and grow.

To grow into an interesting and well-rounded adult, a child must have an interesting, stimulating childhood. The more a child is allowed to expand his curiosity, the wider will be his sphere of expression and his joy in life. He needs outings and experiences—field trips. This doesn't always have to mean a trip to the zoo or the dairy or the park or the cheese factory. You can take a child on a field trip right in your own living room or kitchen by allowing his mind to be stirred and his eyes to fill with wonder. A book, a shared project, a story, a "new" food—anything can whet the appetite of his mind.

Curiosity is the basis for imagination and creativity and genius. To realize that the foundation for genius is accessible to us all should motivate us to direct our children's minds toward new areas. It has been theorized that almost every child is born with the mental capabilities of genius and it is only the roadblocks of insufficient stimulation that keep it from emerging. A baby's mind is new and alive and fresh, and so will a child's be if it continues to be fed with intellectually stimulating things. His ability to cope with everything life has to throw at him will be significantly strengthened with a healthy foundation of imagination, curiosity, creativity, and wonder. This will keep him from being bored, restless, dissatisfied—the earliest symptoms of a dull existence. It is important to remember that these qualities need nurturing in order to mature.

Imagination—The Flower of Learning

As a child meets and wonders at new and curious things, his mind becomes increasingly inventive, questioning, resilient, and fertile. Every new idea he turns over inside (new to him, not necessarily to everyone else) will make him more capable of thinking on his own. A parent can encourage this to happen by getting down on his hands and knees with his son or daughter, to look at life from his often upside-down perspective, and also to point out occasional things to him to expand his viewpoint.

God placed imagination within us all. But in some it never

grows, because it is a fragile quality, a delicate flower that is easily crushed. Yet it is also a plant easily nourished by simply encouraging it to grow. It is nurtured and grows quickly in an atmosphere of great freedom within the boundaries of safety and reason—freedom to climb, explore, create, build, draw, and dream. You can enlarge it yet further with your own imagination which you open toward your child. By walking with him, exploring life side-by-side, you are able to demonstrate in little ways that an imaginative viewpoint makes the minor things in life all the more exciting. As you show him things, ask questions, put visions and choices in his head, read to him, converse with him, and listen to him you will be encouraging the exercise of his productive mind. This can happen through any medium—words, food, magazines, music, sightseeing, animals, plants, or sounds.

Why imagination? Shouldn't our concern be with the realities of life rather than fantasies?

Imagination is not so much a thing to be sought after or passed on to our children on its own. Imagination is an exercise. Curiosity and imagination stretch the capacity of one's mind into areas that might otherwise remain untouched. Intelligence, interest in life, excitement all have their roots in the imagination. A mind that probes the unusual, the new, the curious, the unknown, is a mind more able to know itself and probe the hidden reaches of God's world, His principles, and His infinite character.

Yet imagination is in another way a worthwhile quality in its own right, because imagination adds a certain tangy relish to life, a certain twist that makes reality all the more real. Without imagination and curiosity it is impossible to fully live the command, "This is the day the Lord has made. Let us rejoice and be glad in it." An imaginative mind is the basis of a heart which lives in constant thankfulness to God.

It is possible to enrich your child in these creative areas in a hundred ways, especially through your own attitude. Imagination has a way of rubbing off. But, in addition, in a child's younger years his days should be full of stimuli, from knowing and seeing you talk with people of different ages, to playgrounds to books to toys to outings. Later your child will need more time sharing activities with each parent individually—a fishing trip with dad, making a dress with mom, or a family camping trip.

He needs two kinds of teaching experiences, and he needs them both regularly. The first is outside influences of infinite variety (your emphasis on them will add to their effect on him). And secondly, he needs quality time with mom and dad when life is given perspective through shared activities and discussion. You are seeking ways of enriching his mind from a hundred different angles. This is how God can make of him a unique individual, ready to learn and grow from everything he experiences, ready to love life and those around him with a heart able to thank God for being in it all.

Self-Discovery—The Basis for Learning and Intelligence

Curiosity and imagination cannot necessarily always be equated with intelligence. But they lead to self-discovery. And in the process of discovering, learning occurs.

A parent cannot discover things for his child. But he can provide an environment richly laden with the potential for discoveries. This can be done by providing as many firsthand unusual experiences as possible and by providing the materials (playthings) to learn from.

One of the best ways to set your child's mind in the direction of learning through curiosity and discovery is to take him places where he can see unusual things. Let him actually sit in the seat of a fire engine or a bulldozer and actually pet the nose of a cow or goat and throw food to a monkey or duck. As he grows older, take him to places like a dairy, a factory, a photo-processing shop, a newspaper, a police station, or an airport. When curiosity and imagination are sufficiently aroused, discoveries begin, whether it be from questions or further reading. A child who is interested in something will *want* to learn about it. And he will.

Young children especially need ample "things" to play with and manipulate which act as thinking stimuli. These can be blocks, paints, tools, felt-tip pens and paper, stacks of magazines, scissors, cardboard boxes, a blackboard and chalk, glue, cloth, toys, a bulletin board, and countless other things. For a child (whether a toddler or a nine-year-old) such things are not a waste of time. They are the foundation for thought. They act in much the same way as outside experiences—they lead to discoveries large and small. Later abstract thinking is able to arise out of such early concrete experiences.

Many people are not able to tap the power that God put in their brains for thought because they have not had many firsthand experiences of their own to stimulate their minds into action. They have been filled instead with nothing but the opinions, thoughts, and ideas of others. They have not had practice in thinking things out for themselves and so thoughts and ideas have not originated or been allowed to blossom within them.

There is a lesson here for parents. How important it is that we teach a child to think by allowing him to make discoveries on his own. It is hard to stand back. We always want to say, "Blue and yellow make green." But how much more significant in the child's life to simply offer him the paints and wait—maybe two days, maybe a month—until that excited moment when we hear from the other room, "Hey, I mixed blue and yellow paint and it turned to green!"

Just as God placed within every child an intense curiosity, so He also gave him a desire to figure things out. Children are curious and they must know *why* and *how*. They want to understand how things work. This is how they learn. Children *want* to make discoveries. And they will, if we just stand back to allow them. From the moment they are born, they are bombarded with new information. And from that moment on, they are constantly trying to arrange and organize and relate all this information. They are trying to discover whatever they can about it.

There are several things we can do to help this process along. Games are good at any age to help your child think clearly and rationally. His unconscious and imaginative processes can be developed through learning to make (create) out of nothing—playdough, collage, sand, etc. The fact that there is no structure means the child has to invent something on his own. When that happens, learning is taking place. Reading stories (and making up our own) also encourages a child's use of this imaginative part of his brain. Even toys (from a three-year-old's building blocks to a nine-year-old's Erector set) can accomplish this. But toys are vastly different in what they accomplish. If a toy provides a means for a child to use his creativity, then it is a good toy. A cardboard box large enough for a door and for a child to fit inside, for instance, is something that lends itself to many imaginative uses. It is unstructured enough that many different things are possible. It can be a fort, a playhouse, a hiding place, a bed, or (if large enough) a special place to get in with mommy to read a book. Certain cars and trucks also can stimulate a child in all sorts of directions in his play, as can the many varieties of "construct-o-blocks." This too is part of the value of books in a child's life—to encourage visualized, imaginative thinking.

Contrast this with battery-operated or push-button toys where 95 percent of the "play" comes from the mechanics of the toy itself rather than from the imagination of the child. The more a toy does for the child, the less the child himself is able to develop his own creativity, imagination, and self-discovery. But when a toy actually stimulates a child's mind in new areas, then it is valuable. In other words, toys need to be abstract; they need to lead a child into his own inventiveness. Something specific (like a doll that wets and opens and closes her eyes or a mechanical crane that performs five different functions with various levers) is limited to only those certain uses. Little is left for a child to "make up."

This must be the motive behind much of what we provide for a child, not simply in relation to toys. The more we can encourage imaginative and creative thought which leads to self-discoveries, the more we will help him to *learn,* even though our teaching will be subtle and indirect.

The Increasing Necessity for Direct Verbal Teaching

We are teachers all the time, though often not as we would think.

The more a child is allowed to expand and grow in new directions (under the influence of his parents' wisdom), the more he will begin to express himself. He will ask questions and learn to search for answers. His teachability will be in direct proportion to the roominess of the house you are building for him. The more rooms you introduce him to, the more he will be eager to learn and see more.

Though a baby learns simply by absorbing what is around him in the context of our total love, it is not long before a toddler begins to require more direct teaching. Though it may still be some time before he is ready for us to actually "teach" him information and facts, the preludes to that time are already actively stirring. We begin to set boundaries, slap hands, move objects, and say "no." Direct forms of learning are coming more regularly. By two years, we can look the child straight in the eye and talk to him, confident that a good portion of the message is getting through. His eyes seem to grasp what we are trying to convey.

As the years progress, teaching becomes increasingly straightforward. Little by little we feed our children information about everything—God, bugs, cars, books, jobs, tractors, responsibilities, food, words, sex, toys, school. The list goes on and on. And it is a different list at every age.

The parent is the teacher. The groundwork laid in a child's early years of love and of providing stimuli for his insatiable curiosity now provides the foundation for more informative teaching situations.

As a child grows older our verbal interaction with him becomes more crucial. It is not sufficient for us to talk *at* him. We must talk *with* him, always aware that good discussion is half talking, half listening. When we are talking, presuming him to be attentive, our running commentary about life is penetrating his mind. Our awareness of this mustn't slip or our talk could become sloppy. Therefore, as we explain to him the "whys and wherefores" of everything around us, we must exercise care, always listening to ourselves even as we talk, and listening to him as well. Every word makes an impression. If we plant a running string of critical reactions to everything from taxes to policemen to someone across the street, a child's fertile mind will absorb it all and negative attitudes will be shaped which will leap to the surface later. There is no such thing as an "innocent" word. A child learns from us every moment.

Through our words, we teach our children in two ways. We are passing along information to them about life and the world, information which they need in larger amounts as they mature. We are also instilling attitudes, habits, values, and priorities. Not simply by what we tell them *about* God and life and our responsibility toward others, but also by how adequately we live up to our own words. The brain of a child is always working overtime, taking raw information and words, assimilating it, organizing it, analyzing it, and forming life-molding attitudes and patterns deep in the subconscious. Our children carefully observe not only what we say, but also how we say it and how we live it. They are quick to spot inconsistencies.

We must, therefore, plan family times of learning *about* things, of reading the Bible and discussing it and applying it. As we do, however, we have to recognize that the greatest learning will occur after we get up from the table or once the activity is past. We are teaching primarily as models during their formative years when everything (both heard and observed) has an indelible impression. Habits, reflexes, values, and qualities of character are implanted by our own actions and responses as well as by words. Every moment of a relationship between a child and his father or mother is an essential part of this complex training process.

Side-by-Side Encouragement—Teaching by Sharing Your Life

Though children will measure our words by the consistencies

in our life, nevertheless, words are vital. They provide them with information they might otherwise not receive. And they can motivate to action if we are skilled in their use.

Motivation is a process that has far more than simply talk built into it. As a parent tells his child about something, it is important that he also show him simultaneously. If there is a project we are working on—a fix-up job, a new fence, a bit of weeding, or if we simply need something at the store—this is an invaluable time for teaching. Shared tasks not only teach, they also encourage and can build confidence and deepen responsibility.

Naturally an adult can usually take care of such things more quickly and with less bother himself, without his child's help. But the wise parent will add a few minutes to the job and include his child from start to finish, teaching along the way. It is an opportunity for a child to learn basic skills, gain wisdom about the use of tools, see diligence and good stewardship in action—all from a simple household task. And the opportunities arise daily.

Once a child attains a level of competence in certain areas, you will be able to turn more and more over to him. This delegation of responsibility greatly enhances the teaching process and makes it come alive for the child. Children at all ages (if you have cultivated it) remain remarkably curious. By sharing with them how and why things are done in the midst of a project, you will significantly raise their level of enjoyment, and their competence as well. Your efforts will pay off greatly in their lives.

As we teach them in this manner, sharing our time and our activities, we must rid ourselves of all criticism of their initial efforts. Criticism at this stage will kill their desire to learn or practice further. Appreciation and praise, on the other hand, will encourage them to reach further, to tackle more difficult and demanding assignments. It is important, therefore, to seek out situations where we will have opportunities to give our approval. We must carefully choose our tasks to fall within (and ever so slightly beyond) their capabilities. We must at the same time be on the lookout for those areas where our children may be having difficulty and therefore are in more need of approval, and then find ways for them to experience success in those areas.

As you teach your child by working side-by-side with him on some project, the atmosphere should be relaxed. There must be no pressure to succeed or excel, especially at first. He needs to investigate his own skills as he learns. He knows he will not excel at everything he does. He needs to discover these things without pressure from us to add to his burden.

A parent cannot force his child to learn. But when you provide him with situations where learning is possible and in which he is regarded as capable, and then stand by his side encouraging him, he will learn. He needs to watch you do something, listen to you explain it, and then do it himself. His real learning comes during the last stage, by doing. He cannot be rushed or ridiculed. In all learning there is failure. That is what you must ignore. Then praise the attempts, and especially the new skills. In that atmosphere, your child will learn and will love every minute of it.

Implanting Spiritual Perspectives

Through our experiences with our children, we must deliberately develop spiritual values and priorities. They will not accidentally "pick up" a spiritual value structure and outlook on life; it must be inculcated over the years by us, their constant teachers. From his earliest recollections, a child should sense an awareness that God is someone the family knows and is responsible to, who provides the family with all its needs. Naturally, to begin with, a child will know very little about who God is, but the important thing is that he senses a certain attitude on the part of his parents toward God. As the child grows he should be gradually told about God, not from a doctrinal slant, but from an intensely personal one. All spiritual training must come from this angle—teaching about a God who is very intimately a part of the family. With this foundation, a later introduction to Jesus will make more sense.

Young children take nearly everything they are told as pure truth, rarely questioning its validity. In his pre-teen years, even the child destined to turn from the Lord in the most rebellious ways imaginable often will demonstrate what appears to be a "close walk with the Lord." Parents often are lulled into a false sense of well-being regarding the spirituality of their child. Then when the teen years hit, suddenly the inadequacy of their example faces them in all its vividness. Children will not be deceived by surface or rote spirituality on the part of their parents. When a family lacks a solid trust in God in the details of life and obedience to the principles of living that God has laid down, no matter how angelic the children may be for a few years, their future lives will eventually disclose the inconsistencies of their parents.

Thus, as parents, we must do far more than simply tell our children *about* God and the church. We must do more than simply read the Bible and pray with them regularly. These things are, of course, part of the process. But the most important aspect of our spiritual training must be the example of our own lives. We should teach them verbally about the Lord, truth, obedience, prayer, respect, and faith. And we must recognize that true learning does not come only with telling. It comes later, as they witness those principles coming to life before their eyes—*in our lives*. How do *we* live and react? What do they hear me say and see me do when the hammer slams down on my thumb, when the traffic is snarled, or when the roof or hot water heater leaks?

As a father, I am on the job day and night, filling my children with perspectives on life by my own. If they grow to see my actions line up with those things I have *told* them about God's principles, then they will sense order and will accept what I tell them as reasonable. They will be secure in that consistency and will be all the more likely to later accept the system of spiritual values I have implanted into them as their own.

However, if they hear me *say* a certain set of things but under the stress of the moment they see me *do* other things, they will feel the underlying tension of inconsistency and their lives will ultimately reflect it.

According to the book of Proverbs, the highest spiritual quality we can ask God to allow us to instill in our children is wisdom. And because of the God-given nature of wisdom, it is clear we must make our daily prayer, "Lord, fill my own life with your wisdom that I might pass it along to my child." In the first three chapters of Proverbs, it is made clear that wisdom can be attained by anyone who diligently seeks it. Yet it is given by God.

Wisdom, therefore, cannot be taught in the same manner as arithmetic. It must be demonstrated in the hopes that it will find fertile soil in which to grow. Our own lives lived in submission to God moment-by-moment demonstrate to our children the wisdom of God. Then we can enhance the likelihood that it will strike root by cultivating qualities of character, self-value, and spiritual priorities. We cannot give them wisdom as such, for it comes from God alone. But we can nurture conditions in which wisdom can grow.

When a Child Opens the Door—Be Ready!

As your child's head teacher, you must realize that through the years he has many different teachers. Yet you are the one who is responsible to deliberately expose him to as many different aspects of life as possible—always by his side, always ready to teach when he is ready. Such an exposure to learning will prompt many questions from a child, questions that are as unpredictable in content as they are in timing. But when those questions come, a parent must be ready.

Questions and answers provide the supreme moment for the teaching parent and the receptive child. When a child asks—which he may do in a hundred different ways, not just with clearly verbalized questions that have a carefully measured response—he has opened his mind to you. In that moment he is wide open and teachable. Effective parents must be ever attuned for such moments, ready at the signal to jump in with sensitive, thoughtful, well-planned responses. Though the exact moments when a child's mind will open are unpredictable, still the thoughtful parent can be prepared if he is prayerfully monitoring his child's development.

Such open moments can be created by parents, as well, through the skillful prodding of the child's questions. During a child's younger years, his mind is often open and receptive to such intense interaction. But he is growing fast and the door won't stay open forever. As a parent who desires to make full use of the moment, you must train yourself to be fully attuned to the heart and mind of your child. If you don't enter to teach and mold him in those receptive times when he is most pliable, others will. For your child will be taught, one way or another. His hungry mind will see to that. It will absorb what it is fed. If we do not feed it, it will seek food elsewhere.

Confidence Built by Learning

Through the mixture of growth and learning, children will begin to discover singular interests and go in different directions. These particular bents will be a child's means of expressing himself as a unique individual and should be encouraged and cultivated. One will express himself in music, another with a paintbrush, another with dress-up clothes, and another with a hammer and some nails. Other children may assert themselves in games or sports or may find a personal satisfaction in long solitary walks. Whatever a child enjoys and finds fulfillment in should be promoted. Give him the opportunity to sample every bit of life he can, so he can comfortably discover his own proper niche when the time comes.

This is not to say you let him go off on his own in whatever directions he chooses. You must remain the teacher, in control of his environment, setting boundaries, and so on. You are the one whose responsibility it is to show him the world. Yet you must open him up to as much of the world as he can take without being overwhelmed. You explain to a toddler about the sow bugs in the grass; you demonstrate to your fourteen-year-old the perfect drive and lay-up; with your seventeen-year-old at your side, you help her make the perfect dress for the senior ball. And in between you are faced with a million opportunities to expand your child's horizons.

"All of his activities, as well as his adventures, his friendships and his toys, give his intelligence a tug every day. The mind is not taut like the skin of a drum, but rather like taffy. The more it is stretched, the farther it can reach. Each time you help him look for the nest when he sees a tree and look for the eggs when he finds the nest, he'll be more likely to grow up with a zesty, 'What's next?' view of life. He'll be able not only to see beauty in the world and try to create more, but also to see its problems and try to find answers."[1]

As we discovered earlier, a child's self-confidence is largely influenced by two things: what he learns to do effectively for himself, and the positive responses given his efforts as he is learning to do those things.

Therefore, both keys to a child's self-image originate during our teaching moments. It is vital then that we teach a child to attain skills in many areas, without pressure, for their enjoyment and well being. This means providing him with opportunities to garden, sew, build, make things, use a paintbrush, handle a hammer and nails, play instruments, sing, and draw. If we encourage and praise his efforts, these activities will build confidence immeasurably. And he'll learn more and more on his own as a result. He'll learn joy in his work and accomplishments too.

There is a lasting satisfaction that comes from doing something yourself, especially when you create something that is permanent. This feeling is multiplied many times for a child because it's so new to him. He has had very few chances to do things for himself.

As our children approach adulthood, they continue to need teaching and guidance. This will now take more of the form of side-by-side encouragement and counseling. With the teen

---

[1] Excerpt from *The Mother's Almanac* by Marguerite Kelly and Elia Parsons. Copyright 1975 by Marguerite Kelly and Elia Parsons. Reprinted by permission of Doubleday & Company, Inc. pp. 177-78.

years must come the parental realization that teaching and advice can no longer flow quite so freely; a young adult needs to find things out for himself. He will often ask for help and at such times a parent can give it as always. It may now, however, be about overhauling a pick-up, perfecting a ballet routine, learning to keep your eye on the ball, or getting the Chopin sonata just right for the recital. But at such times, we must sense when to back off and let him try to apply the teaching. Learning will come from his efforts, not our words. If he needs us again he will let us know.

We will also find ourselves discussing with our teen-age children everything from sex to grades to popularity rebellion to church to D's in chemistry. The seeds planted in childhood are sprouting. For a few more years they will need us more than ever, but in much different ways. We must continually retune ourselves to their needs at each particular age. To nag a sixteen-year-old about putting on his raincoat, boots, gloves, and hat before going outside as we had to do when he was six will only alienate him. He needs to know we accept him as an adult. Though he isn't quite there yet, he thinks he is. We must respect that notion even if it is mistaken. Inherent in all teaching is sensitivity.

As with all pupils in all classrooms, graduation day finally comes. There is a time when parental teaching must come to an end as well. We can still hope they will come to us occasionally in the future. But we must resist the urge to continue to go to them with counsel and advice. Our children are now adults. If we have implanted valuable principles through the years into their lives, they will be shaped and prepared for the days they will now face on their own. The priorities we have demonstrated through the years, if we have kept an eye focused on this coming time of their independence, will have found a way into their lives as well. We can now only pray for them, that our training will have set their feet on the path that is guided by God's wisdom.

What we teach our children, as well as the way in which we teach it, will determine how large life is for them, how big the house is, and what the rooms look like.

Therefore teach your child so that his house may be large and so that he will grow to fully, creatively, and confidently occupy all of it.

9

PROVIDING THE ROOF AND COVERING

The Model and Leadership of a Parent's Life

A house requires covering for protection. The roof provides warmth, safety, and security. In the same way, the house we are building for our children needs a tight, secure covering to protect it from harmful outside influences. We provide our children with this protection by the covering example and guidance of our own life, which we live day in and day out with them.

A Parent's Leadership Gives a Child Strength

Everything a parent teaches his child comes to life as the child sees the principles actually lived. If a parent demonstrates by his own example values that are materialistic or hypocritical, he will build him a house with no roof, no shield to defend against later attacks of the world's value system. If, on the other hand, the model of a parent's life is consistent, when the world later says to the child, "Leave those outdated values your parents taught you. They are primitive, unenlightened," the child will be able to respond, "No, I will not leave them. I know they are tried and true for I have seen them lived!" As the walls of self-esteem strengthen a child's character, the model of a parent's life keeps that strength intact, just as a roof keeps the structure of the walls in place.

The model a parent provides his children has two components. First, a parent (with all his values, spiritual convictions, attitudes, and actions) is constantly on display before his children. This gives substance to their future memories. They can look back years later and realize *why* many things were the way they were. If a parent is consistent this will provide a great security, a covering to keep erosion from undermining the values he has instilled into the life of his child.

But the parental model is not merely a static thing. It is intensely active. You are a daily pattern to your children, not just by virtue of the things you stand for, but by virtue of the things you do. You lead them, teach them, walk hand in hand with them through life. You are not only their model, but also their leader. You provide a solidity to their lives by what you are; you lead them and show them life by what you do.

Both perspectives of a parent's role are vital.

In one sense this is more a father's function than a mother's. Though, of course, a wife complements her husband's role, it is uniquely the father whom God has called to be the leader in family relationships. His task it is to institute order and then to maintain it, to guide children through the years into maturity so that they can experience and blossom into the full potential God intended for them. God has given to man this unusual opportunity. And it is a responsibility for which he will be held accountable. If a child is not allowed to thrive, to grow to the very reaches of his potential, it is first of all to the father one must look for the reason. The mother contributes significantly, yet the father provides the foundational drive and momentum to see the job through to the end.

The father is a leader from whom two things are constantly required: one positive, one negative. On the negative side, he is the one who must lay a firm foundation of authority in his child's life in order to stay the rebellion which exists in the heart. But once this foundation is laid, a father is called upon to guide his family on a daily exploration of everything in life God has placed here for us to discover. In that process of discovery, both a child's father and mother become daily models. All of a child's earliest reactions to life, experiences, other people are tightly bound up in the reactions they observe in their parents. All human experience is reflected through parents to their children. This influence continues whether or not anyone is the least bit aware of it, day and night. When a child begins to develop habits, values, and patterns of response of his own, he will largely mirror the early-year demonstrations of his parents. Every single moment of the relationship between a child and his father or mother is part of this complex demonstrative training process.

An old Chinese proverb says, "One picture is worth more than ten thousand words." Numerous Scriptures support this statement. Our daily lives cement into reality what we have taught our children. Our ultimate influence will be decided by what we *are* much more than by what we *say*.

"I Want to Be Just Like My Dad"

From the moment a child can walk it seems he wants to wear his parents' shoes. It is a common childhood pastime to try on a parent's shoes and attempt to walk. But there is more to it than that. From a very early age, children want to copy their parents. They learn to talk by mimicking our sounds. They acquire our habits, speech patterns, interests, and outlooks on issues.

A boy wearing his father's shoes is symbolic of a deep emotional and spiritual process going on. The boy is trying to emulate his father. And chances are he will. Children will largely become what their parents are. They learn behavior patterns from us.

A parent is constantly filling the young impressionable mind of his child with perspectives on life and his surroundings. Patterns are being set into motion that will continue throughout his life. Therefore, consistent instruction and wise choices are imperative. In the flow of daily activities in the home, children are observing things that are being slowly ingrained into their character. By far the greatest part of this modeling process occurs in the home, not on special days. Being "on your best" occasionally won't condition your child with any regularity. Children learn to respect and show kindness to others by seeing it happen around them. They learn to treat one another with dignity by observing such mutual treatment flowing between a father and mother and between brothers and sisters.

They are especially cognizant of attitudes during conflict. They carefully listen to the words we choose. They watch our eyes. They are sensitive to outbursts of temper and bruised feelings. During such times, if they can be shown love and tenderness and how to use the words, "I'm sorry," they will develop similar methods for exchanging differences.

Children will for the most part become what they observe in their parents. They want to wear our shoes. This is how God made them. They instinctively copy us.

In Daddy's Steps

I watched him playing round my door,
  my neighbor's little boy of four;
I wondered why a child would choose
  to wear his Dad's old worn out shoes.
I saw him try with all his might
  to make the laces strong and tight.
I heard him say—his voice so glad—
  "I want to be just like my Dad."
With flopping shoes he shuffled down,
  to await his hero, homeward bound.
When he saw at last the car draw near
  he jumped, rejoicing—"Daddy's here!"
And away to give a hug he ran
  to a happy Dad with open hands.
They walked along with measured stride,
  each face aglow with love and pride.
"What have you done today, my lad?"
  "I tried to wear your old shoes, Dad."
They stopped and stood there, hand in hand,
  he saw his son's tracks in the sand.
His words—a prayer—came back to me:
  "Lord, let my steps lead him to Thee."

Parents Stabilize Life's Rhythm

A family will live out the pattern a father demonstrates. He sets the pace and they follow. In a cross-country race of five or ten miles, if one runner is heavily favored, he is the one who sets the tempo for the other runners. He does not necessarily occupy the lead at every point. He may drop back from the front runners at times, but by reputation, skill, and speed, the others know and recognize him as the class of the field. The rhythm he dictates for the race is emotional as well as physical. He is the acknowledged leader. The others comply with his pace, no matter where he momentarily happens to be in the pack. And when the race nears its conclusion, his leadership will usually have forcefully asserted itself in a sizeable lead.

A father's role is much the same. He is not constantly with his family. In fact, he is gone a majority of the time his children are awake. Yet if he is a forceful and leading father, a healthy model to his children, then he will be setting the pace nevertheless. His influence covers the family relationships and direction. The impressions of his life, made with more than words, guides the course and tempo and rhythm of the race, like a strong runner who is in command every moment.

But because of his frequent absence, a father must maintain an awareness of the extreme importance of his every moment with his children. Today children are acquiring their value and attitude structure out in the world. The role of a father, therefore, is vital. He must forcefully wrestle away from outside forces the right to determine what will influence his children. He must offer them sufficient personal exposure to allow his character, his values, his entire person to rub off. Otherwise, the values of their peers will be assimilated by default, because of the father's lack of sound leadership. This demands of a father quality time filled with rich experiences for his children—rich because he is with them.

Both positive and negative experiences accomplish this. Emotional moments of stress, crisis, disappointment, and inconvenience provide laboratory situations for revealing to a child how to cope with the unpleasantries of life. If a child sees his parent react in anger, he will undoubtedly acquire the identical characteristic. Such times of peak emotion are among a child's most vivid memories. If in his memory you were calm during crisis, loving in disputes, understanding and forgiving, such a pattern will find its way into his emotional make-up as well.

Children are also keenly perceptive of the sort of marriage that binds their parents together. A healthy model here is vital to a child. He observes everything that flows between his father and mother. An exemplary marriage will not only prepare a child for his own, it will also provide the basis for his view of all relationships. Children are quick to perceive how we express ourselves, how we talk, how we disagree, how we express affection, how we listen, how we forgive, how we help one another. They notice when dad helps mom with the dishes or when mom fixes a special meal for dad. They see it, then tuck it away into their brain as one additional factor in a successful relationship.

The rhythm of life a father and mother set is all important. If they set a pace where there is a good deal of joy and laughter and fun in the midst of the need for teaching and discipline and authority, then a child will take pleasant memories with him into his later life and relationships. The inner functioning of a family, between all family members—especially between its leaders, the father and mother—paves the way for a child's discovery of how all relationships should operate.

The Twofold Demands of Parental Leadership—Coping with the Immediate and Reflecting on the Future

Effective parents are constantly keyed toward the model their own lives and relationships are presenting to their observant children. They therefore set out daily to try to insure that conditions will exist under their roof which will allow their children to mature with the covering of a clear demonstration of God's principles always before them. This will never come to parents by accident. For such conditions to exist in a home, parents must make this a way of life. It takes a conscious decision and it will become a preoccupying concern.

Leadership in all its forms requires a similar commitment. Effective leaders do not accomplish their tasks by chance. They are foresighted, prepared, alert, and diligent. Leadership is hard work!

Parenthood is doubly difficult. Not only are parents responsible for decisions, judgments, teaching, and training that will affect their children for years and which, therefore, require much thought and prayer and a high level of preparation, but parents must also deal with their children on the moment-by-moment level of *today*. This alone is a demanding, full-time job for any mother. There is usually precious little time, much less emotional energy left over for the "higher" forms of parental leadership and long-range evaluation. For a young mother of toddlers just to survive each day is an enormous accomplishment.

Parents then are faced with what in the business world would be an impossible assignment: to set policy *and* to carry it out as well. It is a job more demanding than any executive would have the fortitude to tackle. For unlike the executive, the parent has no subordinates to carry out his policy decisions for him. The parent himself is both the planning and policy-making executive *and* the hard-working subordinate who carries it through. The parent faces an impossible task; yet it is a necessary one.

To accomplish this great end, thoughtful parents must train themselves to live on two levels—that of the day-to-day affairs in which their children are involved; and the level of the greater picture in which they view the entire structure which is being built. Always the higher level must be specifically lived out at the day-to-day level. The two levels are separate only so we can distinguish them in our thoughts. In reality they are not separate at all.

Parents cannot build efficiently by simply adding one board after another. Their construction must be a well-thought-out program with frequent reflection and re-evaluation built right into it. As in any successful enterprise, evaluation meetings are necessary between a husband and wife who are concerned that they remain on course toward the completion of the blueprints they have drafted for their children. Then once the evaluation is completed, it must find its outlet practically, on the lower level of specific interaction with their children. Parents who live exclusively on either level—ignoring either planning and evaluating *or* getting down on their hands and knees with their children—will fail to build the house as the plans describe.

The Leadership Vacuum Created by Today's Life Style

We've all experienced leaderless situations. And they're usually uncomfortable. I've been in classrooms where the teacher said, "Okay, now break up into small groups and discuss this." After the chairs are shifted around, there is the awkward silence which comes because there is no one to take charge. Or the same thing can happen during a large group prayer meeting: "Get in groups of three or four and share needs and pray together." If no one strongly asserts himself, most are reluctant to speak out.

In such cases it usually happens that one person does assert himself and take charge. He assumes a leadership role (though no one may define it as such at the time) and in that sense gives the group a bit of direction it wouldn't otherwise have. He leads by default, because there is no one else. He may have few skills and certainly little foresight has gone into his role. It is not an example of definitive leadership.

We've also been in situations of another kind, where a clearly recognized leader was strongly in charge. No leadership void existed. He was in command from the beginning and no one questioned it. And everyone was secure in it.

If a father is to give his family a sense of purpose, direction, and stability, his leadership must be of the second type—strong, forceful, well thought out, planned. Parents cannot hope to train their children properly if they are leading simply because they are older and bigger than their children and "someone has to do it." There has to be a plan of action which is implemented through effective leadership. Parents must constantly train themselves for this crucial aspect of their role.

This is particularly important for fathers. Today many families have fathers who are not strong leaders. Fathers often are not even willing to lead by default. They don't lead at all. So a mother steps in and takes command. Soon the family structure is backwards and confused. Though these parents too are models to their children, they are showing them an upside-down perspective of leadership which cannot help but contribute to an unbalanced perspective during a child's later years.

Effective fathers must do more than make major decisions, they must *lead*. They must train themselves to discriminate between healthy and unhealthy influences in the lives of their children. They must choose those things that will build their children up. Their leadership must be firm and it must demonstrate the principles of God and the characteristics of love.

Often such a life does not come naturally to us. For a large number of today's men, this is a role for which they are ill-prepared. In years past, when families were tied into an agrarian community in one way or another, this leadership was a common thing. A rural family worked together throughout the day. The father was there. His children did not merely get up each morning to say good-bye to him for the day. They observed him in action all day long. The various family relationships did not start and stop, they were ongoing.

I was given a vivid taste of this during two summers in which I lived with a German family and worked with them on their farm. From six A.M. until six P.M. we all worked side by side—the father, the mother, the mother's sister, two children, one daughter's husband, and myself. Though we often were working on separate jobs on different parts of the farm, the father was dramatically setting the tempo for the entire family at all times. The farm was the center of this family's life.

From such constant family interaction, several things emerged. There was sustained leadership, not absentee leadership where mom has to assume dad's role for much of the day in addition to her own, as we often see today. My German friends witnessed their parents under a much wider variety of circumstances. This gave a broader scope to the model their parents set. The home was the undisputed center of life, for everyone.

In most of today's society, however, that is not true. As children grow older, the school takes the place of the home in many ways. For many fathers, their place of work is the center of their world (a center which sadly remains hidden from the view of most children). The daytime hours when a father is most productive and is involved with doing the things he has been called to do are hours totally removed from his children's eyes. His demonstration of life is therefore vastly incomplete to them.

The resultant home life has gradually become leisure-oriented, the place we come to relax after the workday is done, where we gear up for another day on the job—at the office, factory, or at school. Most creative accomplishments, from the first-grader to his father, occur outside the home. Much of the significance of the home and family life has therefore been lost.

Obviously we cannot all immediately transfer our lives to the country. But we must see our enormous need to restructure our thinking. We need to once again make the home the center of the best hours of the day and the best, most creative times of our lives. Children won't thrive on leftover time. They must be given the most exciting chunks of time a parent's day has to offer.

Because today's life style and society contain some inherent disadvantages, our leadership capabilities as parents become all the more consequential. Both a man and a woman must be aware of their proper roles in God's family order and must maintain a firm grip on where they are heading and what they are building. Impulsive, spur-of-the-moment thinking gets parents into situations where it is easy to lose control. Wise leadership, on the other hand, is foresighted, always peering beyond the next turn of the road in ready anticipation. This keeps a family at ease. Children sense a security in knowing their parents have firm control. They need this stable balance to help them over the bumps and bruises of life. When conditions around him become unsure and topsy-turvy, a child is insecure. He needs to know what to hang on to when the boat starts rocking, and your leadership is the rudder that provides a stable equilibrium.

Foresight—An Absolute Essential to Leadership

A parent not taken by surprise by new developments in the life of his child is a parent who is constantly training himself. He must be on the lookout for clues in his child's behavior to indicate new trends, new patterns, new habits, new problems. A parent must learn to spot these tendencies even before a child is aware of them himself. When the time comes for a response, the parent is ready and is not taken by surprise.

A parent, therefore, must know each of his children extremely well. He must know their individual capabilities, strengths, weaknesses, temperaments, traits, fears. He must spend lots of time with each child to maintain this depth of insight, because a child is constantly changing. A parent who isolates himself from his children, even for a relatively short time, will soon discover that he has missed out on a lot of growth. Things change quickly in a child's life.

Each child is different. A parent must listen to each one, observe them at play with others, watch what sorts of stresses they feel and learn how best to guide them through difficult times. He must be very sensitive to the struggles his children face. It sometimes becomes easy to dismiss things a child grapples with as unimportant and relatively harmless because of the child's age and the insignificance of the problem from our far-off perspective. But struggles are never insignificant to a child. Though they may be meaningless to us, they may be earth-shattering to our son or daughter. Our capacity to lead them will largely depend on our focus—our ability to visualize things as they see them. We must *feel* with them. Every young person struggles with a multitude of questions and dilemmas at every stage of his development. As we gently lead them through such times, we need to demonstrate how deeply we love them and feel for them, and then move on to show how a mature person handles doubts and struggles.

By such sensitivity to the development of our children, we will be ready when questions come. We will have anticipated conflicts and uncertainties, will have already given thought and prayer to them, and will simply be waiting for the right moment to gently ease ourselves into the arena of a child's difficulty. No child wants a parent who is constantly intruding with unwanted advice. A parent who is wise and ready when his child summons him, always available, always open, always with a sensitive ear, and never unnecessarily critical is like a spiritual refuge to a growing child. His parents form a rock upon which his life is based.

This becomes especially critical as our children reach the age where they begin to wrestle with spiritual issues as well as questions about themselves. We need to *experience* their questions, trying to remember what it was like when we were in their shoes, battling with self-doubts and questions of value. Children may not always verbalize such things, but their effect inside can often be tormenting. We must face these issues on their level, not on a pat spiritual plane of our own. This is a time when a child needs a strong and mature Christian parent who can question with him, cry with him, listen to him, and then tenderly teach him to pray and discover answers.

This sort of involved family leadership requires the commitment of a parent. Mothers and fathers must remember that as a child is experiencing growing pains he is constantly on the watch to view how they are handling the pains of their own lives. Personal effort is necessary to order your life so that it provides an example to your children. A parental recommendation he has never seen put to use will be an ineffective ointment for a child's hurts.

Much of the necessary foresight a parent must exercise comes by accepting a growing child as someone increasingly capable of making more of his own decisions. This, too, is difficult, even painful, for parents. Decisions must be well thought out, not hasty or premature. Flexibility will need to be worked into our habits and responses as well. As a child grows, more exceptions—reasonable exceptions—will occur. The time is gradually approaching when he will be on his own. So there must be increased freedom in his decision-making process. Even if we think his decision is a wrong one, we are sometimes wise to let him go ahead with it. There is a fine line here. Wisdom must always be our guideline. We do not remove boundaries all at once. It is a gradual process that takes a number of years. If a child is on the verge of making a decision that will do him (or others) harm, it is obviously no time to overlook such consequences. Nevertheless, we do need to recognize when it is time to give our child's rope a bit more slack.

Rules are always necessary for the stability of a family. With no rules there is uncertainty and the resultant home life is one of chaos. As children grow and as you let the line out, it is not that you begin to relax the standards so much that you allow breaking them. No, rules must remain firm boundaries. It is simply that you work the flexibility into your family pattern, which allows your children a greater role in helping to establish and enforce the rules. The guidelines for a family with three teen-agers will certainly be much different than for a family with three preschoolers. Your leadership and wisdom at this point (which is firm, yet flexible enough to weigh options, listen to your children and take their feelings and opinions into account) will greatly determine how your children will later view wise decision-making.

Throughout the years a parent has with his children, his leadership techniques will constantly change. You will be demonstrating one thing to a thirteen-year-old, and another to your six-year-old. Through it all, however, you will be a model of life to them both. You are a model who has also been their leader. The really great leaders are models. Jesus showed His disciples how to serve by washing their feet. He was their leader *and* their constant model.

This dual responsibility of parents is a child's best preparation for the day when he must face life on his own, as his own leader. When this time comes, your child's performance will be the great test of your own success during his early years. Leadership is built upon a model. You do not lead a child by telling him where to go. You lead by taking his hand and accompanying him on the journey, showing him the signposts along the route.

This is the leadership of the parent. It is involvement, a never-ending exercise. We expose our children to life and experiences and they grow from the process to the extent that we have shared it all with them.

10

PLACING DOORS AND WINDOWS

Preparing a Child for the Future

Windows give a house light; doors open a house to all that surrounds it. A person who has no such avenues outward—into the world and into others—lives in a cold and dreary house. Doors and windows prepare our children for what awaits them as well by enabling them to evaluate what they observe as they look outward and forward.

Parents Equip Children for the Future from the Beginning

Each aspect of the building process we have discussed—from the foundation and walls to the floor plan and roof—has been clearly preparatory. A weak foundation, unstable supportive walls, or a leaky roof all signal a decaying structure. Without foresight at every step of the way, our building will have been in vain.

However, even after the precautionary measures of sound building principles have been rigidly followed, there remain several additional preparatory ingredients necessary to fully equip a child for the time when he will be on his own. These are not things we simply tack on once everything else is completed. Doors and windows must be planned and built into the structure of the walls from the very earliest stages of construction. A constant factor in a parent's relationship with his child must be showing him how to look outward, down the road to what lies in the distance. This is not necessarily a verbal communication. A parent must quietly build into his child's character certain traits which will naturally enable him to cope with the changing future.

This is an important role a parent occupies in the life of his child. For in today's almost abnormally *now*-oriented pace, you are one of the few people in your child's life who will ever take his future into account. Nearly every other influence he encounters will either be trying to take from him all it can *now*, or else will be encouraging him to take what he can *now*. From few other sources will he be taught foresight, wisdom, planning, and eternal spiritual purpose.

There will come a time in your child's life when he will be on his own. You will no longer be the favored runner determining the rhythm and pace of his life. Win or lose, your child will set his own tempo and stride. His decisions will be binding. And the effectiveness of a parent's early pace-setting in his child's life will largely determine the skill with which he is able to run the more serious race of his own life later on. Like a trainer, there comes a time in a parent's life to stand back and let his protégé perform. If the child was capably coached, he will have the fortitude to succeed.

A resourceful parent is always conscious of this element in his role. An expert trainer, whether it be for a world-class miler or a prize quarter horse, is always looking ahead. The whole point of training is to prepare for a season, a tournament, a race, a game. The proficient mentor, therefore, has one eye focused on the upcoming event and the other zeroed in on the present conditioning necessary to achieve the goal he has set.

As a parent learns to acquire this double vision of a skilled instructor, certain things come into focus. It is commonly recognized that most adult behavior is set into motion by the time a child is nine or ten (many authorities believe the pattern is set even much earlier). If a child remains with his parents until he is out of high school or college, about all his mother and father can hope to achieve during the entire latter half of his time with them are minor alterations, mid-course corrections. Therefore, the early building, in every area of a child's life, is absolutely vital. Lost ground can never be fully regained. Time is of the essence for solid childhood preparation. So as a child matures beyond ten, approaches adolescence, and then moves well into his teen years, it becomes a parent's increasing responsibility to build upon the various foundations he has laid with more and more attention placed on specific preparation for later life. If a parent has been doing his job wisely all along, this will involve few major shifts in emphasis. Deeper consideration will simply have to be given to new specifics a child must deal with as he matures.

Preparation through Decision-Making

A key area of training in the life of a child is to enable him to make decisions. It is not always something that comes naturally; it takes a good deal of practice and skill, especially to make wise decisions.

By the time a child leaves home, he will be solely responsible for everything in his own life. It is the job of a parent to slowly transfer that responsibility onto his shoulders over the years so that it doesn't come all at once. If a parent reserves this transmission of total responsibility for the moment his son or daughter leaves home, the burden will be crushing. Muscles need to get used to the weight and this comes slowly.

A child becomes comfortably accustomed to responsibility by being carefully and thoughtfully given more slack, more latitude in his movements and decisions. A young child is given some minor tasks. Occasionally he should be given assignments slightly over his head to enable his mind and capabilities to be exercised. As a child grows and learns to do things, his abilities will expand as well. That growth process can be aided by continually stretching him just beyond his normal grasp—always gently and encouragingly, enough to build further confidence and success. Pressure to achieve some predetermined mark will work more ill than good.

When a child approaches his teen years he not only needs to be given an increasing variety of tasks, he needs to be confronted with choices—choices which will affect him personally in greater ways. To release an adolescent in this way is not to abdicate one's parental responsibility. On the contrary, it is one of your most significant duties. A teen-ager needs the emotional recognition that his own choices and responsibilities are beginning to carry more weight. A youth has the right to become an adult and we cannot impede the process. Again, making decisions takes practice! If a young adult is going to capably handle deciding where to go to college, what line of study to pursue, whom to marry, how to spend money, and what job to take, his training begins in childhood with decision-making practice.

Decisions begin with simple choices, for that's basically what a decision is. You should confront a child with choices early, as soon as he is able to distinguish between a glass of apple juice or orange juice. Every time such a selection is offered, a child must use his mind and imagination to recall previous experiences and weigh them to arrive at a verdict. This gives practice in decision-making and also enriches mental awareness. To accomplish these healthy ends, however, a parent must be sensitive to a child's frustration level, which can sometimes be low. You mustn't force choices on a child to the point where he will balk and refuse to comply. A child must sense that his parent remains firmly on top of things, including his decisions. Choices should be fun for a child, not demanding. Remember, a child's emotional frame is weak and decisions are a heavy responsibility for him. Don't weigh him down with them.

A toddler can be given a choice between a snack of dried figs or apricots, a ten-year-old between two TV programs, and a high school junior between going on weekend ski trip with the youth group or a business trip with dad. The older a child becomes, the greater number of decisions he will have to make regarding his own life, how he spends his time, what he will do with his money, whom he will spend his time with. This progression is as it should be. We are slowly training our future eighteen or twenty-year-old to exercise full control. Decisions, therefore, that have an impact on him personally must be worked into his life much sooner. Prayerfully we give his decisions greater consequences. He must learn from unwise choices as well. Better to get practice now, while we are still with him, than later when improper choices will have devastating effects.

All this is not to imply that we allow children to control their circumstances from the moment they are able to choose at all. A child is not capable of being in charge, and does not want to be. The increasing practice of decision-making must fall beneath the covering of our control. The widening of the boundaries of a child's environment must remain firmly in his parent's hand if the entire process is to have a healthy and maturing effect. I've seen (too many times) mothers following their toddlers around a store from one thing to another, unable to exercise even the most minimal control. Their children were completely dominating the situation; this is certainly an unhealthy preparation for later life.

Boundaries remain the crucial foundation. Our leadership, while sensitive and gently easing through the years, must remain forceful for our children to remain secure. The boundaries must remain firm and must be strictly enforced (though in obviously different ways for a teen-ager than for a preschooler). Boundaries will slowly be widening as we turn over to our children increasing freedom and responsibility.

If the foundation and structural elements of the house have been squarely built, it will be a joy to watch this process unfold. As a child matures and learns to accept himself as capable through his increasing responsibility and through our unconditional acceptance, he will learn to step out positively all the more. His increasing independence (in an entirely positive sense, not rebelliously) will be rooted in his assurance of his parents' dependability. As the rope is let out and the boundaries safely extended, he knows we are there to quickly reel him in once there exists the slightest danger or uncertainty. There is great freedom in being able to develop in that security and he will develop all the more solidly.

Preparation by Learning Skills

Children need to develop abilities in order to function capably as adults. A large part of our training, therefore, involves teaching them a variety of skills. The first requirement for learning a skill is an interest in it. A perceptive parent transmits interest to his children by his own. He takes the time to draw his children into his own circle of activities, interests, jobs, and hobbies. He gives them opportunities to watch, and to enter into his work—fixing, repairing, building, and cleaning up. He shares tasks however he can.

As soon as a child reaches an age where he can offer genuine assistance (and a wise parent can inventively find things for even a two- or three-year-old to do) he should be included. Praise is the feature of these experiences which will generate further learning and which will make the tasks fun in themselves. He will enjoy his learning and will quickly acquire dexterity and proficiency. A toddler may just stand and watch and hold your tools, but by the time he is fifteen, if you have taught him well, he could well be tearing into your car's engine while you are standing back holding the screwdriver and socket set. Such proficiency, in a wide diversity of fields, is of enormous benefit as one enters adulthood.

All preparation of this kind, however, is not always self-motivating on the part of a child. Children must learn diligence in areas they'd often just as soon ignore as well. Chores are important. Children must know how to cook, sew, iron, paint, mow and weed a lawn, clean a bathroom, do dishes, and so on. Most children would rather play than responsibly carry out such tasks. Nevertheless, they are a vital preparation for adulthood. Parents must be careful not to load a child down with more than is reasonable. But a child's load should be enough to require a degree of diligence and obedience. A teen-ager will often need to know how to work long and hard, either in school or at an outside job. Such diligence won't just come with age. It must be ingrained through a long series of (sometimes forced) earlier responsibilities diligently completed. Work is often no fun for a child, but it's something he has to learn to do. In addition, children need to learn to handle money, clean a house, buy clothing, maintain a room, and enter into family projects. Authoritative prodding will often be necessary.

Such elemental tasks are the forerunners for later more specific teaching we will work in as they grow older. A child needs to learn budgeting, how to determine a good buy on a car, how to make a dress or cook a meal, how to lay bricks, build a fence, make repairs, or design a cabinet. These are practical things. The child who has never earned money of his own to spend, who has never had household chores, and who has never helped his dad with a major project will find such tasks in his later life to be overwhelming obstacles.

Preparing for Emotional Struggles

At every age, every person faces certain stresses. But ordinarily those of the teen years and early twenties are much more severe than at any other time. Growing from adolescence into adulthood is a demanding, and usually painful, process. Throughout our child's life we should be laying the groundwork for easing these emotional struggles our son or daughter is certain to face.

Naturally, the influence of our own steady and wholehearted affirmation and acceptance of them as worthwhile people will be the foundation for such preparation. But in addition we must consider how to best enable them to cope with such things as insecurity, peer pressure, competition, fatigue, physical changes, demanding schoolwork, frustrations of failure, decisions which regard their future, uncertainties and questions about the opposite sex, insecurities about their own physical development, and a host of dubious suspicions regarding their own self-worth.

All teen-agers wrestle with these very dilemmas. We can ease the burdens they create by seeing them coming and doing two things. First, we must prepare thoughtfully in advance, so that when the time comes, our parental responses are not hasty and unreasonable. And second, we must build into our children's lives the capacity to deal with different kinds of stresses from an early age. By ingraining an approach to doubts and problems (by our own example as well as by our teaching) that is calm and deliberate and is based on a deep trust in God, such patterns will find their way into a child's habit patterns.

There is a certain rigorous conditioning which must be infused over the years: the tough self-discipline to withstand and weather adversities. This is a personal quality that is inbred into a child largely from observing his parents. But we can train our children to deal with challenges they will face as well, through the planned stresses we carefully allow to tug on their emotional equilibrium. This is an area where parents must proceed with caution and must know exactly how much a child can take before unhealthy reactions set in. We must see such a role, not as one in which we deliberately introduce severe pain into a child's life, but instead one in which we recognize that certain natural forms of pain can be beneficial. Most parents instinctively try to shield their children from all forms of pain. But emotional struggles, if encountered in just the right amounts, give a person a resiliency, an ability to face future stress more effectively. God uses this principle thoroughly to bring His sons to maturity.

Through such conditioning, we teach our children that surface feelings can be mastered and conquered, that barriers can be broken down, that limitations can be removed. We thereby increase their self-confidence. No one ever makes it to the top without crises to discipline their spirits and bring out their abilities.

The principles of accomplishment we discussed earlier can also provide a young adult with much-needed defenses against the rough waters of late adolescence. Many times young people feel caught, trapped by their surroundings, by their weaknesses, by their doubts, by their anxieties and frustrations. We can show them that it is possible in a sense to master your surroundings, to control your destiny under God's laws, by applying God's principles of bringing faith-pictures to reality. They need to be more than told about the principles, they need to be shown how to actually do it. You must jump into the process with them and go through it with them. What a lift for a teen-ager to realize that he can achieve whatever he wants to by putting this process into action.

Confidence and self-worth are probably the most forceful traits desired by teen-agers. A parent can greatly enhance the likelihood that his own child will indeed manifest these qualities, through carefully planning out a program designed to build them into his nature over a span of many years.

Preparation for Possible Persecution

As a Christian concerned with the future in light of biblical prophecy, I must realize that the emotional and psychological guidance I am able to give my children are only one aspect of their overall preparation for the days ahead. In addition to instilling within them certain qualities by observing these principles we have been discussing, I know I must provide them with a spiritual foundation for a different day that is surely coming soon to the world—a day in which they could well witness and experience widespread deprivation, persecution, and even martyrdom as Christians.

Admittedly, it is often difficult for me to imagine what sort of life my children may face if what many of the prophetic writers tell us does indeed come about during their lifetime. In the relative comfort and ease of the Free West, it is easy to gloss over the words of men like Lindsay, Wilkerson, Solzhenitysn, and Wurmbrand: A new and drastically different day is coming to the West! A day when many of our present freedoms will be gone; a day of suffering and persecution. Now is the time to get ready!

As I jog about our neighborhood in the early morning hours before most households are yet astir, I often cannot help but wonder, "Everything seems so tranquil; could all this gloomy preoccupation with the future so many writers demonstrate be nothing but hollow fears? Might not man's existence simply continue on as it has for years? Might not my children mature and grow up to live a normal life?

"Most people are ordinary enough," I think to myself. "Of course, I know we're all sinners before God. But most people if turned loose wouldn't instantly throw bombs, burn houses, kill, plunder, and try to destroy everything around them. Won't this great 'normality' of the masses somehow stabilize things in the world?"

In considering it further, however, I find I have to admit that if I'd been jogging in my neighborhood in 1929 I could have well been thinking the same things. Or if I'd been walking the streets in England or France in 1937 everything would have appeared peaceful and "normal" enough.

But I'd have been grieviously wrong.

Doom and crisis and death and destruction and poverty and deprivation were so close at those times that you could have "smelled" them if your senses had been keen enough. The depression and the war were right around the corner. And they were destined to affect everyone.

No, world events are not usually determined by the average, ordinary person living in a tranquil neighborhood. Even though such people may comprise an immense majority, they get swept up in circumstances bigger than they are. Events that change the course of world history have never had a high regard for the composed and undisturbed lives of ordinary citizens.

The forces that mold and shape our destiny do not begin on tranquil streets but originate on a much higher plane.

And all about me, once the restful homes awaken and bustle with life and activity as the day proceeds, I see growing evidence, however subtle, of Satan's determination to wrest control of the world from the hand of God.

We may not always recognize it, but *a war is going on!*

A war destined one day to erupt with more fury and destruction than any world war, and causing greater want and deprivation than any economic crash.

Therefore I must continually remind myself that the relative harmony I often feel when playing on our lawn with my children is not a true measure of the state of the world. If it were 1939 and we were playing in an English village five miles from the English Channel it would be hard to forget. The distant ominous rumble of machinery and roar of planes and guns would serve as my continual reminder that things were happening in the world beyond my limited sights—things that could one day infringe upon the peace of my family and could well destroy my peaceful lawn and home altogether. My heart would pound in constant readiness to sweep my son in my arms and whisk him away to protect him from what might suddenly break out close-by.

But today, in 1978, we play on the lawn and no planes are in the sky, no frightening sounds of tanks and mortar shells come from just beyond our sight. Instead, we look up and point excitedly to the Goodyear blimp, in town for a special promotion, lit with bright colors and a "happy face" and huge letters for all to see that say, "Have a nice day!"

It is easy to get lulled to sleep.

But these are different times than they seem. A new day is on the horizon. A day that for Christians may mean persecution more severe than any people have yet experienced it. Satan's attack will be total and unrelenting and God's people will bear the brunt of much of it.

So when I hear someone say, "Isn't it exciting to be living in the last days?" I often wonder to myself if "exciting" is quite the proper word. God has no doubt blessed us enormously in choosing us to be part of these times. But realizing I could be called upon to give my life because of my faith arouses many, many emotions inside me. It especially makes me pensive in regard to my relationships with my sons.

When I am playing on the lawn with my boys, therefore, and we all point up to the blimp together and laugh and talk about it, inside I have to ask as well, "How can I prepare these boys for the sorts of things they may someday face?"

Knowing they may be martyred as God's servants before they reach my age sobers me. "These are the sons God has given me," I think. "He has given them to me for a short time to prepare them for their future. They could be part of God's army that will one day face the might of Satan himself. An ordinary faith in God will do them little good when that time comes. God has called them to live and serve in unique times.

They are called to be mighty men of God; as anything less they cannot survive.

At present they are but lumps of clay. God has given me the

gigantic responsibility to mold them, according to His purpose, into men who will be called upon to serve Him like no people before.

What can I build into my children, then, that will enable them to face the coming days fully as God's children? If I could mold their lives as perfectly as a skilled sculptor fashions a pliable lump of clay, what characteristics would I choose to give them as a solid foundation for what they may face in the coming years? Naturally everything we have already discussed floods my mind. Yet the priority qualities which it seems would most deeply enable my sons to function maturely as God's people are the elemental qualities of courage, leadership, wisdom, and compassion.

If my life is to have one result in the lives of my children, I pray daily it is this: that all I am as a person will combine with the training and teaching I give them to produce life-long courage, leadership, wisdom, and compassion within them as they submit every moment to God's hand.

As God unfolds the answer to this prayer over the years, my family will gradually develop the Christ-likeness necessary to face the unknown future with heads held high, knowing God to be both on the throne and by their side. Only God knows what my family and I might have to face together. In a moment of trial, I will be looked upon to exhibit courage, wisdom and leadership. The effectiveness of my preparation, for us all, will be on the line at that time. I hope they can look into my face in that moment and see a reflection of God, and I hope I will look into their faces and see angels singing.

I have rarely been so sobered as I was when I read the following account. I think it hit so hard because as I read I realized the day could well come when God would require such courage of me, and of my own sons and wife. Whether it be on the high seas, in a cold dark prison, in a furious storm, in a bloody war, or as Satan unleashes the wrath of his servants upon us, it is for such a day I am preparing my family.

When George Jaeger took his three sons and an elderly grandfather out on the Atlantic Ocean for a fishing trip, he had no premonition of the horror that he would face in a matter of hours. Before he would step on the shore again, Jaeger would watch each son and then his father die, victims of exhaustion and lungs filled with water.

The boat's engine had stalled in the late afternoon. While increasing winds had whipped the sea into great waves, the boat rolled helpless in the water and then began to list dangerously. When it became apparent that they were sinking, the five Jaeger men put on the life vests, tied themselves together with a rope, and slipped into the water. It was 6:30 P.M. when the sinking craft disappeared and the swimmers set out to work their way toward shore.

Six-foot waves and a strong current made the swimming almost impossible. First one boy, and then another—and another . . . swallowed too much water. Helpless, George Jaeger watched his sons and then his father die. Eight hours later, he staggered onto the shore, still pulling the rope that bound the bodies of the other four to him.

"I realized they were all dead—my three boys and my father—but I guess I didn't want to accept it, so I kept swimming all night long," he told reporters. "My youngest boy, Clifford, was the first to go. *I had always taught our children not to fear death* because

> it was being with Jesus Christ. Before he died I heard him say, 'I'd rather be with Jesus than go on fighting.'"
>
> Performance under stress is one test of effective leadership. It may also be the proof of accomplishment when it comes to evaluating the quality of a father. In that awful Atlantic night, George Jaeger had a chance to see his three sons summon every ounce of courage and self-control he had tried to build into them. The beautiful way they died said something about the kind of father George Jaeger had been for fifteen years.
>
> Few fathers will have their leadership-effectiveness tested so dramatically or so suddenly. For most men, the test will come in small doses over a long period of living. But the test comes to all, and sooner or later the judgment is rendered. . . . All five people in that dangerous situation required every bit of strength derived from the relationships they had forged over the years.[1]

No, the Lord may not so dramatically test the effectiveness of my leadership and accomplishment in the lives of my boys. But in the uncertain times ahead, there is no predicting He won't find such a thing necessary either.

"The test comes to *all*, and sooner or later the judgment is rendered."

"Lord," I sigh, "I couldn't face what he did. I love them too much."

"But I love them too," He answers, "even more than you do. And remember, I lost a Son myself. I have Him up for a higher good, a greater love. I may call upon you to do the same

[1] Taken from *The Effective Father*, by Gordon MacDonald. Copyright 1976 by Tyndale House Publishers, Inc. Wheaton, Ill. Used by Permission, pp. 13-15.

thing, because I love you and I love your sons. The days ahead will require sacrifice and giving. You may be chosen to partake of the same cup of sorrow that I had to drink in losing my only Son. If you are so chosen, drink the cup with courage, as George Jaeger did."

Realizing that one day my sons and my wife and I could be standing side-by-side before a firing squad because we all professed Jesus to be our Lord is not a thought to dismiss lightly. In that moment I want to be able to say, "I had always taught my children. . . ." Even if my youngest were only ten, in that moment God would call upon him to be a man.

The growth and nurturing of that manhood is presently in my hands.

Preparing Your Child for the Onslaught of the World's Values and Presuppositions

For the Christian parent, it is clear that the most significant form of preparation he can instill into his child is a deep faith in Jesus Christ and a daily reliance on His Spirit. But such a thing is not automatic because a parent is a Christian. Even a strict adherence to sound training principles and a consistent walk with the Lord are not enough to insure a child's salvation. In the world, our children are confronted with satanic perspectives and values wherever they turn. Unless we forcefully combat that influence, our children will be swept away by it while we watch helplessly.

One hundred years ago if you had faithfully taught your children the tenets of the Christian faith and had lived according to them yourself, the chances would have been better than average that your children would have accepted your faith as their own. The tendency to follow one's parents in matters of belief was much stronger then.

Today, however, much has changed. Children are rejecting the ideas and beliefs of their parents as never before. It is too simple to say that today's children are inherently more rebellious than their predecessors, for children have always been that. There is something much more fundamental at work in our generation, something a good many Christian parents do not understand. They are therefore completely at a loss to explain their child's rejection of the faith on which he was raised. Any parent who seriously intends to provide his child with a Christian base on which to build the rest of his life *must* understand this change that has taken place and must work an understanding of it into his child as well.

(Unless you have already done some reading in this area, this will be a difficult concept to grasp. For it is a philosophical issue which is at the root of this present gulf between generations. I encourage you to make every effort to understand this even though philosophy may not be your interest. Your child's spiritual destiny could well be at stake.)

What has happened these last one hundred years to undercut the transmission of the Christian faith from parents to children is this: there has been a drastic change in the way the world looks at truth. There have, of course, been changes through the years—in every generation. These have been nothing like the fundamental change that has come about in our own time. This change is now evident everywhere and affects nearly every aspect of life. It has come about slowly enough that we have not noticed it; nevertheless its effect has been devastating.

The world now approaches learning, knowledge, values, truth, meaning, and significance in an entirely different way than it did just a short time ago. For nearly all of western man's history until recently, man reasoned on the basis of *absolutes*.

There was an absolute true and it was opposite from absolute false. If something was true, it's opposite was false, and that was that.

Christianity is founded on absolutes. God is the absolute truth, the absolute good, the absolute right. Anything opposing God is false, bad, and wrong. God's principles and laws and commands were right and true and good; opposing principles were not.

Of course this is not to say that throughout history most people have been Christians. Far from it. Nevertheless, this Christian way of approaching things held sway for everyone. It pervaded men's entire mental outlook. Even an atheist would have believed in absolutes and opposites. Though he did not believe in God, he would certainly have agreed that Christianity *and* atheism could not have *both* been true. They were clearly opposite.

All throughout history, men have strongly disagreed about what the absolutes were, about which specific things were right and which were wrong. Yet all men were operating on the basis of the underlying presupposition that absolutes did in fact exist, even though there was disagreement as to what they were. Christians, therefore, could talk about sin and be understood. Their listeners may well have replied, "I am *not* a sinner," but rarely would they have said, "This may be sin for you, *but not for me*."

All this has now changed. Gradually over a period of many years, the philosophers, artists, musicians, professors, novelists, theologians and now the general culture have come to accept an entirely new way of looking at things, based not on absolutes and opposites at all, but on relativism. What this means is that opposites are no longer necessarily opposite, good is not necessarily opposite from bad, truth is not necessarily opposite from falsehood. Two opposing things can *both* be considered true depending on your point of view.

To the Christian, such a thing sounds absurd. How can good *and* bad both be considered good? It looks impossible.

What makes it possible is a concept of relativism: everything is relative to how you look at it. This philosophy tells us that one thing can be right for me (being faithful to my wife, obeying the law, and believing in God), and the exact opposite thing can be right for you (having affairs, breaking the law, and saying God does not exist). There are no absolutes to judge such things by. It is all relative to your perspective, your personality, your life style, your goals, and so on. This loss of absolutes—and opposites being truly opposite—is at the root of the current moral decay in the world. Morals are now strictly relative. *Anything* is okay if it is right for the person involved. There is no universal standard.

This is a tremendous shift in the way we look at truth. And it has particular significance with respect to our Christian children. Because in a Christian home a child is still being raised with the basic premise undergirding family life and values that certain things are right (God's principles) and certain other things are wrong (disobedience to those principles). We know the current trend of relativism to be a lie from Satan, a lie geared to make us think it doesn't matter whether we obey God or not, we can just do whatever is right for us. However, when our children go to school, watch TV, read magazines, play with friends, visit neighbors, and even attend certain churches they are constantly bombarded with the subtle message that everything is relative. You will quickly observe dozens of places this relativism has infiltrated your own thinking as well. So our children are in a place of underlying tension and inconsistency. When we realize the tremendous amount of time they spend away from home, especially once they are in high school and college (where relativism is intensely strong and persuasive) it becomes easy to see why they are often confused. This new way of approaching life and arriving at personal values and choices cannot help but influence them. Confusion can turn to bewilderment and soon they are overwhelmed by the onslaught of the world's supposition that absolutes no longer exist.

Recognizing and dealing with this dilemma our children are caught in is one of our most critical problems as Christian parents.

There are two things you must do as a parent to hold back these flood waters of secular thought. First, you must come to a deep understanding of this change that has taken place yourself. This means far more than simply re-reading this brief section two or three times. One of Christianity's foremost thinkers and writers, Francis Schaeffer, has devoted his life almost exclusively for nearly forty years to this very issue. We must give it some serious thought and intense study as well. It is a complex question that has deep historical roots you need to grasp. I have greatly simplified it here. To be an effective parent who is concerned for your child's future, you simply must study this issue in some depth. That is the only way you will have the basis for influencing your child as you must if he is to be a Christian who can resist the current sway of thought. I warn you, understanding these changes will be difficult; it took me two years to come to an understanding of Schaeffer's message. But if you desire to prepare your child for the future, this is something you must do. I particularly recommend two of Schaeffer's books, *The God Who Is There* (Inter Varsity Press) and *How Should We Then Live?* (Revell). I also encourage you to read my own *Does Christianity Make Sense?* (Scripture Press).

Once these ideas begin to come clear in your thinking, the second way you can influence your child properly is to build into him an awareness of this foundational difference between the world's way of thinking and God's principles, which are based on absolutes. You will obviously not discuss absolutes with your five-year-old. All the while, by your words and example, you should be building into his life an underlying awareness of a bedrock foundation of absolutes—the principles of God are true and must be obeyed; disobedience to them is wrong and must be punished. He needs to see that you live and function and are bound by absolutes as well.

As your child approaches adolescence and especially once he enters high school, you will find daily opportunities to teach him these things more directly, to point out to him the differences in the way people think and reason. It will not be your job to constantly criticize his teachers, friends, and textbooks. That will only alienate him. With the right foundation, he will begin to become aware of these things on his own. Later in college or at his job, rather than causing his faith to wobble and maybe even crumble, his awareness of these differences between the Christian way of approaching truth and what he sees around him will confirm what you and he have long been aware of together. For this fruit to mature, however, your entire homelife and relationship with him must have been built on absolutes from the very beginning.

PART III

MAINTAINING THE HOUSE:

Your Unique Child

11

ACCEPTING AND RELATING TO YOUR CHILD AS THE PERSON GOD MADE HIM

A Brief Study in Temperaments

Two things are essential in the building and training process in the life of a child: that we are perceptive to his needs and emotions as an individual, and that we love him and try to build certain qualities into his life. We do so on the basis of his unique individuality. In other words, formulas won't work. Every principle must be specifically tailor-made to fit a particular child's emotional, psychological, and physical make-up. Unless you are responsive to your child in an almost private and singular way as you apply these general principles to his specific needs, they will fall short of accomplishing their ultimate good in his life. And the basis for this individual love and concern is a deep understanding of your child's nature. This implies a thorough acceptance of your child and a thankfulness to God for having made him the unique person he is.

What Is Temperament?

God has made each person with a special blend of strengths and weaknesses. There is no such thing as a person with predominantly "bad" characteristics, while another has mostly "good." Everyone has a thorough supply of both. Inborn traits which have been given to us by God—and which greatly affect the way we think and respond and act and feel—make up our temperament.

Temperament is different from physical heredity. If I have blue eyes and blond hair and hanging ear lobes, a biologist would tell me there is a precise physical, genetic reason for it. Those characteristics have not come out of nowhere; somewhere in my particular ancestry those genes were present and were passed along to me. If my parents possessed absolutely no blue-eyed genes between them it would be impossible for me to have blue eyes.

Not so with temperament. It is not primarily physical or genetic in nature; it is emotional and spiritual. Heredity can certainly play a role in determining temperament. I may have the tendency toward certain of the traits my parents and grandparents had. But much of their influence is environmental as well.

About all we can say concerning temperament at the most basic level is that it is God-given.

It is often easy to confuse temperament with personality and character, because these are the things people most readily see in others. Your temperament, however, is simply an indication of your particular traits and tendencies. What you personally make of those tendencies becomes the personality you demonstrate to the world. The degree to which we allow certain of our temperamental tendencies to surface and control our actions greatly determines the person we will eventually become. As we will see when discussing specific temperament types, many suicidal persons have characteristics which are similar to some of the world's greatest geniuses. What each individual makes of the strengths and weaknesses God gave him determines the sort of person he eventually becomes. Someone with a "good personality," whose life is full and productive, is someone who has allowed his positive traits to surface and has managed to overcome his negative ones. Similarly, others never do develop those inherent positive qualities and instead allow themselves to be overrun by their negative tendencies.

The most significant thing that must be remembered about all that is that these tendencies have been permitted by God *for our good.* His intention is that we allow Him to build upon the positive while working to eliminate the influence of the negative. This is the role of the Holy Spirit in our lives; as we submit all of ourselves to His purifying, He can use the positive for His ends and to make us more like Jesus, and can give us strength to resist the pull of the negative. This can be viewed in light of our putting to death our "old nature" by willfully laying down our natural, negative, ungodly traits.

Our inherent tendencies cannot be changed, yet they can be controlled by God. Understanding one's temperament is a great step toward learning to accept yourself as God made you and can open the way toward true thankfulness for everything—both strengths and weaknesses—He has placed inside you. Self-condemnation has its roots in an unbalanced picture of one's negative characteristics and can come to an end in the realization that God has provided every trait for some specific reason. Self-acceptance and self-love (which is our basis for being able to love others) have their roots in an understanding of yourself and a thankfulness to God for making you the way He has. Such a humble and thankful self-awareness has a great deal to do with a deep familiarity with your own individual temperament.

This has great significance in your relationship with each of your children. Your acceptance of your child is based upon your understanding of him as a unique individual in the sight of God with particular strong and weak tendencies. By recognizing these you will be able to know those areas you can successfully build upon (where he is naturally strong) and you will be able to strengthen those areas where he is weak. If one child becomes depressed when crossed while another becomes stubborn and obstinate, you cannot obviously treat them always the same. An awareness of their individuality will help you know what their own personal needs are and how to respond in each case. Your own temperament will also illumine many of your own responses to your children. Disciplining a child for disobedience is a much different matter than becoming angry when two temperament weaknesses (given to both by God) clash head-on. But without an understanding of your temperament and your child's, you might not recognize the difference.

About all we can do in a situation like this is to come to a better understanding of temperament strengths and weaknesses. Since every child is completely different, it will be very difficult to examine specifics. You must take this information on temperaments and apply it yourself to your individual child. Your child's self-acceptance will in large measure be based on the acceptance you demonstrate toward him. Therefore, your understanding of his temperament and your total acceptance of him, good and bad qualities alike, is the first step toward being able to instill in him a healthy and accepting self-image.

Though every individual is unique and no temperament is quite like any other, there are nevertheless certain similarities, certain groupings of tendencies that usually seem to fall together. Someone who is moody, for instance, often tends to be a deep thinker; a loud, boisterous, friendly type of person usually tends to be quite emotional as well. These categorizations of temperament traits can prove very beneficial. If we know, for instance, that it is generally true that a person who is a gloomy pessimist (a weakness) is also a person who is creative and a perfectionist when it comes to detail (strengths), we can use this information to help our child in many ways. If we see a lot of negativity in him, we can seek to help him overcome it by building on his corresponding strengths. Knowing him to have the potential toward creativity and perfectionism, we can guide him into certain activities (a hobby, books, etc.) which will draw out of him both his creativity and his attention to detail. Building on his strengths and interests and his emotional traits in this manner will help him compensate in a healthy way for the negativity which is also natural to him. If we attempted instead to lump him into the same category as his brother or sister who is an incurable optimist and who never suffers from low moods, we would only add still further to the moody tendency and would destroy his self-confidence altogether. By treating them both as individuals we can allow them to mature and blossom differently according to the traits, interests, and emotional balance which they have been given by God. Understanding which strengths usually accompany specific weaknesses, therefore, is crucial.

Generally speaking there are four primary temperament types, each of which has a host of strengths and weaknesses. They are: sanguine (lively), choleric (active), melancholy (somber), and phlegmatic (slow). The first two fall roughly into the traditional classification of "extrovert" and the last two are generally classified as "introvert." We will look at the predominant tendencies of each of these temperament types.

Remember, these are only broad groupings. There is rarely a "perfect" temperament type. Everyone is a blend of various tendencies. But there is usually a strong likelihood that many of the strengths and weaknesses fall together in similar ways.

Sanguine

Strengths: happy, enjoying, lively, emotional, able to live thoroughly in present, rarely disappointed or depressed or fearful, optimistic, easily inspired, enthusiastic, outgoing, friendly, loving, compassionate, sincere, personable, carefree, happy-go-lucky, cheerful.

Weaknesses: impractical, unstable, restless, disorganized, lacking in concentration and discipline, half-cocked, unproductive, weak-willed, unaware of limitations, undependable, egotistical, irresolute, easily tempted, has a temper.

The sanguine is the classic extrovert: likeable, emotional, buoyant, lively, and the immediate friend of anyone. He enjoys everything he does and especially enjoys people. He is cheerful, loud, smiling, and friendly and is therefore the "life of the party" wherever he goes. Public speakers, salesmen, and good conversationalists are frequently sanguines. Turn on a quiz show on TV, and chances are the host is a sanguine—and if he isn't, he is undoubtedly acting like one. He is naturally popular and his style of life often appears free-wheeling and exciting and he is therefore often the envy of the more timid temperaments.

Sanguine children are loveable. They are constant talkers, even with perfect strangers. Inhibitions are unknown as they cheerfully skip their way through life. They are not so strong-willed that they are regularly rebellious or disobedient, but they do often exhibit a temper because of their emotional nature. They can erupt with both highs and lows (when crossed) but the lows do not last for long. They can usually adjust to disappointments and changes more readily than others. This is especially helpful during the teen years when emotional changes are often severe for the other temperament types.

In a group, the sanguine is the quickest to adjust to new surroundings and to strangers and therefore quickly becomes a leader. This is evident in any classroom or Sunday school class. He is boisterous, a show-off, and a daredevil with little thought for the future or personal safety. This impulsiveness often gets him into hot water and he can make the same mistake time and again. This is not primarily because he is obstinate or disobedient but because he is so totally ruled by the emotions of the present.

A sanguine is anxious to please and genuinely likes people. Moodiness does not last long in him; long depressions are unknown. He is too cheerfully optimistic for that. Though he has a short attention span, the sanguine is rarely bored. He has difficulty with schoolwork because he is undisciplined. Self-discipline is not natural to him in the least. This weakness of the will has both positive and negative features. It makes him relatively easy to get along with, but it also makes it hard for him to stick with anything long enough for any permanent and long-range accomplishment. Finishing what he starts, sticking to a plan and deadlines are most difficult. He tends to overestimate his abilities with an initial burst of enthusiasm which quickly burns itself out.

Sanguines, therefore, though they are well-liked and friendly, can experience difficulties throughout life because of this lack of the capacity to see jobs through to completion. Christian sanguines are very responsive but lack deep thought and discipline and their Christian walk can be an up and down affair.

This lack of discipline is probably the most serious weakness of the sanguine. Children with this tendency must be trained from a very early age to discipline themselves, for two reasons: so that they will be able to consistently follow God's principles without wavering, and so that they will acquire the perseverence and stick-to-it-iveness to develop skills and abilities which are so vital to their self-confidence. Parents of sanguines need to concentrate on several things for their child's sake: instilling self-discipline, teaching that emotions are an inadequate base, and training in skills that are thoroughly acquired. None of these things will come to a sanguine who is left on his own. And these things must be instilled by developing his corresponding strong qualities.

Choleric

Strengths: self-disciplined, aggressive, confident, tenacious, single-minded, determined, highly accomplishing, practical, organized, strong leader, forceful, quick and bold, optimistic, adventuresome.

Weaknesses: self-sufficient, stubborn, hard, angry, impetuous, uncompassionate, unsympathetic, quick-tempered, revengeful, bitter, cruel, unyielding, unfeeling toward others, proud, blunt, sarcastic, cutting, disapproving of others, independent, domineering, obnoxious, hard to please.

A choleric's predominant characteristic is an active, strong will which gets things accomplished. He is disciplined, practical, and independent, often hot and quick in his responses. Life is activity to him. He has endless ideas and plans and has the practical and disciplined mind to carry them out. Adversities goad him on to even greater successes. Unlike the sanguine who buckles under pressure, the choleric becomes even stronger. If you want to get a job done, get a choleric behind it. He possesses the most productive temperament by far.

The choleric is a born leader, but not a people-oriented "Mr. Nice-Guy" leader as is the sanguine. His motivation comes from within. In fact, he is independent and often uninterested in others. His mind and activities are well organized in achieving his goals. He can often be domineering and is often accused of being an opportunist.

His strong will and self-sufficiency make it difficult for the choleric to trust Jesus in the details of his life. Repentance and forgiveness do not come naturally to him. He is a less intense extrovert than a sanguine, but he is still an attractive figure to those who follow him. He can be a good executive; many well-known generals (and dictators) have been cholerics. Though he finds it hard to submit to God, his strong will power can nevertheless be a great strength when harnessed for Christ with singleness of purpose. Paul is a notable example of a choleric whose will was tamed and redirected, but whose fire was never dimmed.

Choleric children have independent spirits and quickly learn to do things for themselves that other children often will not try. They are even insistent about doing things for themselves. Their strong wills and determination exert themselves early and a parent must recognize this and take steps to break it before it permanently solidifies. (The stubborn, self-sufficient, unyielding will must be broken while the drive and energy and discipline are developed and properly channeled.) Even very young cholerics will be leaders, dominant in the neighborhood and in the classroom, because of their ability to organize and take over and accomplish things efficiently.

A choleric child has many rough edges, sharp speech, and self-assurance that can be sarcastic, cool, and even cruel to others who do not in his estimation "measure up." He will often speak out or act with no thought about the effect on anyone else. He invites conflict as a result of his iron will. From a very early age he will feel the need to be boss and woe to anyone who stands in the way. Submission comes very hard.

Since God has given the choleric a natural leadership gift, it needs to be (and should be) developed, though to do so implies a sometimes frustrating mellowing of the will. A choleric child is able to assume responsibility at an earlier age and in some ways matures more rapidly. (His selfishness, however, also matures more rapidly in the process.) He thrives on productive activity and his drive and energy need healthy channels in which to flow. Sensitive parents will provide him with opportunities to be fully himself as a choleric who is driven to *do* things. But they also need to teach him to relate to others in a gentle and understanding way. This will be very difficult for him. He thinks that everyone possesses the same drive and determination and abilities he has. He will often bluntly reprimand others for what he considers shortcomings even though they are but differences of temperament. Parents of a choleric need to give their child great amounts of love and tenderness while seeking ways to curb and soften his strong will. Throughout this process he must be given outlets for his unceasing energy and activity. Throughout his early years he needs to be shown how to submit to Christ and to love and serve others. Even though such things are not inherent in his nature, if you give him a model, he can learn them.

Melancholy

Strengths: sensitive, emotionally responsive, creative,

inventive, appreciates life's finer things, perfectionist, detail-oriented, analytical, genius-prone, faithful, dependable, self-sacrificing, aware of limitations, precise, reserved, thorough, thoughtful, organized, practical.

Weaknesses: self-centered, overly contemplative, easily offended, suspicious, takes everything personally, persecution complex, pessimistic, indecisive, fearful, critical, proud, moody, depression prone, gloomy, despairing, unforgiving, expects a great deal from others, negative, judgmental, perfectionistic, complaining.

The melancholy is the introverted version of the emotional type. But whereas the sanguine's emotions keep him buoyed up and happy, the melancholy's keep him moody, sad, and withdrawn. His emotions (like those of a sanguine) can propel him to great heights and depths. But often a period of ecstacy is followed by a bout of depression. It is interesting that this temperament which has some of the most severe weaknesses is also the one with the greatest strengths. The melancholy is the richest of the temperaments, highly sensitive, gifted, always striving toward perfection, and self-sacrificing. Yet this perfectionism is the very thing that causes him such emotional struggles. For he is always disappointed, always perceives that he has fallen short. No other temperament can be right 98 percent of the time and be depressed about it. This greatly affects his relationships as well. Many melancholies are responsible for serious problems in marriage because their spouses cannot measure up to their perfect expectations. The melancholy's critical eye and constant negativity further compounds the problem. The melancholy parent can destroy a child with his constant expectations which a child will never achieve. Especially if the child is himself a melancholy, he is doomed to consider himself a failure no matter how great his achievements.

Though melancholies do not make friends particularly well because of their reticent nature, they are very faithful to the friends they do have. Their relationships are usually very deep. They prefer to let people come to them because extending outward to others is difficult. They do like people and are dependable, but they are very self-conscious.

The melancholy has great analytical ability which makes him able to see the potential in anything at a glance. He will usually, however, focus his attention on potential problems in any project. Whereas the choleric also can analyze an undertaking, the melancholy often will not take on a task because he pessimistically interprets everything in the worst possible light. When he is able to overcome this, however, his great creativity and inspiration produce great accomplishments (though they may well be followed by depression, doubts, thoughts of failure). He is self-sacrificing, thorough, and persistent in seeing successful accomplishments through to their conclusion. He has almost unlimited potential when he allows God to harness the gifts He has given him. Melancholies have been great artists, scientists, writers, and inventors. Most geniuses (as well as suicides) are melancholies. They have the potential either to excel or to sink lower than their peers. Melancholies are rarely "average." They usually demonstrate one extreme or the other.

The child melancholy usually has a brilliant mind and the ability to be a deep and creative thinker. But his pessimistic and depressive tendencies make it easy for him to get his feelings hurt, feel inferior, and think he is not liked. He needs great love and understanding. He may be the most talented of all, yet suffers from the greatest doubts and feelings of inferiority. It is difficult for him to handle criticism and in many ways he needs it the least. For he will always be engaging in (sometimes morbid) self-introspection. He will be more aware than anyone of his own shortcomings and deficiencies. Unless it is checked, this negative self-analysis can destroy his self-esteem and wreck his spiritual life altogether.

A child who begins early to demonstrate such mood changes for no apparent reason especially needs many esteem-building experiences if he is to enter adulthood with a normal attitude toward life. He has such high potential, so many gifts and abilities and insights, yet he needs much help to come to understand himself and to achieve his full personhood. He especially needs tenderness and acceptance, for his tendency will be to feel imperfect and unaccepted. If left to himself he will often grow up pitying himself and complaining. He will be the last person to ever recognize the gifts that lie dormant within him and will need to be taught to give thanks to God for them. It will not come naturally.

The self-image of the melancholy is naturally low and he will often consider himself a failure despite many outward successes. This is largely because the goals he sets for himself are high—impossible to achieve. Anything he does is never quite good enough. And not good enough implies failure.

Disciplining a melancholy is a knotty assignment for a parent, especially if he has secondary temperament characteristics of a strong will or temper. His sensitivity will require much more love and compassion than most children, yet his wilfulness must still be broken. It is no easy task for a parent. "Breaking the will while preserving the spirit" of a melancholy requires much prayer and a great deal of love.

A parent's key responsibility toward his melancholy child is to teach him to give God thanks. If this is deeply ingrained early it will do wonders in overcoming his inherent negativity. He will also need little criticism (particularly if the parent is also a melancholy) and must be shown how to focus on the positive. Melancholies should make Philippians 4:8 and 1 Thessalonians 5:18 their daily food. Finally, parents need to recognize the special gifts of their melancholy child (and teach him to recognize them too) and give him opportunities to creatively learn and express himself in those particular areas.

Phlegmatic

Strengths: easy-going, good humor, witty, good listener, objective, thoughtful, dependable, cheerful, good-natured, faithful, practical, neat, efficient, high standards.

Weaknesses: slow, lazy, unmotivated, teasing, stubborn, selfish, conservative, indecisive, uninvolved.

The phlegmatic is known for his calm, cool, slow, easy-going approach to life. He is happy, content, unexcited, pleasant, and tries to stay as uninvolved as he can. No matter what happens he seldom gets ruffled. His emotions are well under control, very consistent. He too is timid, but unlike the melancholy it is not the result of self-centeredness and fear. The phlegmatic just likes to keep his distance. He likes people and makes friends easily though he does not seek people out like an extrovert. His mind is sharp but he is not usually motivated to succeed greatly as is the melancholy or choleric. He is a spectator of life and sees humor in the idiosyncrasies of the other temperaments. He is kind and likeable but he keeps his true feelings and emotions submerged well beneath the surface. He will rarely take leadership on his own, but he does have leadership ability when it is placed upon him. He is a natural peacemaker, gracious, and efficient.

The child who is a phlegmatic may be the most enjoyable of all to raise and have around because he is so easy to get along with and undemanding. He may appear to be slow developing in certain areas; this is not because of any deficiencies, but simply because he is unmotivated and inexpressive—content with things the way they are. Because of his relaxed style and lack of variant emotions, the phlegmatic's weaknesses may not surface too visibly. Parents, therefore, have to watch him closely. His individual problems and stresses will require just as much love and help even though he does not appear to be overly bothered by them.

His lack of motivation can cause him to have difficulty paying attention to your instructions. He will not be quite as strong-willed in his disobedience as the choleric, but he does have a stubborn streak. His gentleness can fool you into thinking he is more cooperative than he really is. He also has more of a problem with selfishness than the other temperaments, especially when young. He is a great tease as well which can lead to making fun of others and insensitivity unless it is checked early. He often must be encouraged to participate with other children rather than merely being a spectator. He always has many things to offer but has a difficult time entering in. He is a genuine introvert.

A phlegmatic has a deep need to learn responsibility because it is his natural tendency to shirk it. Many things are unimportant to him so being responsible concerning them seems unnecessary. But when taught responsibility and when motivated to carry through, he usually does an outstanding job.

For the parent of a phlegmatic it is important to teach two things above all: compassion for others and diligent responsibility. Since self-motivation to make these changes will be low, a parent must begin to ingrain these values from a very early age.

The Effect of Temperament on Your Child

These characteristics have obviously been very brief and simplified. Most people are a mixture of two or more types. Especially common is a sixty-forty blend (there are twelve such combinations). You must know your own child well; your understanding of his predominant traits will affect your specific application of every principle we have discussed in this book.

I strongly recommend you read two books in order to grasp the effect of temperaments in your child more thoroughly. They are *Spirit Controlled Temperament* (Tim LaHaye, Tyndale House Publishers) and *How to Develop Your Child's Temperament* (Beverly LaHaye, Harvest House Publishers). They will help you come to see ways you can work an understanding of strengths and weaknesses into your child's life.

The crucial thing about an understanding of temperaments is that it enables you to fully accept your child as he is (weaknesses and all) and thank God for him. It is naturally frustrating for parents to deal with problems in their children. And all children have them! The normal tendency is to try to discipline or love or pray everything out of a child that is unacceptable. But often these methods don't work and both parent and child are left worse off than ever. An understanding of your child's God-given weaknesses (in addition to the principles we will discuss in the following chapters) will often illuminate areas that require a special sort of attention, a special sort of understanding, a special kind of love.

Remember, God gave your child his strengths and

weaknesses. He has them for no other reason. They are God's special gift to him. It is therefore very important to thank God for *all* the child's traits, good and bad. It is especially important that a child not be punished simply for being the way he is (unless it leads him into wilful disobedience). To punish a melancholy for not being happy all the time is absurd. He often cannot help in the least how he feels. He is as confused about his behavior as you are. He needs understanding of the way he is made. Each of the temperaments have weaknesses which can confuse a child in his early years. He needs you to help him come to know the way God put him together. Understanding him yourself is important, but then you must lead him into a self-awareness that is able to give God thanks, for both strengths and weaknesses. Only then will he possess the means for combating his negative traits.

We have an interesting alignment of temperaments in our family. It is complicated by the fact that our identical twin boys have vastly different temperaments. One is a classic extrovert, the other a more withdrawn introvert. On the surface of it this is fine. They both have strengths unique to their own special personalities. We would not change either of them one iota, even if we could. As parents we are deeply aware of the potentials, the glories, of each of these two temperaments. We see such amazing things going on inside the mind of our introvert. He is becoming a tremendously capable and gifted boy. And we know our extrovert has real gifts and needs as well. We try not to take his good nature for granted and thereby ignore his deep needs and the emergence of the development of the special gifts and qualities God has given him.

But around other people this sometimes presents problems. Because society has dictated that a certain type of personality is more generally "acceptable" than other types. It is much more acceptable to be outgoing and friendly than it is to be soft-spoken and shy. Neither is better in God's eyes. But through the distorted eyes of society, the sanguine is seen as being better. People *like* a sanguine. They subtly expect everyone to be friendly, responsive, and warm and subconsciously others often take offense at personalities who do not exhibit these characteristics.

People, therefore, cannot help comparing our boys and in many subtle ways they try to make them fit the same mold. At church, for instance, the extrovert is more quickly accepted because it is simply his nature to enter in with others more easily. What then happens is that his brother is expected to behave in exactly the same manner. When he can't, or when he gets his feelings hurt (which is more common to an introvert) most people don't understand and further aggravate the problem by allowing a negative picture of him to form in their minds. There is a constant false value system influencing us all which tries to make everyone fit the same predetermined and arbitrary mold of acceptability.

So we realize we have a real problem as we try to allow them both to mature exactly as God made them. Their own uniqueness and our understanding of their temperaments dictates that we are constantly working on different things in each of them. When it might be best to encourage one to expand outward toward others, it might be for the other's best to hold him close. We find in this process of constantly seeking those influences which will build upon each boy's temperamental strengths, that we have to often shield them from other people's sometimes damaging reactions to the individualities of their very personal natures. Hating to do so, but often sensing we have no alternative, we even find ourselves making excuses for the introvert's inwardness in the hopes that people will think of him as more outgoing than he really is. We have no need ourselves to do this but others are so geared toward external forms of behavior we feel we must help him put on "a front" to keep their reactions of him as a person from being negative. Out among people, it seems he is continually forced to be something he can never be. Society is fickle in its expectations. This affects both our boys. When a problem is thought to be present (such as the inwardness), change is expected. And the other boy's good nature causes people to often take him for granted and not look beyond the surface to those areas of his personality needing special nurturing. It is difficult not to be forced by these mistaken norms of acceptability to try to "make up for" things that need no making up for.

With all three of our boys, therefore, we have determined to ignore the responses of people (and avoid encounters where such responses can be expected) which fail to take into account each boy's unique individuality. We know there is no need to overcome shyness in our introvert. God gave him that shyness for our son's good and His glory. So we try not to subject him to people who expect him to do just that. And we want always to see beyond the surface good nature of our extrovert (yet praising God for that cheerfulness as a special gift from above) into those areas where needs may be present which are not expressed. In each case we want to respond to what C.S. Lewis has termed "the central part" of each boy, not the external manifestation that comes across to the world through a certain temperament. And to do this requires the constant realization that what one needs for his personality at a certain moment may be directly opposed to what the other needs at the same moment. We know that we must genuinely and continuously transmit to all our boys our deep thankfulness to God for them and our deep acceptance of them exactly as they are, as God made them.

Relating to your child's weaknesses in the perspective of his overall, God-given temperament is one of your primary jobs. And along with this is the development of the particular strengths God has placed in him. Since self-esteem is largely built on what capabilities we possess, you must discover what your child has the innate capacity to do, then provide him with the opportunities to practice those things. Build upon the strengths while you seek to help him understand and overcome the weaknesses. In accentuating those positive qualities, you will give him the most priceless gift possible, the capacity to live to the full potential God placed within him by virtue of his inborn combination of qualities.

This will require a diligent effort on your part. You must know your child well. Memorizing a list of strengths and weaknesses won't do. Your son or daughter may be 35 percent sanguine, 20 percent choleric, 30 percent melancholy, and 15 percent phlegmatic. He will obviously fit no pattern but his own. Therefore you must find what his particular qualities are, then build upon them.

When very early in his life, one of my sons began to exhibit a strong will and a degree of moodiness, my first reaction was, "We'll have to discipline it out of him!" I had temporarily lost sight of the effect of his temperament. I began to find myself mentally critical of him and losing my patience. Then suddenly I stopped to realize, "Why, we've probably got a melancholy on our hands. . . ." And that opened the door to a new attitude on my part. It made me much more sympathetic to his frustrations and fears and moods. It led the way to a much closer relationship, because I too have many similar tendencies.

When I was in my late teens I went through a period of deep depression that lasted nearly two years. I exhibited nearly every one of the melancholy's negative characteristics although at the time I had never heard of temperaments. I was a Christian at the time but everywhere I turned for help the counsel was the same, "The old nature is dead, brother, just claim victory in Jesus. A committed Christian will not be depressed. We have new life in Him!" That just added guilt onto the rest of my burden and I sunk lower and lower.

Somehow I stumbled onto LaHaye's book on temperaments. When I got to the chapter about Mr. Maestro Melancholy I could hardly believe it. Here among the list of negative characteristics was a perfect description of me! I manifested every single one. Contrary to what might be expected, that chapter on gloom and depression gave me the first real hope in years that I might be normal after all. I had come to the point where I thought of myself as a neurotic Christian. I was excited to think that I was the way I was (depression and all) simply because God had created me so.

And what was even better was that alongside all the negative traits (which I was already far too familiar with) was a corresponding list of positive traits. Though I had seen few of these in my life as yet, the fact that I so perfectly matched the negative melancholy characteristics gave me great hope that the others must be there as well—somewhere! Through this understanding, the way out of my long depression was underway. In the state I was in, simply an elementary understanding of myself caused my heart to lift and give thanks to God. It was not long before I felt truly blessed to be a melancholy. No longer did I envy other people; I was thankful for how God made me. I became excited about my own personal God-given strengths and was willing to put up with the weaknesses knowing that they were part of the package God had given me as well.

This has given me great insight into my role as a parent. My boys are certainly going to have to cope with weaknesses of their own. If they can learn to accept them and overcome them by using their corresponding strengths, they will be in a position to allow God to use and bless them greatly.

Understanding temperaments is not a doctrinal thing; it is a tool. And like any tool, it can be mishandled and used destructively. Two of the most serious negative results such an understanding of your child can have are causing you to judge him and giving you a negative faith-picture of him. Anything overstressed can lead to problems. Both these things will come about from overemphasizing the negative qualities while failing to accentuate the positive. Jesus' words are simple: "Don't judge lest you be judged" (Matt. 7:1). Understanding his temperament is meant to help you understand that your child's weaknesses are innate in his being (and therefore not his fault and not something you have a right to judge and punish) and help you to form a positive and glorious faith-picture of him on the basis of the strong qualities God gave him. This is so important because as you visualize him, so he will become. *If you dwell on his weaknesses, they will grow; if you dwell on his strengths, they will grow.* It's just that simple.

You must never forget that there is unlimited potential (for good and bad) in all temperament types. They can all be used mightily of God. The Bible is full of all sorts of men whom God used—Peter, the sanguine; Paul, the choleric; Moses, the melancholy; and Abraham, the phlegmatic. Who wouldn't want his child to be used like any of these men? In the same way, strong will and rebellion and pride are not limited to certain temperaments. If your child throws tantrums and exerts a strong rebellious spirit he may not always be a choleric. Strong-willed rebellion exists in *all* children (naturally the degrees vary) and must be driven out. Having a phlegmatic child is no excuse for sloppy discipline just as having a choleric is no justification for overly harsh punishment.

Finally, these lists of strengths and weaknesses won't always be found in every sanguine and phlegmatic and so on. A melancholy will not exhibit every one of these characteristics. This is cause for rejoicing and caution. Rejoice in the strengths, including the ones that may not yet have surfaced. (You *can* look for all the positive qualities on the various lists, but beware of looking for or anticipating the weaknesses.) As you visualize, anticipate, and form images your child will grow to conform to them. Use an understanding of his weaknesses to help you love and understand your child more deeply. Beyond that, don't dwell on them. Dwell on his strengths, and teach him to do so as well.

A child's individual temperament will have a strong impact on the manner in which his emotional and psychological subconscious develops. His temperament will greatly determine the lens through which things go (and which colors them) on their way to his brain. It will also have a great deal to do with the methods Satan uses to attack your child. Understanding your child's individual nature and emotional disposition, then, is vital to instill wholeness on a deep psychological level, which is the subject of the following chapter.

12

INSTILLING AND MAINTAINING EMOTIONAL AND PSYCHOLOGICAL WHOLENESS

Positive Programming of Your Child's Memories

As we've noted throughout, from the very earliest stages of a child's development (many psychologists maintain this process is underway even before birth) the brain is being programmed. Everything he experiences makes an imprint there. By the time he is three or four, when memories are being formed that will be with him for some time, this programming is in full swing and is daily influencing the sort of person he is becoming. Our lives today are but "an accumulative expression of our yesterdays" which have been recorded one after the other in the memory bank of our subconscious. It is from the millions of things a child hears, feels, sees, and experiences that a good part of his eventual personality is made up.

A child's brain is like a computer with infinite storage capacity. It forgets nothing. Feelings, thoughts, words, fears, experiences, relationships, and all emotions fed into it are not simply "run through." They are imprinted into a child's brain and remain there. Nothing leaves that vast computer. Naturally, most are not remembered. Probably 98 percent of everything which enters our brains is quickly forgotten on the conscious level, especially during the very early years of our lives when everything is forgotten. Actual remembered memories do not begin for some time; even later in life we continue to consciously remember very little. Nevertheless, it all remains stored and has its effect. That is why such things are called subconscious memories—they exist below the level of our conscious memory.

But as psychologists have long known, such programming of the brain, though it may be stored so deep in the memory of our inner man that it could never be recalled, has a very significant, ongoing, lifelong effect on a child's personality. A child is constantly forming impressions, attitudes, and images of himself and how he relates to people and the world, and how they relate to him. Especially consequential in this process are the emotions he experiences, particularly the negative ones which press themselves deeply into his memory. Every pain, every sorrow, every guilt, every bit of loneliness we have ever felt is subconsciously recorded. So this multitude of input of various kinds affects a child doubly—it has an immediate impact at the time it occurs, and it has a permanent impact on him by being fed into his memory. It contributes to the overall "program" of his computer's storage memory bank.

A parent's enormous responsibility, therefore, is to feed his child positive impressions. Self-image is one of the most important results of this constant programming process, but it is not the only thing at stake. A child's entire character, personality, and emotional make-up are largely determined by the way his brain is programmed with respect to his inherent temperament. Parents are in a position of responsibility unparalleled by the most brilliant and highly skilled computer programmers in our nation's largest corporations. Childhood builds into our memory banks millions and millions of impressions from which we draw every day of our lives. All we are has its roots in the early years of programming (which lasts until adulthood but has its most profound impact in the first five years). Where we have been fed healthy and positive emotional input, we enjoy life and are reasonably happy and well-adjusted. In those areas where we have experienced hurt or anxiety or pain or rejection, we tend to repress our true emotions and ignore them as much as possible.

The Ways in Which Children Are Programmed

At conception a child's computer is blank; the memory is completely empty. From the moment of birth the brain begins to store information at a positively furious rate. There is no limit to what it can hold so it holds *everything*. There are a number of different ways in which the subconscious mind accumulates data to later feed back through the personality.

Emotions

The memory's foundation is built upon emotions which affect a child from even before birth. The love he feels, or doesn't feel, is primary at first. Security, tension, fear, anger, hostility, rejection, and so on are all emotions which quickly find their way into the subconscious storage unit of an infant's memory. Emotions are deeper than many of the other programming aspects because they are rarely remembered, even much later in life. I do not "remember" emotions I felt as recently as five or ten years ago (much less those of my early childhood) in the same way that I can recall relationships, conversations, and teaching. Therefore the impact of emotions is often more difficult to detect as well. Yet physicians, psychologists, and psychiatrists tell us that the potential for many negative emotional attitudes have usually been formed during the first five or six years of life. If during this time there has been an experience of traumatic fear, then there will be a likelihood that we will be fearful for the rest of our lives of something which arouses similiar feelings inside. If we have a strong attack of guilt in our early years, we will have the tendency to feel guilty later. If we experience rejection, we will have the tendency to feel rejected all our lives. Our individual temperament and the sensitivity of our parents will often determine how much we are dominated by these tendencies. But even though we may, for the most part, conquer them, often the tendency, however invisible, will remain with us. A child who reaches six is by no means suddenly protected from further hurts. A man or woman of twenty can still have experiences that will scar him for life. But the emotions we feel in those first six years go the deepest and hold onto us the tightest.

Words

It does not take long before a young child begins to respond to words. He understands far more than most parents give him credit for. By the time a child is three he understands nearly everything that is said. And he is quick to take the millions of words he hears inside. He is especially anxious to listen for any word concerning himself. He is seeking his own identity and this is one of his most significant ways of finding it.

The foundation of the subconscious, remember, is built on emotion. Even the words a child absorbs need emotion to stamp them indelibly into his brain. The emotional sting of a critical word is the heat (like that of a branding iron) which burns it into the subconscious.

Every word his parents say contributes to the programming of a child's inner computer, because nearly all words a child hears about himself are taken inside through emotional ears. He is learning about love and acceptance and values and esteem and worth. So if he is told over and over, "You are stupid," his computer is programmed accordingly. He grows up to fulfill that statement because his brain has been programmed to be stupid. If a child is told, "You are lazy . . . fat . . . clumsy . . . dull," his computer will see to it that he grows to fulfill that program. He was born with a blank tape and such programming tells him what sort of person he is to be. His later personality is but the "replay" of the recording on the particular machine of his individual temperament. It matters not how subtly the message may be disguised—as with electronic computers, the program is always followed. It is as impossible for a child to act independently of this program as it would be for an electronic computer to ignore the programmer's data cards.

Parents unaware of this principle often tell their children such negative things, having not the slightest idea they are actually determining a negative outcome in their child. They do not want their son or daughter to be stupid, dull, fat, clumsy, or lazy. Yet they are programming his brain to become those very things. They are making inevitable something they do not want, by the sheer carelessness of their words. Most young children are not as stupid, lazy, or clumsy as their parents (who are not paying close enough attention) would often think. God has placed almost incredible intelligence and coordination inside young children when you consider how new to life they are. Their efforts are usually highly praiseworthy; they are launching into new realms daily with strength and confidence. Yet this excitement with life and this ability to learn so rapidly is only sufficient to sustain a child until his parents can adequately program his computer. This instinctive intoxication which so stimulates him at first will eventually wither and die when overridden by a parent's thoughtless words and careless programming. As his brain is programmed, his personality and emotions will obey the instructions they are fed.

On the other hand, if a child is constantly told, "You are a child of God . . . you are capable . . . you are loved . . . you are skilled . . . you are intelligent . . . you are significant," he will grow to manifest these qualities. A child's brain can be programmed positively or negatively. All of us have many aspects of both.

Example

As a child witnesses the way those about him behave, impressions are imprinted into his mind. If he grows up in a home where selfishness is the byword, he will grow with the mistaken notion that life is a matter of putting yourself first wherever and however you can. If he sees service instead, and sees living examples of Jesus' words, "Those who would be first must be last of all and servant of all," he will grow with the deep implanted memory of Christ-likeness to influence him. Such a subconscious awareness will often do much to overcome other more negative impressions. Jesus often stresses the purifying nature of giving yourself for others.

Relationships

All interaction with others has an impact on us, but especially important are our early relationships with our fathers and mothers. It is just impossible to overemphasize the magnitude with which a young child views the importance of his father and mother, particularly the mother who is his ultimate reference point for several years. Any pain, rejection, frustration, or overdependence experienced in those relationships in the first five years are devastating to a youngster. Probably 90 percent or more of psychological and emotional problems (which we *all* have, though many are so deeply buried we are not aware of them) stem from hurts in these family relationships. We have the tendency throughout life to expect out of everyone we meet what we experienced as a child with our parents. And we retain the subconscious tendency to always revert to those elemental relationships as well, even the painful ones. A child who is overly controlled and dominated by his mother will have the tendency to feel dominated by everyone. The child whose mother did not provide sufficient affection and worked at an outside job during her child's first five years will forever be subconsciously seeking that missed time with her and yet will at the same time internally expect to be rejected by others. The effects of these relationships are intense and strike right to the very core of our deepest memories.

Trauma and Fear

Specific childhood episodes of fear and unusual trauma have a much more lasting and deep effect on the tender spirit of a child than normal occurrences. The reason is that young children are tender; they wound easily. Fear of the unknown—the dark, the wind and rain at night, strange sounds, the bogeyman—can petrify a child.

An intense moment of fear can strike so deep in a child that it can cause the emotional computer to "short out." Sometimes pain that is too agonizing to remember is repressed even deeper into the subconscious and the door is locked behind it. It cuts a deep wedge into the brain and though the conscious mind may bury the incident, it is logged into the computer and the subconscious mind never forgets the emotions that were felt. As frequently happens, a child who has thus repressed a moment of intense trauma will forget it altogether and will go on to lead what appears in all outward respects to be a perfectly normal life. But at some point in his adult life, something happens which registers the exact same emotion in enough intensity to trigger that repressed trauma and release all that previously repressed emotion back out into the consciousness once again. This is often the case when a nervous breakdown comes seemingly out of nowhere or when something which seems simple to observers causes another to "go to pieces."

Emotional hurts are worse in their effect than physical hurts. God has given children an amazing capacity to bounce back from the bumps and bruises and cuts they acquire throughout childhood. But the trauma involved (whether or not there has actually been a physical hurt) is not so easily dispensed with. A second grader who is beaten by two fifth graders on his way home from school will be over his black eye and bruised knee in a week or two. But the deep impression of fear which his subconscious has recorded will probably never leave him. He may grow to be a six feet four inch Golden Gloves champion and still suffer a childhood fear which has its roots in that early episode.

Rejection

One of a child's most far-reaching needs is to be loved unconditionally. He is fragile in every way and the love of his parents allows him to grow without his emotions being permanently scarred. When a young child experiences rejection (or even thinks he has been rejected) his memory bank is programmed to feel rejection throughout his life. Depending on temperament and depending on the extent to which a child feels secure in his parent's love, just about anything can trigger a sense of rejection—death of a parent, an inadequately affectionate parent, a brother or sister who seems more worthy of a parent's time and affection, a too-busy parent, a divorce, a father who is away from home excessively, a mother who works. Nearly anything will do it if the child has the tendency to react that way. It is not even necessary that he actually be rejected at all. If he emotionally *feels* rejection or *thinks* he is rejected, then even though his parents' love may be great, his computer will program his brain for rejection regardless.

Such a person will be caught in a lifetime bind. For he will always be trying to regain that childhood love he missed and will therefore seek out loving relationships. But his childhood conditioning will at the same time cause him to subconsciously expect to be rejected and so he will withdraw from others as well. The thing he needs most, he constantly withdraws from.

Guilt

Guilt is ordinarily a by-product of something else. Some tragic or painful memory is held long enough that we begin to blame ourselves for it. A child's guilt is often imagined, but, like rejection, its effects can nevertheless be devastating. A child's response is often not reasonable. He will often assume guilt or rejection and allow his computer to program itself that way though there may be no basis in fact for it. Parents can instill a false sense of guilt for many things that God in no way condemns. High expectations, rigid rules for behavior that cannot be met, excessive blame always dealt out for wrongdoing, and unforgiveness can develop a highly guilt-ridden conscience in a child who blames himself for everything. Melancholies particularly are prone toward this tendency to feel guilty and inferior no matter how hard they try and though they may perform to the maximum. Guilt can also be assumed by a child for something completely beyond him.

Many children blame themselves for a parent's illness or for other family problems or setbacks. Once such guilt is imprinted into the memory, no amount of reason can dislodge it.

Unhealthy Programs and Their Hindrances to Wholeness

As we've seen, a parent occupies a significant place in the life of his child's inner emotions. And daily a multitude of things can go wrong with the programming effort, which leads to a lifetime of emotional hurts. Most prominent, of course, is the double curse parents inflict on their son or daughter with carelessly-spoken critical and negative words—being saddled with both a low self-image *and* the negative traits themselves.

But other misdirected programs can be fed into a child's brain as well, often by well-meaning and loving parents. Sometimes a totally positive program ("You are beautiful . . . you are good . . . you are smart . . . you are talented . . . you are successful") can backfire into a vaunted sense of pride and egotism if not tempered with a godly awareness of humility and sinfulness.

Most adult personality deficiencies, as well as many physical ailments, have their beginnings in childhood. Ruth Carter Stapleton identifies five root causes of adult emotional suffering which are fixed in the first five years of life—fear, frustration, guilt, inferiority, and rejection. Sometimes these can have nothing whatever to do with the fault of a parent. If a vivid hurt or trauma is deep enough, the child's consciousness usually represses it—shoves it into the furthest reaches of the subconscious, where it is covered over and forgotten. This is a simple act of self-defense, getting rid of the hurt so it can't wound still further.

But many times this repression of emotions is brought on by

parents themselves. There is much anger and frustration inside most young children. Coping with life simply produces these emotions. They are a part of childhood. When a parent places demands upon his child which do not allow for the least bit of negative expression or when he is totally insensitive to the emotions felt by his son or daughter, the child will eventually learn to repress these feelings into the subconscious. An example might be a man who is convinced that his Christian witness would be hurt if anyone in his family acted sad or depressed and who therefore forbade any of his children ever to express anger or other negative emotions but insisted they always "put on a happy face."

The result in such a case is a child with two programs being entered into his personality simultaneously. On the subconscious level the child is angry or frustrated or sad or fearful. These emotions are becoming part of his being on this deep level. But on the conscious level he may be quite well-behaved. He may indeed conform to his father's expectations. But what is often developing is a Dr. Jekyll—Mr. Hyde sort of double-programmed personality. It is never suspected, of course, because of the pleasant and agreeable exterior. (There are other exterior manifestations besides good behavior. Some children's repressed emotions will eventually come out—notably in the teen years—as extremely hostile and angry rebellion. All children rebel. But when a lifetime of repressed emotions is released it becomes much more severe. This sort of behavior is not limited to teen-agers by any means; it is simply that in those years it is much more extreme.)

Whenever a child is in a situation where (for whatever reason) he is unable to release and express these emotions inside at the time they occur, he usually has no choice but to repress them. The trouble is, the emotions still exist no matter how deep they may have gone. They remain there lurking below the surface, and continue to seek an outlet. They are much like the "repressed" violent gasses below the earth's surface. If a fissure of sufficient size opens above them, a volcano is the result. Nervous breakdowns, fits of temper, and even heart attacks can be evidences of long-repressed emotions suddenly escaping to the surface.

When there is no outlet, these emotions seethe and boil underneath the surface (where no one ever sees them) and occasionally escape in small amounts that go undetected. Many so-called "physical" problems (some doctors even say *all* illnesses) are emotional in nature. They are outlets for long-repressed emotions. They are the result of the two opposing emotional "programs" warring against one another for supremacy. Severe and regular headaches, arthritis, asthma, and many sorts of marital difficulties all have their roots in unexpressed emotions in the past. Of course, they usually go undetected as having originated deep in the subconscious memory and are treated in the physical and surface realms. Since the symptom is dealt with rather than the cause, many times there is no visible progress or explanation.

Emotional volcanoes can erupt when repressed emotions are touched off by a new high intensity of emotion similiar to the first. Often no one has any inclination what is wrong, since the first experience is completely unremembered—only the resultant emotion lingers. A woman may live quite a normal life and be unaware there is any problem in her past whatsoever. But then something happens between her and her husband which the subconscious remembers in relation to her father. Suddenly problems exist in the marriage which have no explanation.

There are an infinite number of things that can program a child's memory with wounds from which he cannot fully recover. A child continually spurned by his father may spend the remainder of his life seeking his father's acceptance, even after his father's death. A woman with an inadequate relationship with her father (for whatever reason) will tend to carry her subconscious hurts, as well as her expectations, into all her future interactions with men (especially her husband). She will tend to respond to all men throughout her life as she was programmed to respond to her father. And she will subconsciously expect all men to treat her as her father did. If this father-daughter love was inadequate, it will be very difficult for her to give and accept total love from her husband.

Similarly, a man is usually most deeply affected by his early relationship with his mother. If there has been strain or rejection there, he will often place expectations on his wife that have nothing whatever to do with her or their marriage but have their origins some twenty or twenty-five years earlier in childhood. Husbands and wives are often occupying the roles of displaced mothers and fathers.

Such repressed negative emotions are not the only things to generate unhealthy memory programs. There are certain very necessary memories we all require in order for emotional balance, stability and peace to exist. We all need a strong male and female image burned deeply into our subconscious by loving parents who exhibited their proper roles toward one another. Where a mother is domineering or a husband is cruel to his wife or one particular parent is missing altogether, those very healthy and positive and necessary male and female images never have the opportunity to mature. Such missing memories often have an equally significant impact on the later adult. During the years between nine and fourteen, for instance, when the emphasis of a boy's emotional needs shifts from his mother to his father, the father-son relationship becomes very crucial. If this relationship is weak during these years when he needs to learn how to properly adjust to manhood, his program will be weak as well. He will not have sufficient memories to form a thorough masculine picture.

Both boys and girls at every stage in their development have very critical emotional needs. A host of memories are needed to build a positive self-image. Between the ages of three and six, for example, children are for the first time trying to discover what it means to be a "boy" or a "girl." This process (known as "gender identification") provides the basis for later images of masculinity and femininity acquired during adolescence. Sensitive parents and strong mental images are needed.

No one, however, has a perfect self-image and a whole and pure collection of memories. We have all been imperfectly programmed. This is one of the results of the Fall. Feelings of self-condemnation, guilt and fear often just naturally develop where there should instead be feelings of self-respect and peace. And such unhealthy programs are passed along from parent to child down through the years because we all have the tendencies both to become like our parents and to expect the same things of our own children that our parents expected of us. Surely this is one of the ways the Scripture is fulfilled, "I am a jealous God who perpetuates to the third and fourth generation the iniquity of fathers upon their children for their sins" (Exod. 20:5; 34:7). This is no reason to despair. And it is especially no reason for parents who may already be aware of their failings and shortcomings to heap further guilt upon themselves for their humanness. For as we will see, there are ways to stop this trend, and there are even ways to retrace our steps into the past and undo much that has already been entered into the memory. Jesus is Lord even over those areas we have long since forgotten.

Generating Wholeness

The parent facing the awesome responsibility of raising a child must come to two primary realizations if he is to become an effective "programmer." He must come to grips in a deeply personal way with the impact his own life will necessarily have on his child's. Then he must frankly admit that he is bound to make mistakes. This is no license for laziness. It simply gives him a guiltless base from which to begin. He must then proceed to make a full commitment to the wholeness of his child's growing emotional memory bank, which he is able to positively influence in a number of ways.

Giving Love and Understanding

A child's *most basic need* is to be loved. Without this memory implanted from the moment of birth, a child faces an uphill struggle the rest of the way. Love gives every other memory its true meaning. As a child grows and enters his childhood years, he needs the compassionate understanding of his parents. Childhood is a fearful time, uncertain, often cruel. There are often greater fears for a child to face just in spending a day at school than you have to face in a month. He does not need sermons, he does not need lessons in self-defense, and he does not need for you to disinterestedly buy him all sorts of "neat" things to compensate for the rough time he's having. What he needs to cope with the anxieties and pressures of being a child is *you*. He needs you to understand it with him, to live it with him, to feel with him. This is the greatest protection and the greatest maturing influence you can give him.

Instilling Self-Esteem

The most important ingredient of an emotionally whole

memory bank is a healthy dose of positive self-esteem and a proper godly and balanced self-image. It is only in so loving and understanding ourselves that we are released to love and understand others. God did not create us to ignore our inner selves. He designed our *selves* as the foundation for our ministry to others. How to achieve this has essentially been the subject of this book. All the various factors we have discussed combine together in this regard. Its importance cannot be minimized.

Absorbing the Pain of Childhood

Childhood is an emotionally painful time. If you can't remember it, observe schoolchildren closely sometime. Listen to their words, how they treat one another, how they make fun, call names, ridicule, and even physically abuse those who do not fit in or whom they do not like. This is not imaginary, it is intensely real. Children can be cruel, and your children will suffer. They can hardly escape it.

A child with no one to share the pain with him, shield him from some of it, and then help him to understand it is a child who will have no alternative but to repress the painful incidents into the subconscious where they often will come back to haunt him later. A parent can do a great deal to generate emotional wholeness by absorbing some of this pain for his child. This will often mean simply understanding it with him, talking about it, and especially loving him very strongly through it. This is a far different thing than cushioning what are sometimes very necessary falls of childhood. Just as there can be a healthy sense of guilt that convicts of sin and leads to repentance and there can be a very devastating form which does nothing but harm, there can be both healthy childhood pain (which ingrains in a child the capacity to cope with life) and an emotionally unhealthy kind. Once again, the call to parents is sensitivity and discernment.

"He comforts us in all our troubles, so that we in turn may be able to comfort others in any trouble of theirs and to share with them the consolation we ourselves receive from God" (2 Cor. 1:4 NEB). This verse implies that through Jesus it is mystically possible to share in other people's sufferings and thereby relieve them of some of the pain. I take this to mean that a parent can actually prevent emotional scars from becoming imprinted so deeply onto a child's memory by "taking on" his pain for himself, in much the same way that Jesus did when He died for us. I offer no theological or doctrinal proofs that this is so. I just somehow feel God has miraculously transmitted a little of this aspect of His life and power to parents with respect to their children.

When I entered the fourth grade I was transferred from one school to another and entered a class in which I was treated with all manner of contempt. I was given deriding nicknames, hit by those bigger than myself, and treated with cruelty. My only two friends at school were in the first and second grade. Emotionally and physically, I was unprepared to compete with my peers. Such a thing could have permanently wrecked my self-image.

However, it somehow did not seem to affect me as negatively as it might have, largely because of my mother. She shared this time with me completely, feeling every bit of pain, I think, actually more than I did. I can recall seeing her weep over things I told her that went on at school. I can't tell you how and why such a thing was able to happen. I only know that her sharing of that burden—not just talking to me, loving me, understanding me, letting me unburden myself in tears as I told her of the day's events, but also in assuming a large share of the burden herself—somehow relieved me of the depth of pain I would have otherwise experienced. It is as if a certain fixed amount of anguish and emotional hurt was to be generated that year and my mother's acceptance of much of it kept it from falling to me.

I recall other instances of such "shielding" as well. I was always small, not particularly gifted in sports, and usually socially "on the fringe." On the junior varsity football team in high school, I sat on the bench throughout every single game of the entire season until the final forty-five seconds of the last game when I was put in the defensive backfield (the equivalent of being put in deep right field when a bunt is expected) for two plays. We were ahead thirty to seven at the time. Yet even though sports and social acceptance are so important for a growing adolescent, somehow I always knew that in the eyes of my family I was tops. My dad had been a first-string football player and I'm sure he would have been proud to have a star for a son. But he applied no pressure. Never was there the slightest hint that I had not measured up. My parents had confidence in my abilities, in my gifts, in my personhood even though those qualities may not have shown themselves at this early stage to anyone. Consequently I was kept from having to face lifetime hurdles of self-doubt and the pain of failure which so often dominates others who have faced similar obstacles.

Such a task for a parent is not always pleasurable. By absorbing your child's pain through compassion and understanding and prayer implies a willingness on your part to take the pain that would be his onto your own shoulders. I'm certain my mother still hurts when she recalls my fourth grade experience. There is a cross she has had to bear all these years in order to remove that pain from me. But as I look back and recall that year and those people in that class, I feel no pain whatever. She succeeded in generating emotional wholeness in that part of my being through her willingness to carry my load. Had she not done so, I could well have been scarred by permanent feelings of rejection. She was able to short-circuit that negative program and substitute a positive one instead.

Allowing Emotional Outlets

One of the key ways a child can be kept from repressing emotions into the deep subconscious is to let him express those emotions outwardly. At the time emotions are generated they *must* go someplace. They never just fade away. They can either go upward to the surface, or they can go downward into the subconscious. Emotions are something like air bubbles that suddenly appear in the midst of the ocean or a lake. As long as they remain in the water they will never be *gone*. In order for the bubble to be burst it must surface. Only in surfacing can an emotional bubble be healthily dissipated—eliminated.

So one of the vital ingredients to your child's wholeness is that his emotional bubbles surface and are therefore dealt with. Whether a child learns to allow his emotions to rise to the surface or instead forces them downward depends largely upon his parents' attitude toward those emotions. A parent who is insensitive to what his child is feeling or who is unable to allow his child the freedom to let his feelings out will teach his child to squelch his emotions.

A child needs freedom to express what is inside. This can come about in many ways. Young children often express themselves through noise, rambunctious play, yelling, running, tumbling, laughing. Just being able to yell as loud as you can is a tremendous "release" of pent-up tensions and frustration for a young child. A parent who puts a tight lid on such behavior and always insists on quiet, calm, "proper" behavior may indeed raise a very "well-behaved" child who is very well thought of by everyone who sees him. But inside that child may be suppressing many emotions. Sometimes the most well-behaved children are in fact the angriest down deep inside. There can be a high price parents pay for quiet, well-mannered children if they rigidly insist upon such behavior all the time.

In this light, then, a wise parent will draw his boundaries for behavior loose enough to allow this emotional release to take place, though it is sometimes boisterous, disorderly, impetuous, and loud. A child *needs* a certain amount of what might even be called "bad" behavior simply as his way of getting rid of the childhood frustrations that accumulate inside. This does not mean we relax our standards with respect to obedience. It simply means that we set our behavioral boundaries out far enough to allow a child freedom to fully be himself. A parent who cannot take a great deal of plain noise and childishness is simply in the wrong business. Children need it to keep their emotional system flushed out and clean.

The older a child becomes, the more he needs to be able to genuinely communicate to his parents without having to feel guilty for what he is feeling down deep inside. He needs to know that it is not wrong to have feelings and he needs to be able to share them, to let them out. Certainly part of your responsibility is to teach him what to do with those feelings, how to deal with the negative ones, how to commit them to the Lord, and so on. But your child must be able to let those feelings surface without fear of your condemnation. When this cannot take place, two things happen to him. He begins to repress the emotions themselves. And then he eventually adds guilt to the list.

Inherent in this sort of parental stance is a fairly relaxed atmosphere with a low line of differentiation between acceptable and unacceptable behavior. We need to save our heavy parental artillery for the really important issues and let our child have plenty of leeway in those areas where perfect behavior is not necessary. The fewer the demands we saddle our child with, the healthier will be his emotional state.

Providing Physical Outlets

A growing child is flooded daily with emotions. Many times these emotions have chemical and hormonal origins and usually there is a high energy level associated with them as well. Therefore, physically demanding exercise can often be therapeutic in releasing some of this emotionally stored energy. Physical exercise can let off the emotional steam that builds inside a child. It is almost impossible to separate the emotions and physical activity of a youngster. They are very closely interrelated.

Athletics, therefore, and other forms of demanding exercise are beneficial, even necessary. Playing an instrument, collecting stamps or coins, reading, and so on can be valuable esteem builders. But they lack the ingredients of release of energy and tension. (A boy with a drum set certainly *can* relieve tension with his drums, however.) They should not be eliminated. But whatever else your child does, he should get exercise. Young children must get outside as often as possible without an overprotective parent guarding their every move. Boys and girls should be encouraged to participate in sports. This need not always be competitive, simply physical and active.

But as children grow older, you must watch these activities closely. Sports today, even at the grade school level, are frighteningly competitive. So many things are linked into athletics—self-esteem and emotional release. The boy who is not a gifted athlete often lacks feelings of self-worth and a desire to do anything physical again. Little League and Pop Warner coaches make this all the more serious with their Vince Lombardi imitations. I have my doubts about participation in these things at all. But simply take it upon yourself to teach some fundamental skills, to play hard with your children often, and to raise them so they enjoy being outside, playing vigorously. And if your children do participate in athletics make sure you apply no pressure. Give them the freedom to develop along the lines of their aptitudes. Your main responsibility should be to see that your children get enough exercise frequently to release their energy and in teaching them sufficient skills (throwing, hitting, running, etc.) so that they are able at least to enjoy playing with their peers. A boy who cannot hit a baseball or throw a forward pass (however wobbly) is a boy whose esteem is bound to be low in his classroom. Being the best in sports in not necessary; being average *is*.

Encourage Esteem-Building Activities

The destructiveness of repressed negative emotions can often be diffused through an interest, activity, or hobby which the child is able to throw himself into successfully. This is one healthy way in which suppressed anger or frustration can rise to the surface. It is called compensation. A child compensates for a deficiency, a problem, or a feeling of inferiority by excelling in something he is interested in and good at. Very often highly successful adults in some particular area have achieved great levels because this principle is at work.

There is, however, a grave danger here. If we "put on" an almost phony form of surface spirituality rather than the loving nature of Jesus, our children will grow to subconsciously compare themselves with a standard they can never meet. And we ingrain subtle guilt patterns in many of our "spiritual" exercises. A child goes to Sunday school and learns songs which say: "I'm inright, outright, upright, downright happy all the time. . . . Are we downhearted? No, no, no. . . . Every day with Jesus is sweeter than the day before. . . . I'm so happy, tell me why you're happy. . . ." The whole Christian consensus, especially as it is communicated to young children, seems to be, "If you're a Christian, life is all joy, happiness, smiles, friendships, and wonderful times. Being a Christian takes care of all life's problems."

But what about the child who is sad, lonely, fearful, unloved? What is he to think? (And all young children experience these emotions, Christians as well.) He cannot usually figure out that there must be more to the messages than the songs seem to indicate. So he interprets it to mean that there must be something wrong with *him* individually. *He* is out of step with everyone else.

Guilt eventually is the result. Guilt because he does not measure up to the standards he hears about all around him.

Certainly we must be positive about our faith. But we must be realistic as well. A child must learn from us that being a Christian involves our negative emotions just as much as it does our positive ones, maybe even more so. The "imitating" we do of Christ must be as real people with real lonely spots, not as hollow shells. *No one* is "inright, outright, upright, downright happy all the time." Our children must know this or they will falsely accuse themselves of falling short of a mistaken Christian ideal. There must be no hidden pressures for them to be something they can never achieve.

Putting On The Nature Of Christ

C.S. Lewis talks about the transformation that can occur by "imitating" Jesus. This is what obedience to God does; it gradually makes us more like His Son. While a child cannot obviously be expected to be like Jesus in very many aspects of His life, nevertheless, when the atmosphere in our home is one in which such is our goal, emotional health will often result. Obedience to God clearly results in wholeness.

Even in the face of emotional and psychological pain, therefore, we do our children a great good by founding our home life on God's principles and teaching them, without applying pressure and thereby causing guilt. We must encourage our children to found their personal lives on these principles as well. Such obedience, or simply "goodness" in the life of a child, can have a healing effect at a deep level. God can "fill in" much deep solidity when we obey on the surface level. This is why He commanded us to obey regardless of how we feel. Because if we obey He can take care of the rest.

Providing a Positive Spiritual Self-Image

Our self-image, rather than our surroundings and circumstances, is the primary source of our frustrations and anxieties. And it is mostly determined by our parents' perceptions of us. The child whose father frequently says (or even implies), "Can't you do anything right?" gradually comes to view himself as a person who can't do anything right. It hardly matters whether that father actually does view his child in such a negative manner. His child may in fact be unusually gifted and the father may think a great deal of his accomplishments. No matter. If what the child hears is, "Can't you do anything right?" his mind registers the program: *I can't do anything right.*

The conscious mind hears words, feels emotions, has experiences and relationships, and watches reactions. It then feeds this information down to the deeper level of the subconscious where it is imprinted permanently onto a child's memory. Anything that is consistently repeated on the conscious level will be fed right along to the deeper memory to become a permanent part of the personality. Verbal repetition is so important in this process, because anything repeated long enough becomes emotionally imprinted.

So a negative program can be continually fed into the brain of a child unknowingly and it will eventually surface in the child's attitudes. This principle can be used by knowledgeable parents to feed positive programs into their children as well. They remember what they hear often enough. It is therefore extremely important that they frequently hear the right things—affirmation, praise, and other verbal expressions of the child's positive personhood and capabilities.

In our locality there is a Christian organization which ministers largely to young people who have come out of backgrounds where they have had to battle failure, despair, broken homes, drugs, and lack of purpose. One of their primary tasks is to train these young Christians in new and positive thought patterns. The Christian life is one of hope and victory, yet it becomes very difficult for a Christian to appropriate all that can be his in Christ when for twenty or thirty years his computer has been negatively programmed and is filled with rejection, guilt, fear, and selfishness. It's like taking a tape recording made on a forty-nine-dollar recorder under the worst conditions imaginable and then replaying it on a brand new $1500 system. Though the machine may operate flawlessly, the recording will sound as bad as ever. The defective tape needs to be erased and re-programmed. It is as Jesus said, "New wine is for new wineskins." Both a new life and a new program are necessary for wholeness.

So the leaders of this organization have written a lengthy "faith-picture" which they instruct the new Christians to read each morning while allowing their minds to creatively imagine the fullness of the life that is now theirs. They want to re-program their minds with spiritually positive and scripturally sound input to replace the negative programming that has been fed in for years. They are using the principles of locking onto a vision in the imagination (the conscious mind) until it actually becomes implanted in the memory (the subconscious) and thereby begins to work changes in the personality and emotions. The life of Jesus cannot have a full impact until the computer begins to be re-programmed in this manner.

This "program" begins as follows:

> Today because Jesus lives within me, I am a son of God. This great miracle has transformed me. Today I am a king and priest unto God. Today I confess that I have the mind of Christ. I confess that my old self is dead, and that Jesus has created inside my same body a whole new me. This whole new me is in reality Jesus continuing his life through me. God is fully living in me and through me. Through the Bible, which is the written expression of truth, channels are continually being opened and enlarged in my being. These channels allow the life of God to flow perfectly and abundantly. This life manifests itself by such words as love, joy, peace, patience, kindness, goodness, faithfulness, gentleness, and self-control.

It is easy to see that a daily reading of such a positive affirmation of God's work within would gradually re-orient one toward new ways of thinking and approaching life.

Parents seeking to build a positive set of emotions and spiritual attitudes into their child have two things working against them which they must be aware of and overcome. First, children will believe *anything* negative they hear about themselves, whether true or not; second, children will *not* believe positive things they hear about themselves unless they genuinely come from a parent's heart and are heard often. Even if a criticism made in a rash moment is in fact untrue and is even later retracted by an apologetic mother or father, the memory bank has already stored the statement and it cannot be erased. (This is not to undervalue the need for forgiveness to flow between family members because it does usually help. But it often cannot undo what has already been said.) But a child will *not* automatically store a corresponding positive statement such as, "I love you," for all time. It must be restated over and over and proved conclusively through actions.

It is a result of the Fall that we all tend to let ourselves readily believe the most negative things possible. We naturally assume the worst about ourselves. A child will quite naturally place guilt upon himself even when innocent. This is the way we are. A parent must therefore counteract this tendency with positive input. This can be no flinging about of meaningless words; words (however positive) that are dished out with no proof to back them up and with little feeling will not be remembered. A child is constantly listening to the spirit of the words, to our state of mind. If we harbor an underlying fear that our child is turning out badly in some particular respect, by trying to gloss it over with shallow positive words, we will fool no one. The inner message of our anxiety will still get through to his subconscious. Positive programming must be genuine.

It is possible for Christian parents to work toward providing their children with a wholesome and positive self-image in a way similar to reading a strong affirmative statement of our relationship with God. We need to construct some definite affirmations of our vision of our child that we build into his subconscious memory both by repetition and by action. I regularly tell my boys, "You are special . . . God loves you and I love you . . . thank you for being unselfish and considerate . . . thank you for being obedient . . . I thank God for you . . . God has given you special gifts and abilities."

Ruth Carter Stapleton calls this a "positive portrait list" and recommends writing down a specific list of qualities and characteristics which you would like to have manifested in your inner life as well as your relationships. She says to aim as high as you can, and then to read it daily, affirming everything in faith. In constructing such a vision for each of my children, I try to recall those specific characteristics I see in them through the eyes of faith. This provides me with a strong faith-vision and keeps it constantly alive in my heart. For I know that the way I see my child in my heart and mind by faith is the way he will ultimately become. My vision of him is so important.

I do not simply recite my certain vision for each child at given intervals and thus sterilize it. And I don't try to discover whether the ideals are being lived up to. I just keep it before me, pondering it, giving the vision and my boys to the Lord in prayer. I make modifications as they change. And I let the words come out to them as well, sometimes one part, sometimes another. When I am quietly holding one of them or when we are talking is a good time. I especially try to look for opportunities at bedtime when all is quiet and when their minds are more receptive. When we pray I work various words of my vision into my prayers for them. And I especially do so when I pray for them while they are asleep. I say these things over and over, knowing that though their conscious minds are asleep, their subconscious minds are still responsive to my emotions and thoughts and prayers. Such repetitive input will find its way into my boys' permanent memories and will contribute to the program which will become their entire person. I want to so thoroughly infiltrate their memories with "You are special, loved, helpful, significant, important . . ." that those thoughts will penetrate much deeper than the pains and hurts they repress along the way.

Praying For Your Child

Most Christians pray for their children; to do so is natural. Prayers, however, are often too general. We must pray specifically in ways that will contribute to a healthy memory bank in their subconscious. Our prayers do two things: they give our children insights into how we view their lives before God, and they focus our love (and therefore God's power and love and healing) toward certain key aspects of the inner beings of our children that we feel require a special touch of His Spirit. It is not that God needs us to tell Him what needs attention. He knows our child far more intimately than we do. But it has always been one of the mysterious aspects of prayer that God's part and our part go hand in hand. God could certainly have set it up differently, but for some reason (which has our good at its core) He always says, "Ask, therefore, that you might receive." A child holding a magnifying glass to focus the sun's rays has no power of his own; the power is all in the sun. Yet his positioning of the glass determines the extent to which that tremendous heat will be focused and therefore the power it will have. Prayer is like holding a magnifying glass. The power is all there, we simply must focus it properly. That is our part.

In praying for our children, then, we must pray knowledgeably and specifically, focusing God's love and power and healing directly at potential problems and hurts. It is often best to pray for problems when the child is asleep and pray positively (affirming God's great work in him, asking God to make ever more alive the characteristics of our faith-vision) both while he is awake and asleep. In this way he benefits from positive works and does not have to be aware of the problem area where we are asking God to touch him.

When I pray for my boys, I first of all ask that God would act as a shield between their subconscious minds and the emotional hurts they experience. I ask Him to purify and cleanse their memories and to supply them with all the healthy memories they need. Realizing that I make countless mistakes and often negatively program my sons' minds unknowingly, I ask God to make up the difference between the love and acceptance they need and what I am capable of giving them. Then I review the day or week or afternoon and bring before God those areas I feel might require His healing touch (this can be anything from a cold or a physical hurt to some deep pain in the inner subconscious). If there has been a strong bout of rebellion or disobedience during the day and I have found it necessary to do a lot of spanking, I bring it all before the Lord for cleansing. I ask that there be no permanent scar from the emotions generated; I ask for humility and purity for myself and total love in handling such situations; I ask for healing of the memories regarding the incident, and I ask that the discipline will have its full effect in curbing the disobedience and breaking the rebellious spirit. This is hard to go through, because I am aware that my child must be disciplined and that rebellion must be driven far from him. Yet I hurt for him as I am carrying it out. I often have to just trust God that good is going to come of it.

When there has been some influence (either something regarding my own relationship with him or some fear or traumatic incident which was independent of anyone) that I sense could potentially result in a lasting emotional wound in onc of my sons, I pay particular attention in my prayers to that. I adjust the magnifying glass, as it were, to focus God's love and the healing power of His Spirit right to the precise point of inner pain. I know the incident cannot be undone. And I know that no matter how positively I try to counteract its effect, the emotion of the moment will still remain imprinted on my son's memory. Therefore, I know the only thing that can be done is to ask God to somehow heal the resultant wound so that no permanent scar will develop. This sort of memory-altering or healing prayer requires some additional discussion and will be dealt with in the following section.

The Healing of Subconscious Memories

No parent can prevent his child from experiencing hurts that penetrate his subconscious. We are imperfect and occasionally lash out, saying and doing things we do not really mean. As parents we are largely the products of our own parents. Their flaws and emotional scars have been passed along to us, as ours are to our children. This is no cause for either guilt or dismay. The reactions of a child, even to his parents' sins and weaknesses, contribute in a positive way to God's creative process within him. God gave us the sort of parents we had because He knew what we needed to become His completed child. We needed their unique love and care; but their particular sins and weaknesses and even mistakes also contributed to the eventual maturing of the potential God placed inside us. And this same principle is at work in God's present molding of our own children. The Bible is filled with passages that say: out of bad comes good, out of darkness comes light, out of pain comes joy, out of hurt comes healing, out of defeat comes victory, out of sorrow comes happiness.

The key to God's work in the life of our child, therefore, is not our perfection, but rather our submission to Him of those areas that require His touch. Emotional hurts as well as physical ailments can be given to Jesus and, through the healing touch of the Holy Spirit, wholeness can be regained. A parent's first responsibility in this process is to acutely tune himself to his child's emotions. A child has to learn to verbally express himself and often will not volunteer such information. We must know how he feels in spite of what he tells us. Particularly important are feelings of rejection, guilt, fear, and self-doubt. These can be the most devastating of all to a child's memory system. You must learn what sorts of things signal the infiltration of these feelings in a child (a car accident, being lost in a department store, losing a parent or friend or dog, a humiliating school experience, a fearful and stormy night, being bitten by a dog, having a close friend say he doesn't like you any more, having to go outside after dark alone, feeling responsible for someone else's pain). Some moments of trauma are major and (though repressed) could lead to a lifelong emotional imbalance; others are relatively minor. But all have their effect and should therefore be dealt with. The Lord desires to touch every area in our lives that has been damaged, no matter how minor it may seem. It is always possible for a child (or adult) to adjust to pain and learn to suppress it or live with it. Children are remarkably versatile at this. Yet how much better to allow God to remove it altogether.

When a parent is in tune with the emotions of his child, he can then regularly (whenever he sees a potential memory problem developing) submit those areas of his child's memory bank to the Lord for healing. Praying for healing of the memories of the subconscious is no different than praying for physical healing, you simply ask the Lord to heal your child's memory of his fall, his grandmother's death, or of being made fun of at school.

Because the original moment of the hurt is still *now* for Jesus, you can ask Him to go back to that moment and take on your child's pain himself (which He in a sense has *already* done at the cross). Jesus acts like a lightning rod. As the hurt is transferring itself from your child's conscious mind down to his subconscious, Jesus can intercept and ground it into himself. Obviously you cannot do this for your child, and your child cannot do it for himself. In our time sequence, the hurt has already implanted itself in the memory—but since that moment is still in the present for Jesus, He can keep the memory from becoming deeply lodged in the brain. It is miraculous and I can offer no better explanation than that.

Remember your position as a parent. You are much like a computer programmer. When healing is necessary it is because an incorrect program has been entered. It must either be removed or else it will forever disorient the rest of the total program. God is the only one who can remove the incorrect program, but you are the programmer who must diagnose the problem and bring it before God for His healing. Another way of looking at it is that you are asking God to feed an erase program into your child's memory at the particular point of his hurt. You ask Him to make your son or daughter remember the hurt no more (on the deep level) and to replace it with a positive memory by His Spirit. However you choose to view the process, God is able to remove, erase, ground, or short-circuit the negative memory, heal whatever scar it may have caused, and replace it with loving, positive and healthy memories instead.

The longer a memory remains lodged in your child's subconscious, the more difficult it is for it to be removed and replaced by God's love, just as the repetition of words and emotions deeply stamps them into his brain. And the longer they remain the more they will begin to affect other memories. A negative chain or pattern can quickly be set into motion that can become almost impossible to extricate after several years.

Therefore it is crucial that parents pray for such healings as quickly as possible after hurtful experiences—even during them if it is possible. You can continually be asking the Lord for spiritual insight into potential problem areas. As an example, imagine that your family is planning a move and you know the displacement is going to be very difficult for your first-grader. In this case, you need to give him extra doses of love and assurance as far in advance as possible and throughout the move itself. In addition you can pray during the entire time for his emotions, memory, and subconscious. Pray that God will keep hurts from penetrating too deeply, will allow you to absorb a measure of his pain, and will heal any emotional scars that do develop. In this final prayer for healing, be as specific as you possibly can—pray that God will heal your son's memory of having to leave his best friend. This is far more effective than a generalized "shotgun" approach. (Of course when you do not know the specifics, general prayer is necessary.) Keep in mind that you are focusing the lens so that God's power can penetrate right to the precise point of pain and surgically remove it.

You will usually not be so fortunate to have advance warning of memory problems. You must just keep on your toes and pray immediately when you do become aware that healing is needed.

When our twin boys were born, both had to remain in the hospital longer than normal—one for five days, the other for nine. In addition, one had severe lung problems at birth and for two days had no human contact at all, just the tubes and lights and needles and monitors of the intensive care unit. Aware of a newborn's acute emotional need for the love, warmth, and security of a mother's arms, we prayed regularly for any emotional scars that could have developed during those first crucial days after birth. Similarly, we have prayed for the healing of their memories regarding a hernia operation both underwent at five months of age. And whenever they now suffer falls or accidents or hurt feelings, or whenever I have to discipline unusually harshly, I pray for healing of any hurts that could be caused.

I know that a certain amount of pain is healthy for a growing child. I do not want to shield them from the positive effects of it in the life of one who is trusting God. Nevertheless, I always ask God to use such pain for their ultimate good and to keep it from adversely affecting their capacity to love Him and themselves.

Healing of Long-Repressed Memories in Older Children and Adults

The longer a certain memory has been repressed, the more deeply ingrained into the subconscious it is and the less likely it becomes that it will be able to be extracted quickly. The older a person grows, the more complex becomes the relationship between repressed memories, the will, personality, temperament, and even physical manifestations. Everything that makes up a person becomes more tightly interwoven with each passing year. In small children it is often possible to pray for healing in one specific area and know that God has miraculously erased the memory as if nothing had taken place. Unfortunately, it is rarely so simple as we grow older.

Every emotional wound is linked together with every other one. There is a chain of emotional memories all tied together. Removing one won't eliminate the rest of the chain. In addition, there is usually guilt and rejection and a badly damaged self-image that have come about as a result of this progression of negative programming. So even if a particular link in the chain is dealt with and a certain memory erased, the feelings of guilt and worthlessness resulting from it remain. We learn through the years to erect defenses as well which allow us to further repress our weaknesses. Healing is therefore needed, not only for the initial hurts of the past, but also for all the defense mechanisms, guilt feelings, and further negative emotions that have become part of our psychological programs through the years as a result.

Why Many Experience Frustrations As Christians

Small wonder, then, that so many Christians—well-meaning, committed to the Lord, faithful and obedient to His principles, good people trying to submit to the Spirit of God in their lives—seem unable to experience many basic aspects of the Christian life (joy and peace and self-love) and appear to be so fruitless in their growth. It is often said that such Christians are simply not totally committed to the Lord and are inwardly disobedient. One popular tract implies that there are but two types of Christians—the "spiritual" Christian who has the fruits of the Spirit and everything in life in perfect order and harmony; and the "carnal" Christian who exhibits disorder, sin, lack of fruitfulness, and inconsistent growth because Christ is "not on the throne of life."

This, however, is an overly simplistic explanation. What about the Christian who genuinely has submitted to Christ and put Him on the throne of his life and yet still suffers (he knows not why) from inner (deep, past) psychological and emotional hurts that affect him today? Will power is often not sufficient for such persons to overcome these difficulties. Neither are a host of other formulistic answers dished out today by well-meaning, yet nonunderstanding, counselors. When I was depressed for so long, I tried with all my might to apply the words I heard from my reading and counseling with others: "Just praise God in the midst of your depression . . . be filled with the Holy Spirit . . . be faithful in your daily devotions . . . witness to others about Jesus . . . ask forgiveness for your sin. . . ." These things are, of course, good advice and they do help, but often they will not provide complete solutions. In my case, an understanding of my temperament was what I needed. For many others who find no way out of the emotional and psychological effects of the deep past through the traditional terminology of the church, inner healing is often necessary to release them to experience the Christian life as Jesus said we should.

For long the church has floundered to find a workable answer to give such people. Often psychologists with no Christian base have been able to offer more help than the church. We are now beginning to see that God not only sets us free from our sin and separation from Him, He also sets us free from the effects of that sin on a deep emotional level.

Memories Are Linked Together

Since emotional scars and their resultant effects grow more complex and intertwined each year, the healing of the subconscious is increasingly involved as one grows older. The first necessary step is that the root cause of a memory hurt be located—to find the first link in the chain. When the painful or ungodly memory or the void that should contain a healthy memory can be found and dealt with, the door will be opened for a whole series of domino-like healings that will bring a person toward wholeness, with each healing leading into the next.

If a child fails to go through certain stages in his physical development, he can develop brain deficiencies. If he skips the crawling stage—during which time his brain is learning certain things about coordination and how to move his legs separately—those particular circuits in his brain will never have been developed. This process is very complex; it continues throughout childhood and involves many different aspects of learning. Such an omission in his physical development will have an effect on the child's mental growth as well. It is widely known that crawling, for instance, has a great impact on later reading ability and that certain other muscular skills control the extent to which a child can distinguish between right and left. Any stage that is cut short or omitted will result in insufficient mental programming.

It is similar for emotional growth. A child needs certain key subconscious emotional experiences and memories in order for him to develop emotional wholeness. We've already mentioned the need of preschoolers to discover their sexual identities through strong male and female models. Another key emotional need of this period involves a child's gradual (and painful) separation from his mother. Unless this early form of independence is achieved properly, the later independence of adulthood will either be missing or distorted. A child has hundreds of such emotional needs.

When any of these are missing, healing is necessary also, just like when there are negative memories present. God can either remove unhealthy memories or instill missing ones.

To visualize this, imagine a young boy whose father is away from home often and somehow just doesn't take the time to play with him, talk with him, wrestle with him, and so on. As a result this boy grows up with certain unhealthy feelings about himself—doubts about his importance as a person, low estimation of his skills and abilities. He has a double problem. He has negative memories of low esteem, and he is missing the healthy memories of a strong, positive, masculine relationship with his father. Both problems contribute highly to the personality of this boy as he grows and they begin to surface in more noticeable ways (perhaps through rebellion, poor grades, or an unbalanced sexual relationship with either boys or girls) as his subconscious seeks to compensate for what he missed from his father.

Hundreds or thousands of such influences—positive and negative—combine together to become the composite personality that we demonstrate to the world. A parent who punishes his twelve-year-old son for his surface behavior may quite possibly be adding to the root problem. Usually things that happened ten, fifteen, or twenty years earlier are behind what surfaces as fear of heights, homosexuality, rebellion, anger, bitterness, depression, and a need to escape through drugs.

God Can Heal in the Past by Making It a NOW

God, however, can delve back into the distant past and can make our memories whole. It is *all* the present for Him, it is only the "past" for us. Jesus can walk back in our memory and actually be with that little boy or girl who experienced some hurt *right at the time it happened.* But in order to submit such deep, inner memories to the healing of His touch, we need to get at the root of the problem. The memory of the subconscious must be opened and gently probed. Psychologists employ all sorts of devices to get a person into his past. It does not matter so much how you get there through questions and conversation, but you must gradually uncover the deep emotional past in the person who needs healing. It is important that the original link in the chain be discovered and then many emotional scars may have to be dealt with—one at a time. If the primary cause cannot be unburied, it is possible to start in the middle somewhere and later trace the wiring back to defuse the original emotional time bomb.

Often merely a deeper awareness of the effects of one's past upon the inner emotions can prove therapeutic in itself. When my wife was uncovering some emotions in her distant past which were affecting her physically, often just a simple insight into why she felt as she did was enough to lighten her load considerably. This was before any prayer had yet taken place. Just knowing there is a reason can be a big help.

In such a time of deep spiritual and emotional interaction, it is vital to sensitively and lovingly listen for deep inner needs and hurts. Don't play the role of a psychoanalyst. Jesus is the healer, we are but the instruments to open a person to his own past. A lonely person in deep need of healing will often be the first to feel negative emotions from us as well. Sometimes just a ventilation of the past is helpful. Love and understand him and pray for sympathy, understanding, and guidance. When dealing with your child, pray especially for an awareness of how you felt at his age. Step into his shoes and wear them for a while.

Prerequisites for Healing

Several things are vital if a person is to experience a significant healing. For one thing, there must be a willingness on his part to be whole. To say to your child, "I've discovered some things in you that need to be taken care of. We're going to pray for your inner healing," will undoubtedly accomplish nothing. It must be a mutual thing. If your child is unwilling, then just continue praying over him while he is asleep. God is not limited to the conversational method. Until the subconscious inner child gives his approval to a "session" of conversation and prayer, pray privately.

Secondly, forgiveness (particularly self-forgiveness) is at the root of such deep healing. Often a parent will have to be forgiven in the heart of the child to release the necessary healing. You may need to ask your child to forgive you for your mistakes. When experiencing healing in your heart you might need to begin with forgiving your own parents. Forgiving and accepting yourself is vital since guilt (in many forms) is often to blame for many later side effects. Forgiveness must be coupled with thankfulness—to God for creating us as we are, to our parents for their love, and even for our hurts which are allowing God's love to touch us. Nothing can block healing more thoroughly than a root of bitterness which has a source in an unforgiving spirit. If we are unable to forgive—but are willing to do so and are willing for God to make us able—we can ask Him to go back in our memories to heal the bitterness (and help us to find its source) as the primary cause of our other hurts. God can heal anything if we are willing.

A final prerequisite for wholeness is the necessity of obeying the principles God has established for living. Where there are deep-seated emotional hurts, often the Christian trying to be obedient will still suffer from frustration. In such a case, inner healing will help. But the person who submits to inner healing while disregarding God's principles in his life will find the healing does not "take." Disobedience to God always involves consequences. Healing is required for those hurts in our past for which we are not primarily responsible, which occurred when we were emotionally too vulnerable to defend ourselves. Hurts from disobedience and our own rebellion require prayer as well, but of an altogether different sort. In those cases, we need to pray for forgiveness and must repent before God. Inner healing may still be necessary, but for a different aspect of our behavior.

How Healing Can Take Place Through Creative Imagination

Healing in the deep subconscious can take place in many ways. Two methods are primary. One is through private prayer.

We must often employ this when praying for the memories of our children, especially when they are young, but we should continue to pray for deep wholeness and healing throughout their years with us. We can pray for ourselves and for others in this manner as well.

The second method is through the use of what Ruth Carter Stapleton and others call "creative imagination." Through conversation or prayer or reflection on the past a root cause of emotional hurt is discovered. Healing can now take place. But instead of simply saying to God, "Lord, heal that memory," we visualize in our imagination that incident just as it happened so long ago. You can do this for yourself and you can instruct your child or another adult as well. You reconstruct the original moment of pain and then ask God to erase the negative memory and replace it with a new and healthy one. A new program must be entered into the subconscious. Imagine the time just prior to the painful incident and then step by step vividly imagine a parallel memory which is positive and happy and which completely fills the particular need of that moment. It often helps to imagine Jesus in the mental picture as being a part of that past time of life—holding the hand of the child who was hurt, fully loving the rejected child, filling in any gaps in the relationships that existed. When there has been death or intense fear, Jesus can be imagined there right in the midst of it, taking it all away. Such "creative imagination" acts as a new program in the subconscious. By focusing intently on that new image, it is able to register into the memory in much the same way the original negative memory once did. Remember, you have asked Jesus to go back into the past and make that memory a *now* in your subconscious. We are not playing with doctrinal descriptions here; God has the power to *do* this, to erase and to permanently and positively re-program the memories. Merely recalling events does not promote healing. It is when we re-experience them (in our imaginations) that we allow God's healing love to burn new emotions into the memory in place of the old. And in subsequent imaginative times of prayer and healing God can heal not only further hurts, but also the guilt and pain caused by the primary incidents. Each incident must be exposed and dealt with individually.

In the case of missing memories rather than wounded ones, God is able (through the same process) to build into the empty parts of the subconscious memory bank whatever is needed for wholeness. Though a young child may not have had a certain experience, Jesus can go back into the child's past and build a memory of that experience even though it did not exist in the actual life of the child.

Psychologists have taken back into their childhood adults who have suffered from various physical, emotional, and mental handicaps which resulted from insufficient physical stimulation (such as crawling). Many times a grown man who has suffered with reading difficulties for years can be taken back imaginatively into his infancy and taught to crawl. By experiencing this missing physical experience (even as an adult) those particular undeveloped sections of his brain can be energized and his reading problems often cleared up. His brain was simply missing something it needed in order to function properly.

Jesus can do the same thing in the area of our emotional memories. If a strong male or female image was missing in the life of a husband or wife, thus causing marital difficulties, He can go back to the original causes and build in those needed, strong images. The process is the same. In the imagination you vividly visualize either Jesus or your parents or someone else giving a strong dose of love and affection and then visualize missing relationships and activities which would have provided that strong father or mother image. This is not a "wouldn't it have been nice if . . ." sort of daydreaming. This is a genuinely joyful experience which causes a response such as, "Wow, what great fun this is!" To be effective, in your imagination you must genuinely be a child again. The more vivid the imagining, the more deeply God can stamp the new memory into your subconscious.

Some Examples

For years I have been afraid of dogs. When running I will go miles out of my way to avoid one. When I was about twelve I was walking home and was bitten by a German shepherd. It was nothing, really, but it was frightening. For years afterward, I went far out of my way to avoid that house. It was because of nothing my parents did or could have avoided. In fact, they gave me a great amount of love and sympathy afterward. Nevertheless, the image of that big black dog slowly walking up to me and very quietly jumping up to sink his teeth into my jeans and thigh has always remained vivid to me. I recently realized there is no reason for me to be in fearful bondage to that incident for the rest of my life. So in my imagination I frequently go back to that day and picture myself as a little boy of twelve walking along that quiet country road toward home. But there is a difference now. Jesus is walking along beside me. We are talking and laughing and all the dogs along the way seem to know Him and bark and come up to greet us. But they are like little puppies, friendly, tails wagging, tongues all over us, positively delightful. As we approach the Wolverton house, the big German shepherd barks and comes running toward us. But there is love in his eyes. He bounds forward and jumps up into Jesus' arms and the three of us roll and tumble in the grass, barking and yelling and laughing in fun. And every time I go by the house on my bike or walking we have a great time. I picture him like my old dog George with whom I used to roll and tumble and run. Whenever my mind reverts back, I try to visualize it in this way.

I cannot give you a bubbling testimony of my healing. I am just trusting God to work in my memory a bit at a time. When dealing with repressed emotional incidents such as this, you are often unaware that anything is going on (at the feeling level). But later the negativity which had once been so a part of you begins to stop recurring. A healing like this is rarely a one-time event. There are usually perceptible results, but healing is progressive and does not happen all at once. Keep in mind that we are working on a long succession of memories and in God's gentleness He often only uncovers things that need dealing with one at a time. (Mrs. Stapleton compares it to peeling off ever-deeper layers of an onion.) In adults, especially, there are many factors involved. In addition to a need for inner healing, there is often a need for repentance and sometimes a need to resist Satan's influence. Many times there are more basic emotional wounds that must be uncovered as well. Observing changes and establishing new patterns of behavior through obedience is a long and slow process. Re-programming the memories is but the first (yet very necessary) step. Determined will power to follow God's principles and continuing prayer for healing must accompany it.

You can have a significant impact in the life of your child once you become aware of his needs and how you can help. If your son or daughter is old enough to go through this process with you, it is possible for you to guide him into new memories in specific areas. Of course, your most significant part will be to provide him with the healthy memories he needs in the present and pray for him often. Nothing can compare with giving your child genuine memories for which there is no need for healing. And even teen-agers are still forming many lifetime images in their subconscious minds.

Programming of the inner mind takes years. Root causes are often buried so deep they take much prayer to dig out. Even after prayer for healing has occurred, building strong images takes time. A parent's job does not end with a prayer for such healing; in a sense it only begins there. A continuous new supply of healthy images must constantly be fed in to supplement the healing of the old, especially with respect to those emotions that have either been damaged or insufficiently developed. Even though such healing and such programming does take years—a lifetime in fact—with each negative memory that is rooted out, with each positive memory that is inserted back in, with each new positive memory that is provided in the present, additional wholeness is achieved. Fortunately, parents dealing with a child of ten or fifteen are in a much stronger position to positively focus the healing of God's Spirit than a person dealing with forty or fifty years of memories to probe and re-program. Such a ministry to one's children can be a major step in providing them with wholeness which will enable them to enter adult life.

For many specific examples of the healing of memories through creative imagination, I recommend Ruth Carter Stapleton's *The Gift of Inner Healing*. But I caution you, as you think and study inner healing further, to think of it primarily as a way to minister to your children and to achieve wholeness yourself. We are all in need of emotional healing at certain points and we mustn't suddenly think a little knowledge about the subconscious enables us to embark on a campaign to "minister inner healing" to everyone we meet. If God leads you that way, fine. Otherwise, let this insight draw you closer to the

Lord before you begin to expect it of others.

I'd like to provide you with an in-depth example of this sort of memory re-programming from Mrs. Stapleton's book so you can see some of these principles in action.

"Every inner child has an image of a man and woman formed by his relationship with mother and father. When mother lives a joyous fulfilling role as a woman and mother, the child within develops a positive female image. If the father is emotionally strong, responsive, and loving, the child forms a positive male image. When either masculine or feminine image breaks down, the child's response to his adult role is affected. If the inner psychic child has been abused, we sometimes find an inner battered-child syndrome. 'As a man thinks in his inner-child heart so is he.'

"Turning to Mary Ann I said, 'You may want to try to see what kind of image of a woman, and of a man, you brought into your marriage. . . .'

"Mary Ann said . . . 'My father was a good man; he was just always busy. I can't remember his showing me affection. I mean putting his arms around me or kissing me. Gosh. I can't even imagine his doing that.' She hesitated, 'Could this be a problem in my relationship with Nick?'

" 'Well, yes, it certainly could be,' I responded. . . .

" 'Mary Ann, in all honesty, who do you think has been more at fault in your unhappy marriage, you or your husband?'

" 'Nick,' she said without hesitation.

" 'Is Nick affectionate toward you?'

" 'He was when we were first married. But never any more. Except when we go to bed. Then he gets all lovey, and I resent it. I feel like he's just using me.'

" 'He may be. But would you be willing to be as much at

fault as he is? Possibly without even knowing it? Dr. Missildine, in his book *Your Inner Child of the Past*, says, "There are four people in every marriage bed: a man and a woman, and a little boy and a little girl." What he means is that we bring to marriage our adult selves plus what our childhood has been conditioned to feel. . . . Could it be that what you're doing in bed, and out of bed too, is sending two messages to your husband? The adult message is, 'I want your love and affection.' The second is the little girl message, 'I don't expect you to love me. I expect you are like my father. I expect you to be distant and unaffectionate.' And your inner rejected child resents this expectation. The unhappy truth might be that the last message is more powerful because it comes from your deep emotions. If this is true, is it any wonder that your husband has turned you off? Can you imagine how he feels when you are verbally saying all the right things, but the message he gets from the subconscious inner child—from your gut level—is an ugly put-down? . . .'

" 'So how do I get my inner child to cooperate?' Mary Ann was approaching the healing point.

" 'If you want to follow this through to healing, Mary Ann, I want you to go back in your memory, or in your imagination, to that age where you can recall wanting your father's affection, when you remember most deeply the pain of not having it.'

"She looked down . . . she was trying not to remember a hurt she hadn't allowed herself to feel for years. She didn't want to dredge up those feelings.

" 'It's hard to say when I felt the need for his love most. I guess when I was eleven, twelve, maybe thirteen. I just don't remember that well.'

" 'Can you remember an incident during that time?'

" 'Let's see.' We sat in silence as she thought. 'I remember when I went to my first dance. I was thirteen. My mother and I had made my first evening gown, and I was really excited. I felt not-so-drab, almost pretty. After I had every hair in place, I walked out into the living room to wait for my date, and daddy was reading the newspaper. Although I don't remember the boy's name or much of anything about that night, I remember I felt for weeks the hurt that daddy didn't say a word about me or my pretty dress. He just kept his head buried in that . . . newspaper.'

" 'That's helpful, Mary Ann. Often it's not that a parent is so terrible. Your father certainly intended no harm. But after many little hurts we begin to suppress them. Then there can be big trouble in the repression of the memories related to hurts. Close your eyes now and go back in your imagination to that living room on the night you described.' I silently prayed, 'Lord, heal her heart.'

" 'All right, I'm there,' she said.

" 'Do you see your father reading the newspaper?'

" 'I sure do. I want to tear it out of his hand and say, 'Look at me, daddy!'

" 'Before you do anything, Mary Ann, look toward the front door. See it opening. See Jesus walking in.'

"As quickly as I set the scene she said, 'I see him.'

" 'You see Jesus?'

" 'Yes,' she responded quickly, 'He walked in and is standing over by the oil stove.'

" 'Let him come over to you and tell you how lovely you look.'

" 'Oh, my soul, what a beautiful man he is.'

" 'Yes, he is. What does he think of you?'

" 'He says I'm beautiful. He says he's very proud of me, that he would be proud to take me out.' Tears were flowing from Mary Ann's eyes. 'He kissed me on the forehead.' . . .

" 'Now, Mary Ann, let Jesus go over to your father. See a radiant light flow from Jesus into your father.'

" 'Daddy's put the paper down. He's looking up at me!

" 'If your daddy was flooded with the Spirit of Jesus, what do you think your daddy would do?'

" 'He'd come and tell me he loves me.'

" 'Let him.' Then came that moment of reconciliation and understanding I had seen so many times before, but it is always new, always sacred. . . .

" 'Daddy, I forgive you,' Mary Ann said through her tears. 'I know you didn't know, but I just couldn't help how cheated I felt.' . . .

"I said to Mary Ann, 'Just see your daddy embracing you and telling you how lovely you are.'

" 'O yes.' . . .

"While Mary Ann was still emotionally responding to the prayer, I suggested that she imagine her husband, Nick, coming into the room. Then, as she had experienced the forgiveness with her father, I suggested that she forgive Nick and that Nick forgive her.

"When the two, the husband and wife, were reconciled in Christ's healing love, I asked the group to join in a circle around Mary Ann.

" 'Jesus, you promised that whatever we bind on earth will be bound in heaven. We bind this experience of reconciliation of father and husband to Mary Ann's heart. May it bring a new experience of love to her, and into her marriage. Amen.'

"After the circle of friends had returned to their chairs, I told Mary Ann, 'Remember, this is only a crucial beginning. Your inner child is going to have to build, by daily faith, that strong image of a man you saw tonight in your imagination.

" 'Try to spend a little time each day visualizing Jesus coming in the door from work. Then see yourself walking up to him, embracing him. Say to Jesus, "It's good to have you home, Nick."

" 'If you do this each day, you will condition yourself to respond to Nick as you would to Jesus. Months could go by before you observe any visible results. But each time you do it, you will nourish and strengthen that inner child. This is the most powerful prayer you can pray for your husband.' "[1]

---

[1]*The Gift of Inner Healing* by Ruth Carter Stapleton, 1976, pp. 13-23. Used by permission of Word Books, Publisher, Waco, Texas.

PART IV

A LIVING AND GROWING STRUCTURE:

Stages in a Child's Development

13

THE PRESCHOOLER

Birth to Age Five

Knowing everything about child development won't make you a good parent. But to be a good parent you must be aware of your child's growth. You have to know him—what he is going through emotionally and physically at various stages as he matures. There is no other way to apply the preceding principles, which have been largely general, to him specifically.

Keep in mind, however, that these stages are broad categories. We will not go into depth about folding diapers, making toys, diagnosing sickness, or talking to your child about sex. For specific answers to the infinite questions that come up about a child in *any* age you'll have to go to other sources that provide such thorough information. (I particularly recommend *How to Parent* and *How to Father* by Fitzhugh Dodson, Signet Books, for much more detail on the various stages of development.)[1]

It is hard to believe, but it is true: nearly 75 percent of a

[1]NOTE: The majority of the material on stages in a child's development found in chapters 13 and 14 has been adapted from Dr. Fitzhugh Dodson's two books: *How to Parent* and *How to Father*. Dr. Dodson's writing backs up Dr. Arnold Gesell's very thorough research studies on child development carried out in the 1930's, 1940's, and 1950's. His three pioneering works are: *The First Five Years of Life*, *The Child from Five to Ten*, and *Youth: the Years from Ten to Sixteen*, all published by Harper Brothers in New York.

child's intelligence is determined by the time he is six. Obviously, he has not gained that percentage of the information and specific knowledge he will eventually possess in this short time. But his brain's basic ability to process information and to manipulate, retain, and organize what it receives is set during his earliest years. This is true emotionally as well as mentally. His emotions, his self-concept, his way of viewing things, his ability or fear of self-expression are largely cemented into place during those first six years. His potential, in a hundred different directions, becomes locked on course in this stage.

The preschooler, then, whatever else he may be, is first of all a *learner*. He is learning and absorbing more things than you can possibly imagine, and at a faster rate than he ever will again. He is especially gaining a foundational outlook on life—one of trust and happiness and security and dependability, or else one of instability and distrust. And this learning process travels through several very distinct stages where certain key kinds of learning take place, all of which are vital to future balanced growth.

Before examining these, we should all remind ourselves how completely unique every child really is. No child will completely match these generalizations and time schedules, or those you find in any other book. There is no "typical" or "average" child. Someone has said that each child is writing his own book on child development. A key word to parents is, "*Let him!*" He will never be exactly like everyone else so don't place that expectation on him. Just because a book says, "A six-year-old will usually do such and such," you cannot construe that to mean that *your* particular six-year-old "ought" to do it exactly in the same manner. There is no "ought" here except that each child ought to be allowed to be himself.

This diversity is one of God's greatest gifts to us. And just as each child individualizes these stages for himself, they cannot be expected to come precisely "on time." Though all children will pass through the same general stages, each child will pass through them in his own way and at his own time. Walking can come at ten months or at eighteen months, and puberty can come at ten years or sixteen. It is the same regarding every stage.

Certain things will be felt more keenly by some children than others. Occasionally a child will seem to bypass a particular period altogether, only to pick it up later as needed. As a parent you must avoid using these insights as a basis for worry. They should help you to love your child more individually. They should make him all the more special to you because of the unique creation he is.

No stage can be hurried, and none can be held longer than normal. To do either will only cause emotional uncertainty, because each period in a child's life provides the emotional, physical, and psychological basis for the next. You can imagine it as a skyscraper which must be erected one story at a time. Every level is foundational for what comes next. Each one supports another. Each stage, therefore, must be fully lived. If a child is rushed into one thing before he is ready for it or is hurried along before he has had his fill of what has come before, he will not have the strength at that particular stage to properly support and undergird what is to come later. Such a process is often the source for either damaged or missing memories in the subconscious. A child must obtain all the memories he needs on one level before going on to the next.

The Baby

Basic Outlook—Positive or Negative?

One of the most difficult things for parents to see about their baby is that through the preoccupation with physical things the baby is acquiring his first bit of self-concept. This self-concept will come to him by degrees and will be the eyes through which he will continue to view the world, God, himself, and his relationship to all that is around him. The most significant thing a baby learns during his first year is what life is like. He learns either that it is a warm, healthy, trustworthy place which he enjoys being a part of or he learns the opposite. He is acquiring a very generalized outlook on life. He is feeling some very basic things about what it means to be alive. Is it happy or is it sad? Can I trust others or will I have to fend for myself? Is the environment basically friendly or hostile?

Of course it's hard for a parent to be aware of this sort of learning in the daily, twenty-four hour, non-stop grind of taking care of a baby. But it is through these primal, physical needs that this basic feeling of trust and security comes to a newborn. He has certain key needs which must be met: food, warmth, elimination, sleep, exercise, stimulation, and cuddling. The way a parent carries out these physical tasks for his child determines to a large degree what sort of early life-philosophy that child develops.

A baby has relational and intellectual needs as well. He needs a strong relationship with his mother and father—which will ordinarily come about in the natural process of attending to the physical needs. (If a father does not involve himself here—with smells, mess, drudgery and all—he will deprive his child of that initial interaction with him upon which a further deepening relationship will be built.) The intellectual stimulation needed by a child at this stage is not being told facts and given information. He simply needs to have his senses aroused. He is slowly trying to grasp what the world looks like, feels like, smells like, sounds like, and tastes like. So anything he hears, sees, feels, and so on helps him to clarify it all.

He needs to be talked to; he needs to be around people; he needs to be rocked, touched, moved; he needs to be played with; he needs toys; he needs to laugh. Certainly, he is unable to grasp the exact specifics—what the sound is, who is talking, what he sees, what the object is used for. Nevertheless the stimulation is somehow being registered in his brain. And this stimulation does two very important things: it teaches him a little about the world of his surroundings, and it makes him eager to know and learn and investigate further.

It helps to realize what a baby is learning in this process. The world to him is nothing but a gigantic blur at first. It does not just look like a blur; it feels like a blur. It is blurry in *every* way—emotionally, physically, relationally, socially. And during his first year he is gradually trying to bring it into some sort of focus. Everything he does and everything which touches him in some way contributes to this adjusting of the lenses of his senses. Being mentally stimulated is the key to his focusing ability.

A baby then is acquiring a basic "either—or" outlook on life. Life is either going to be a positive or a negative experience. And at the same time he is being mentally stimulated and motivated toward learning. The more you can blend together his various needs—physical care, a close relationship with you, and mental stimulation—the more solidly you will be able to give him a positive base from which to build.

When his basic needs are fulfilled and when he is emotionally and intellectually stimulated, your child will develop a sense of optimism about life. It *is* a positive experience. This will be the most solid foundation you can give him for developing to the maximum the strengths and potential God gave him.

The Toddler (Ages One to Two) Exploration

The moment a baby learns to walk, he is transformed into a toddler. Never was there a more inquisitive scientist. His curiosity is full blown now and will take him everywhere. It's been said that a toddler is just an oversized, mobile baby. And that's quite true. His judgment and discrimination are still very immature. He is suddenly physically able to do much he wasn't able to do a few months ago. He has great quantities of physical energy and drive and enthusiasm and the physical capacity to unleash it. But intellectually there has been no corresponding transformation.

It is therefore very important not to misinterpret a toddler's behavior (not doing what we've said, constantly getting into forbidden places, breaking things, climbing dangerously, and so on). He is not primarily hostile, disobedient, or destructive. He is just possessed by curiosity. And it's generally an overwhelmingly good thing: it's his means for learning.

As he learned basic trust or distrust as a baby, the toddler goes a step further and learns to trust in *himself.* During his second year, he is acquiring either self-confidence or self-doubts. Just as a parent instills trust through the meeting of physical needs during the child's infancy, the toddler learns whether or not he can trust confidently in himself from the physical world around him.

He has impulses and feelings and physical drive which all compel him to investigate—*everything*. If he is continuously hindered from looking closely at the things he wants to know about, two seriously detrimental things will begin to happen deep inside him. He will begin to interpret every "no" as a statement regarding his own personal worth and ability. As his movements are curtailed, his self-doubts are increased. Secondly, this constant squelching of what is natural in him quenches his curiosity, which is the basic God-given motive for all learning. Both self-esteem and learning ability have their earliest origins in a parent's responses to his toddler's activities. An unrealistic judgment of what is allowable to a perfectionistic parent will greatly constrict a child's natural growth processes and will saddle the innocent youngster with inhibitions, fears of future investigations, and guilt feelings—all because he simply did what he was compelled to do as a child.

On the other hand, if this exploratory urge is allowed to express itself and if a parent even helps his toddler along and shares it with him, he will begin to subconsciously develop a self-concept which has a feeling of worth at its core. The toddler feels good about himself because he is trying new things every day and succeeding at them. He enjoys investigating. Mommy and daddy are sharing it with him and are giving him approval for what he is learning. Confidence and curiosity are heightened still further. A solid piece of his growing self-concept is put into place, building upon the basic trust he acquired as a baby.

A toddler, then, needs things to investigate, to be allowed to investigate them, and interested parents who enter into the process with him. Upon these will be built his self-esteem. A toddler cannot function as himself in a thoroughly adult house. He needs to be able to explore, to *move* freely without constant fear and the need for continual oversight. Parents must put his budding self-confidence as a priority above the neatness of the house.

He needs toys, objects, *things* to play with, carry, collect, hold, and throw. Play is his means of learning; it is the essence of toddlerhood. It is not a frivolous thing but altogether healthy. We may call it "play," but when we watch a toddler we discover he is hard at work. He is fully expressing the nature God gave him. Unless childhood is filled with an ample amount of it, a child will not develop fully. And the objects of play are an essential ingredient. Not simply store-bought "toys," but anything your child enjoys *having*—lids, junk mail, paper bags, odd pieces of wood, a cardboard box, and even traditional cars and trucks and dolls. Don't give your children many expensive things in which they will quickly lose interest. Toddlers arrange to find plenty to play with.

Not only are such things necessary, so is an environment (outside when possible) that allows running, climbing, jumping, crawling, pounding, hauling, and throwing. He is developing physically in this stage, too, and needs *much* exercise. He is still limited to physical means of expressing what is deep inside, so his aggressive make-up is closely linked with his emotions. He needs daily physical outlets for these emotions. They are trapped and must be released through exercise. Without plenty of it he will become emotionally run-down, bored, edgy, and irritable. However you can participate in this play, giving him positive responses to his new skills and insights, you will strengthen his self-concept.

The amazing activity of a toddler, however, introduces a new need into his life, one that is not altogether a tolerable one from his perspective. That is the need for boundaries.

A toddler needs boundaries for his own safety first of all. His physical ability is more advanced than his wise judgment. He also needs them as part of his growing awareness of authority. A toddler is so busy that he can hardly be expected to remember the boundaries with any regularity. And learning to obey is a long, slow process that does not come naturally to anyone. Nevertheless, the boundaries he is forced to confront as a toddler are the forerunners of more direct training through later discipline. If the process is not begun now with the first "no's" and gentle spankings and boundaries that cannot be crossed, later conformity to boundaries and obedience to authority will be much more difficult to teach. Therefore, discipline gradually begins in the second year with some carefully thought out limits and consistent enforcement.

Don't forget the stage he is in, however. Basically we try to keep restrictions to a minimum. The boundaries we set at this point are not intended to curb his willfulness. His stubborn and rebellious spirit has not yet surfaced, so his stepping across the boundaries must be kept in perspective. He is not disobedient nearly so much as he is simply active. Discipline at this stage is largely preparatory—introducing him to the fact that boundaries exist and that mom and dad are in charge. This foundation is necessary as a base for the strong discipline to "drive out rebellion" which will come later. The boundaries you set, then, though firm, should be as few in number as possible. Remember to encourage his curiosity in every way you can. And when you do set a boundary, enforce it.

Because of the confusion he experiences during this exploratory stage—an insatiable physical and emotional urge to go everywhere at once, coupled with parents who say you cannot go everywhere at once—a toddler needs security. He is now viewing the world in more of its hugeness, and it must be awesome to him. His growing self-confidence needs a secure base upon which to grow. This comes during toddlerhood in three ways: from mother, from a routine, and from an underlying sense of his parent's strong leadership and authority in his daily life.

For several years, a child's mother provides his ultimate reference point. He needs all of her she can give him. For this reason, just as you cannot "spoil" a baby, it is almost impossible to over-mother a toddler. That is, as long as a mother is aware of the need for boundaries and a strong sense of authority in her child's early life. For the most part, spoiling comes later, when a mother without a sense of authority begins to give in to every demand of her defiant two-and-a-half year old. This spoiling is further aggravated when the mother of a three- or four-year-old does not recognize his need, along with firm boundaries, to have the first mother-child cords gently cut, and tries instead to hold him to her. There is a time for a child to be weaned from his mother, but the toddler is not ready for it. A mother who tries to instill independence too soon will not provide her child with a strong and secure base from which later independence will be able to grow.

A great security-builder at this age is a firm daily routine. This does not imply that nothing unusual (drives to the zoo, walks around the neighborhood, visiting friends, and so on) can be done. The routine must have a degree of flexibility built into it. But a child of this age feels comfortable and "at home" with a set order for lunch, naps, snacks, playtimes, story times, daddy's arrival home from work, etc. Knowing what is coming next is something for him to hold on to. Emotionally he is not yet able to deal with constant uncertainty. A child of this age can be given further emotional security if he is eased gently from one activity to another, especially when unusual activities are happening. Change is difficult, unnerving for a toddler. He is comfortable with established order and predictability. So it often helps toward the end of one activity to tell him gradually what is coming next and ease him into it gently. His emotions cannot handle abrupt breaks and providing these times of transition makes him able to adjust. For him to later want to venture out into the unknown, he needs a home base that is firm and orderly and predictable. This foundation is built largely in his toddler years with a routine he comes to trust.

Underlying both the routine and his relationship with his mother, a toddler needs to deeply sense being under strong leadership and authority. This is not something he primarily feels just because his parents make the rules and his hands are slapped when he crosses a boundary. It is more than that. It is a deep sensing of their total control. His parents are totally "in charge," in command of all situations. He does not feel on his own. Later, of course, this authority will have to be proven by the parent, but at this point the toddler accepts it and is comfortable with it. He knows they know when to get up, when to eat, what to do next. He does not want to make these decisions. He simply wants to investigate and let them worry about regulating the affairs of life.

The toddler usually experiences for the first time the devastating demoralizer of being expected to act older than he is. If his parents are insensitive, he will often have to face this the rest of his life and a hopelessly crippled self-image will be the result. A child at any age has certain capabilities, both emotionally and physically. He must fully experience the developmental tasks of one stage before he is ready to move on to the next. When a two-year-old is expected to understand and behave like a three-year-old, he is unable to fully *be* the two-year-old that he really is. The frustration of not measuring up is the damaging forerunner to self-doubts and criticism, and such expectations can easily lead to unreasonable discipline as well.

If a toddler is given plenty of room to go and grow, the stimuli to grow with, and the security to go from, he will mature feeling positive about his worth and his abilities. He will be ready to leave babyhood and enter childhood. But to make the transition, he must first pass through an intermediate stage.

The Rebel (Ages Two to Three) Transition

A rebellious two-year-old is not really rebelling against his parents, their values or their authority, but against his babyhood. For the parent who is unaware of this difference, the "terrible twos" really can be terrible. And even with this understanding, it will probably be one of the most exasperating and trying periods in a parent's relationship with his child. But down at the bottom something very necessary and good is going on—the baby is becoming a full-fledged child.

Fitzhugh Dodson calls this stage the "first adolescence" and compares it with the teen-age time in life. The teen years act as a transition from childhood to adulthood. A child between six and ten has established a fairly steady psychological equilibrium as he relates to himself, his family and his surroundings. He operates comfortably within the limits his parents have set for him. He's not yet mature enough to fully stand on his own, but to become an adult, he must "throw off" the patterns which have served him throughout this period of childhood. He is in the process of discovering a positive self-identity—who he is as a mature and grown-up person. But in order to move into this higher level of confidence and poise as an adult, he must first break up the lower—the former identity of childhood—which means a break with the ideals of his parents.

Those crucial years, then, are a time of stress and storm and doubts and emotional upheaval. A rebellious and negative teen-ager seems to be a different person than before. It can be a dreadful time for the parent who doesn't see that to acquire a solid self-identity requires that the child first lay aside his immature identity. This is emotionally trying for a young person to accomplish because down deep he has enjoyed his childhood identity. Part of him is not anxious to see it pass. So for several years his emotions sway back and forth. He is going through a crisis time. And often what finally surfaces is rebellion against all that has come before, including his parents.

This must not be misinterpreted, however, to mean the past ideals and relationships are in any way being permanently rejected. The teen-ager is rebelling against himself, not his parents (although this is what it looks like). He is rebelling against being a child any longer. He is rebelling against accepting certain values as a child would. He needs to discover them for himself. And the first step toward this highly positive form of reaching out independently into the future as an adult is to throw off the limitations of childhood. The negative paves the way for the positive.

A very similiar thing is happening inside the life of a two-year-old. The "runabout baby" is slowly becoming a child. And to acquire his own personal identity of selfhood as a child, he must first break up the equilibrium of toddlerhood. This process too involves a great deal of storm and stress, but it is necessary. For without it the baby cannot become a child who is attaining the level of independence he needs.

In the process his emotions are violent. He is demanding, disobedient, inflexible, and often has a terrible temper. This is natural, for he is trying to learn how he as a person is to conform socially to those people and situations around him. As a toddler he was content to be himself in a world all his own, but now he must learn how to fit in and function as part of the family unit which will carry him through childhood. Having had no background of experience in social conformity, he must (as the teen-ager does) learn his positive role at first through a negative one. He must throw off the past.

A two-year-old needs very patient and understanding parents who are flexible enough to make allowances for what he does, knowing it is a confusing time for him. In the life of the toddler there is a naivete, a movement outward that is one-dimensional in a sense. He is capable of many things, but he is still a baby. The two-year-old has lost much of that innocence. Life is becoming more complex. He is struggling to understand and cope with it, and trying to fit himself into it somewhere. One moment he wants to revert back to being a baby, the next he wants to push out and forward toward adulthood. "Who am I?" he is asking. He is going through an identity crisis, like the adolescent. This is why he is so likely to revolt against rigid rules, because he is trying to find out what he can do for himself. He is full of conflicting feelings and urges and desires. He needs boundaries. While discovering who he is and what he can do, he must also learn to conform socially—but lots of rigid rules concerning every aspect of his behavior will only frustrate him all the more.

This can be a confusing time for a parent, too, for along with the question, "Who am I?" come the questions, "To whom am I responsible? What is authority? Must I obey? Can I force mama to back down? Does daddy really have the backbone to back up his words?" It is during this year that the solid right of parents to set and enforce boundaries and exact obedience from their child must be established. At the core of the child's identity crisis lies the question of authority and his response to it. The defiance he openly demonstrates is not only an attempt to throw off his babyhood, it is also a definite attempt to discover the nature of the authority of his parents and whether he must in fact obey it.

This challenge must be met. This is the stage when discipline will have to be defined. Authority will either come to be respected and obeyed or it will be disdained—and no parent can lose sight of the scriptural fact that teaching a child to obey is one of our key priorities. A large part of a child's eventual attitude toward authority will be established during his third year.

Therefore, a parent is called upon to exhibit two very necessary qualities during this year: understanding and firmness. A child's emotional ups and downs and his need to do as much for himself and decide as many things for himself as possible must be patiently taken into account. Flexibility and understanding must be worked into the routine. He needs great freedom to move about without constant rules everywhere he turns. On the other hand, his rebellion (surfacing very distinctly now) must be curbed. His defiance must be met head-on. Disobedience must be punished. A parent must set boundaries that are wide enough to allow a child to move about freely and to make decisions on his own, but when openly challenged they must be firmly enforced.

There is a great security for a child in such a widely-drawn rigidity, for he is still too young to want to be left alone. He wants the boundaries and the comfort and security of knowing there is control all about him, but within that control he wants to run and jump and scream and find out everything he can do. *He needs to be allowed this freedom.*

There are two serious mistakes a parent can make at this point. One is exercising such strict control (by drawing the boundaries too tightly) that his child is prevented from having the chance to rebel in a healthy manner against his babyhood and throw off its shackles. A parent who will not tolerate an ounce of typical rebellion and ruthlessly crushes it will make his child passive and fearful. Without the opportunity to blow off some of the emotional steam trapped inside, a youngster will not have the opportunity to discover his selfhood fully. He will have no base on which to build his childhood.

The opposite mistake comes from establishing boundaries that are too wide, or establishing none at all. There is too little control and a parent is soon at the mercy of the child who becomes known as "the little terror." But his open rebellion, which grows worse and worse, is simply an attempt on his part to find those firm boundaries he can depend on and trust. He needs to sense a control that is overseeing his life. Without it, he is in limbo. He continues to grow, having no basis for authority and (especially critical at this particular age) learns no social conformity whatever.

Too much control and too little control lay the groundwork for problems a child will have to cope with the rest of his life.

A child between the ages of two and three is also going through another major change that affects him in every aspect of his life—he is learning to talk. He is usually emotionally ready to communicate and be understood far sooner than he is physically capable of doing so. This can be a source of major frustration for him. He needs to communicate. He is growing into a child and is ready for more advanced relationships. But often he simply cannot make himself understood. This can be fuel for his emotional fire and requires understanding and patience.

When one of my boys was two-and-a-half, we were getting ready to walk outside to the car. It had been raining and the ground was wet. I took his hand and we set out, but he would not budge beyond the edge of the porch. Nothing I could do would get him to come. His insistence grew and soon it began to look as though a tantrum was on the way. I debated about whether or not to spank him for what looked to me like disobedience of my requests. My wife entered the ''drama'' at this point and finally realized what he had been trying to tell me all along. His shoes had tiny holes at the toes and he was afraid the wet walkway would get his feet wet. All he wanted was for me to carry him across the wet area.

His reactions were simply a normal effort to be understood. Mine were the unreasonable ones. Of course, it was simply a misunderstanding. But it vividly points out the need to listen to the needs and wants of a struggling two-year-old on his level.

Many things are trying to surface at this time. The desire to communicate is a universal need at every age. If stifled it can cause deep inner turmoil and frustration. Children, therefore, need nonverbal outlets to express their inner selves. Playing in a sandbox, arranging a row of cars, or stacking blocks can still be a personal statement of *me*. In the life of a two-year-old, this need to express oneself often vents itself as an explosion or a tantrum. But remember, he is trying to learn *how* to express himself. It is new for him. Deep emotions sometimes feel strange. He has never had them before. If he is not allowed to express even his negative emotions (except outright belligerence and defiance) he will be that much more stifled in his learning about self-expression. To learn to express feelings of love and positive forms of expression, he must first learn about self-expression and feelings in general—of all varieties. He must, therefore, know that he can express negative feelings without fear.

A two-year-old is experiencing his first major thrust toward early forms of independence. Part of a parent's responsibility over the years is to train his child to stand confidently on his own feet. But this comes very slowly. If a child is rushed into more independence than he can handle, or if he is kept from the independence that he is ready for, his emotional muscles will not mature properly. The legs upon which he will later stand will not be able to support him confidently.

Independence must come at a child's pace, not ours. He needs to have his fill of each stage, complete with temporary reversions. Only in this way will he mature and gain independence at the exact pace that is right for him. A child who is thrust out too soon will later be fearful. He needs first to develop a total confidence in his security. From that solid base he can then take his first timid steps outward. He can move outward and back as often as he likes. When he is controlling the process rather than being pushed out, there is adventure and growth involved, not fear and uncertainty.

When our boys were two, we could see this out-and-back process vividly at work. They would occasionally ask to have a bottle (which they hadn't had for a year) and be put in the playpen to "play baby." We felt this temporary relapse into babyhood was entirely positive. It was a healthy way for them to regress for a while so that they could then choose to move on and out of that stage. Had we not permitted this, they could have always subconsciously wanted more of being a baby. Letting it come at a comfortable pace insured that they had their fill of each stage. Their memory banks needed a certain amount of programming in each stage—no more, no less. When it has had that proper amount, the child will know and move on.

And our boys' regressions had corresponding surges in the other direction. For instance, when a stranger would come to the house, they would walk up confidently, take him by the hand, and lead him away to show something. When in a crowd, one of them would seem to completely forget us altogether, behaving as independently and as self-assured as an adult. We, therefore, never worried about attachments to blankets or teddy or "childishness" or a flow of tears which seemed too "immature" for his particular age. We knew that all these displays of total dependence had to run their courses in order for true independence ever to come.

Many things are vital during this time for your child's intellectual development. As a toddler he was learning "passive" language skills (understanding what words mean). Now these skills are becoming more "active." (He is learning to express verbally what has earlier been registered internally.) The vocabulary he has, the clarity with which he speaks, and the evolution of his overall speech patterns will be largely based on what you have been feeding him through your own speech. Though you do not sense that a toddler is grasping what you say, nevertheless it is being registered in his brain. Your efforts begin to be rewarded between his second and third years. As he is learning to talk and put into words what has been built up in the storehouse of his brain, he needs a great amount of your attention and interaction. He needs talking to even more, discussing, listening to—always with respect. He is not only gaining pure intellectual skills but self-confidence through his new abilities as well.

He requires books and reading at this age in ever greater amounts. He needs to be drawn into an ever-increasing number of your adult activities, for he is rapidly learning to do many new things in a semi-skilled way. His intelligence is going to depend in large measure on the stimulation he receives during these early years. But as you are involving him in activities often over his head, it is vital that a child not be expected to perform at a level that is impossible for him. It is generally a good practice to assume you are expecting too much from him. In that way you can genuinely praise his efforts for how significant they are rather than always thinking they might have been better.

The two-to-three-year-old is going through many complex changes. It is not an easy age to understand, with any child. Finding the balance between discipline and understanding is not only hard, it is usually nerve-racking. It is a stormy time, but like all storms it eventually blows over, as the overgrown infant finally accepts the fact that he is a baby no longer.

The Preschooler (Ages Three to Six)
Integration into Life

Three-Year-Old

Just as adolescence ushers in adulthood, the rebellious twos usher in childhood. The beginning of the first phase of childhood is a very pleasurable time for most parents. In the three year old many of the transitional anxieties and perplexing questions of the two-year-old are gone and a new level of self-confidence emerges. Reasoning and conversations mature rapidly and intellectual growth is amazing—words, ideas, sentences, concepts seem to come out of him from nowhere. You think he is beginning to behave like a genius. And he *is* a genius who is always anxious to cooperate and please, a genuine joy to have around. He especially needs companionship during this time as he is learning to join in with others in a new way. He continues to be very receptive to all sorts of intellectual input—books, ideas, conversations, and a rapidly increasing number of rather complex concepts.

Parents with three-year-olds who are in this pleasant time should enjoy it to the fullest, because toward its end the child will be readying himself for another period of "break up."

Four-Year-Old

A child's fourth year is another one of instability, uncertainty, and testing. (They seem to alternate—one, three, five, and seven are harmonious; two, four, and six are tumultuous.) The four-year-old is not so much in a period of transition from one major stage to the next as he is simply being loosened and unsettled that he might move on to higher levels of maturity.

The four-year-old is in many ways like he was at two, only vastly more mature and sophisticated in his frequent antagonism of his parents. His friendships with playmates are a significant part of his life, but the relationships have very selfish, primitive, and stormy qualities. Through them, however, he continues to learn to be a social being. He suffers from the same emotional extremes, self-doubts, and strong will that characterized the two-year-old. He therefore needs understanding and much self-esteem. He is fascinated with his developing language and will talk incessantly whenever allowed. So he also needs attentive ears.

The four-year-old child is really the first one to seriously challenge his parents in a series of nose-to-nose confrontations where, in certain ways, he is on equal footing with his mother and father. He was very disobedient at times when he was two, but his four-year-old testing of authority is much more knowledgeable and his will has become like iron since that time. If the four-year-old is cagey and if his parents are lax in their discipline, he has every chance to emerge from most encounters as the undisputed victor.

This is the time when, possibly more than any other, the principles of firm discipline must be put into practice. This is a focal year in the child's growing concept of authority. This is the year which will set into motion many basic patterns. If not disciplined wisely, the four-year-old will continue to consider himself to be the center of the universe, whose every command must be obeyed. Wise parents have laid the foundation for this discipline when he was two and three. And they will need to continue to reinforce it, especially when he is six. But four is a pivotal year. His rebellious will is in full control and *must* be broken through wise and consistent discipline.

This does not, however, negate the need for understanding and the child's need for esteem. It is odd that those years of upheaval in his life are the times he needs the strongest discipline *and* the most assurance about his self-image. But that's the way children are. In the very midst of conflicts of wills that you as the parent must win, your child needs a tremendous amount of your love. He is rebelling, not against you, but (like the two-year-old) oftentimes against himself. The view of authority you demonstrate must be like God's—firm but with a foundation of love.

A four-year-old, too, is driven with unquenchable energy, which makes him a handful when no secure boundaries are provided. He needs freedom (like children of every age) to grow and mature and blow off emotional steam through unlimited physical exercise, but the boundaries must be there, and be secure, to let him feel safety and the sense of control over all and through all.

Five-Year-Old

The five-year-old is once again secure, at peace, self-confident, and enjoyable. The seeming "delinquency" of the four-year-old is gone and again there is stability and calm and your child appears to be "well-adjusted." He does not look for conflict as the four-year-old does. He is very much a *now*-oriented person, his thinking is almost too practical. When asked, "Do you like horses?" he will undoubtedly reply, "I don't have a horse."

Although he is still very much mother-oriented and home-oriented, he is feeling the need for expansion and does need an enlarged range of experiences. He is laying the foundation for the great leap out into the world which comes with first grade at six. He is intellectually ready for much more than most adults would give him credit for. Whereas the four-year-old's greatest need was to be trained in the ways of authority (while keeping his childhood zest for life intact), the five-year-old greatly needs intellectual exercise and stimulation. He is ready for kindergarten; if he doesn't go to one, his parents should provide an equivalent level of teaching.

Between the ages of three and six there are obviously great differences—yet there are many parallels as well. There are a number of physical and emotional developmental stages that all preschoolers go through. Though they will have different specific qualities for each age, each of these developments and areas of awareness run pretty much universally through the entire preschool period.

Though there was but one primary concern facing children in the three stages prior to age three, there are now a host of concerns. There are ten areas of growth which a preschooler must go through during these three years in order to enter his middle childhood with well-rounded physical, emotional, and intellectual capacities and with a strong concept of himself and his role in the world.

Muscular Development and Coordination

There is in every young child a God-given and never-ending drive to release energy in any way possible. He is frustrated any moment he cannot be on the go, every minute of every day. This is sometimes difficult for a tranquil adult to take. But the child has no choice. It's biological. That's how God made him. He needs plenty of hard, vigorous play and should not be deprived of it.

There are three things accomplished by such biological release. First of all, it strengthens the child physically by building his coordination, strength, and muscular skills. Secondly, it helps him emotionally by building confidence. Without this background he will be at a great disadvantage in physical activities later on and will come to feel poorly about himself as a result.

But many are unaware that this physical exercise provides a child with the foundation for his intellectual skills as well. There are many key areas of the brain which affect both physical and intellectual aspects of the same thing. The area of the brain which controls depth perception, for instance, works basically the same whether you are reaching out for a glass with your hand (physical) or are looking to judge the relative distance of two objects (intellectual). The area of the brain which distinguishes right from left works when you are walking or coordinating right and left hands playing a piano (physical) in the same manner it does when you are reading and moving along the page from left to right (intellectual).

In many aspects of the lives of children, the physical precedes the intellectual. In a young child's life it is usually the physical activity and exercise which "energizes" or sets in motion the particular part of the brain which will later be used for a corresponding mental ability. If insufficient physical exercise related to that specific function of the brain is not achieved, the brain will not be strong enough to fully master the development of the intellectual functions either.

Therefore, physical activities of all sorts—organizing

blocks, throwing a ball, swinging a bat, kicking, climbing a tree, jumping off a fence, and digging in the dirt—contribute not only to muscular coordination but also to the growing intellectual capacities of the brain. A child learns right and left, for instance, from crawling, walking, and working with his hands. Those areas of the brain activated through such activities later play a significant role in learning to read. If he has not had enough physical exercise of the right sort (crawling seems to be critical in the reading process, as are other activities for other mental processes) he may have a hard time with right and left when it comes to letters and words and reading. He may not be able to distinguish b from d or p from q because of the lack of exercise of that particular right-left section of his brain.

The preschooler then must be given many opportunities (daily when possible) to play and run and tumble and climb and throw and jump as hard as he can. The results will be very healthy.

Respect And Obedience

The Bible teaches that respect for and submission to authority is at the heart of God's dealing with man. It also teaches that children are to obey their parents so that they will later be able to obey God.

There are two separate aspects of life in which God is training us and in which we are training our children. The first thing necessary to live in a relationship with God is learning to obey Him. We must learn to submit to God's authority and obey Him simply because of who He is. There is a similar role parents occupy in relation to their children. They must teach them to obey and respect their authority as parents.

Secondly, children need to learn to live and function normally, safely, and independently in today's society. A child needs to learn to eat with a fork, dress himself, add sums of numbers, make choices, interact peacefully with others, carry out responsibilities, and ultimately provide for himself. He needs to learn behavior patterns and habits that will give him a basis for a normal life. This sort of practical education ordinarily has little to do with discipline as such. It is purely a practical matter of learning to function adequately in the day-to-day affairs of life. There are thousands of such things a person must know and a good many of them become ingrained in the habit patterns of a child during his early years at home.

In each of these two arenas for training there are distinctive tools a parent uses to teach his child.

TEACHING BEHAVIOR	TEACHING OBEDIENCE
Training Tools:	*Disciplinary Tools:*
Praise, encouragement	Spanking
Logical consequences	Punishment
Self-regulation	Pain
Reasoning	Toughness
Positive reinforcement, rewards	Inflexibility
Conversational feedback	Strictness
Extinction of undesirable behavior	
Patience, flexibility, leniency	
Practice	
Verbal instruction	
Parental model as example	

Each of these tools (and there are many others as well) is

designed for use in one of these areas of teaching. But the tools are not interchangeable. You cannot ordinarily teach your child behavior using the disciplinary tools and you cannot ordinarily teach your child to respect authority using behavioral tools. For instance, if you are teaching your child to tie his shoe or set the table or cook a chicken casserole, an inflexible attitude where shortcomings were met with a spanking would only create lifetime psychological problems and a child fearful of trying anything new. In such a case, you are teaching behavioral skills and need to use the appropriate tools—praise, rewards, patience, instruction, and positive reinforcement.

But on the other hand, when you are dealing with a rebellious and disobedient attitude in your child, to attempt to effect a change in heart by using reasoning, feedback, leniency, or self-regulation will only prove fruitless and will heighten the child's disobedience. When dealing with rebellion you must use an appropriate disciplinary tool—strictness, pain, or punishment.

To use a tool in the wrong area of training will make the problems worse and will cause rebellion, confusion, and fear.

The need to train a child to function in society is universally recognized. But many parents and most modern child psychologists are completely oblivious to a child's need to learn to respect and obey authority. Parents try in vain to fit spankings and discipline into their teaching of their child to function normally in life, not realizing that discipline is primarily a concept having to do with learning obedience. Modern theorists condemn harsh measures such as punishment and pain as ineffective means to alter behavior. And of course to a certain extent they are right.

But modern psychology has failed to take into account the difference between teaching behavior and teaching obedience to authority. Using their methods to deal with rebellion is like trying to talk a lion out of pouncing on you. Your arguments may be very convincing, but they will prove of little use. Words can do little to change a rebellious heart. Something stronger is necessary.

There is a corresponding problem in the opposite direction. Many Christians who have taken up the banner of discipline fail to realize that discipline is not a tool intended primarily to alter behavior patterns but attitude patterns. Focusing in on either area, to the exclusion of the other, will lead to an ineffectively trained child who is confused about right and wrong. A total response must be a thorough recognition of *both* types of training and both needs in a child.

A parent must recognize that both these types of training are going on constantly and must wisely choose responses using tools that either teach behavior *or* exact obedience, whichever is necessary at that moment. But responses cannot be random. For instance, if a child habitually spills his milk, he has a need to learn a different form of behavior. There could, of course, be many different ways of teaching a child to handle his milk glass more carefully, but a spanking in this instance would be a mistake because discipline and authority have nothing whatever to do with the incident.

If, on the other hand, the child is reminded a couple of years later to be careful about his glass, then looks you in the eye and defiantly knocks his glass on the floor intentionally, you are then dealing with a situation in the second area of learning. He has defied your authority and disobeyed and needs to be brought to obedience. To try to reason with such a child would prove equally as fruitless as a spanking would have in the first case. Your parental responses must be determined by which type of training you are dealing with.

Of course rarely are things quite as simple and distinct as this. In reality these two areas of training fuse together almost completely and blend with other approaches as well. A child, for example, may disobey you by knocking his milk onto the floor and to all appearances it may seem you are dealing with rebellion. But the child may actually be disobeying as a way of seeking your attention, which has been lacking. A third need may have entered the picture—the need to deeply love your child. His disobedience may not call for disciplinary tools at all, but a change in your schedule which would allow you to spend more time with him. There are many such areas which require different responses—the sphere of temperaments, your child's age, the realm of his frustrations. The existence of these additional factors does not make disobedience allowable, but it increases your need as a parent to know what is affecting your child's behavior.

This is why confusion and misunderstandings are so common. It is usually very difficult to isolate exactly what type of parental tool is most needed. Many factors usually come into play.

The preschool years are the most significant years in both these key areas—teaching obedience and teaching behavior habits. And parents are not conveniently provided with actions which clearly fall into one category or the other. The interplay between them is total. The only truly desirable behavior comes from an obedient heart—and obedience leads to good behavior patterns. Unchecked behavior that is allowed to go any direction it chooses will lead to selfishness very quickly. A parent is hard at work in both these arenas at once all day long.

The tools sometimes overlap as well. It is sometimes necessary to use spanking to teach behavior. You obviously cannot talk a two-year-old out of being curious about a hot fire.

As we saw in chapter five, teaching behavior through the discipline of boundaries is an intrın   part of a parent's responsibility. We must not become legalistic about this. We must, however, be aware of the difference. It helps to visualize that there are two separate areas of training even though they blend together and are tightly intertwined on the daily level.

Recognizing this is crucial for the parent of a preschooler. During these years he is forming both his lifetime behavior patterns and his lifetime attitude toward authority. You must constantly recognize both aspects of the training process. And in many instances of teaching behavior, a child's stubborn will comes into play. Therefore, you will not be afforded the luxury of being able to teach behavior one moment and respect the next. In the very act of teaching your child to brush his teeth or go to the bathroom or dress himself or share with his younger brother (using the behavioral tools), his will may suddenly rise up and you will have to deal with him in the other way (using disciplinary tools). You must have the full range of tools at your fingertips and use them properly. Much prayer for wisdom and discretion is needed. Much love for your child is a vital prerequisite.

Learning to Control Himself

A toddler often does anything he wants. Many of his needs are taken care of by his parents. He is incapable of making a distinction between "good" and "useful" or "unacceptable" behavior. But a six-year-old has learned to curb certain impulses and to do many things for himself. During the time between two and six a child must be slowly taught (it will not come naturally) to do things for himself and to control his impulses and desires. This takes time; results do not always come quickly. When it comes to self-restraint, a child may intellectually understand what "no" means. But until he has a reasonable control system established, he often doesn't have what it takes to restrain himself.

Teaching a child in this manner is in the area of teaching behavior as opposed to teaching obedience to authority. His lack of restraint at first is physiological and emotional rather than outright defiance. Repetition is vital in this learning process. He needs practice to learn to govern his impulses and to learn how to do necessary things himself (getting dressed, table manners, going to the bathroom, etc.). This practice should lead to self-regulation—but like learning to talk, it will come a little bit at a time.

As we discussed earlier there are all sorts of techniques and tools a parent can use to teach a child to control and determine his own behavior. In applying these techniques, it is vital to remember that we are simply trying to train a child to control his behavior. This has little to do with our parallel responsibility to see that his rebellious will is broken. We mustn't confuse a child's need to conform his behavior to certain social codes with his deep inner need to have his attitude of self-will curbed. They are distinct needs and require vastly different methods. Make sure you know which you are addressing at a particular time.

In training a child to control himself and to take care of some of his own needs, parents can make the mistake either of placing no demands upon him, or of making too many. A child with no demands placed on his behavior behaves at the age of four in the same way he did at two. He grows more and more demanding until he has no self-control. (When this happens, the behavioral sphere grows so large that it eventually encompasses the disciplinary circle. If behavior is not taught, it will eventually lead to disobedience and rebellion.) The opposite mistake is to pressure a child too quickly, expecting control he is incapable of—expecting a three-year-old to behave like a five-year-old. It is a simple fact that a five-year-old will be capable of much more than a three-year-old, in every way. We must constantly individualize this teaching and training process to our own child and his rate of growth and progress.

Separation from Mother

Independence is necessary for a child, and deep inside he wants to achieve it. Nevertheless, it is painfully achieved. A child is not ready for separation from his mother until at least three, and then only in small doses at first. At three he is emotionally ready for outside companionship, but will still feel anxieties throughout the process. He will need some occasional nudging but should not be forced until he is definitely ready. You must be sensitive to his subtle leadings. In a sense this means to allow him to move outward willingly on his own.

If this is not coming by four or five, you may have to encourage it along more vigorously. Separation from one's mother, even only if for an hour at a time, is a gigantic emotional step for a preschooler, like a voyage into the unknown. And it *is* unknown to him! He is still young and everything is new and his emotions are still so very tender. You are gradually preparing him for school, where he will be away from home for enormous slices of time (in his estimation). Make sure his broadening independence is a wholly positive influence, not a traumatic one. The wrong kind of deep injury here could easily be interpreted as rejection and remain with him for life. This separation must come and sometimes you must help it gently along. Keep an eye on the potential need to pray for healings throughout it, for whenever a child is tentatively extending himself outward into the world, there is a chance of getting hurt.

Learning to Express Emotions

The preschooler is flooded with many—often conflicting—feelings. Some of these seek expression simply through his actions and attitudes—things like anger, frustration, uncertainty, loneliness. Others come out through his still rather clumsy vehicle of verbal expression. As he talks more and more these feelings and responses begin to surface in statements such as: "I like that cake. I hate rain. I don't like you. I enjoy this book. That man is ugly. I wish you'd go away. That's a pretty picture. I'm mad at Suzie."

To an adult, some of these feelings and emotions are acceptable and can legitimately be expressed while others are negative and are therefore best left unsaid. A young child, however, is unaware of these distinctions. He only knows he feels certain things rising up inside him which make him feel a certain way and sometimes come out in words.

So during these years, depending on how his parents respond to his various expressions of emotion, he either learns to freely express himself and feel generally positive toward his emotional self, or he learns (what so many, many people learn) that to express one's inner feelings is unacceptable and can be painful and get you into trouble. It is much more comfortable to *repress* them instead of allowing them to surface. When this constraining of natural impulses becomes regular, a lifelong trend is set in motion. These repressed emotions have all sorts of negative results over the years, from physical ailments to subconscious memory wounds which remain deeply implanted. How a child learns to deal with his feelings determines in large measure his attitude toward his emotions. He's either going to learn to feel comfortable about them or he's going to suffer as a result of them.

Young children have no idea that certain feelings are good

while others are bad. They do not yet understand that some of these things rising up out of them can hurt other people. But parents who are perfectionists and who are more concerned about what other people (or themselves) think can begin right off to place unreasonable demands on their children. They begin to convey to their children, too young to grasp it, that it is "wrong" to be angry or to dislike someone or to prefer one thing over another. Repression and a confused self-concept are the results.

It is desirable to eliminate value judgments like "good" and "bad" altogether from our descriptions of emotions to preschoolers. They can hardly keep from interpreting such labels as comments on their personal worth. It is a wise tactic to allow a preschooler (especially a three-year-old) to give vent to as many of his feelings as possible. This will teach him in a positive way that there is nothing to feel guilty about in them. This does not mean we allow a child to *do* anything he chooses. But there is a great difference between feelings and actions. Through the self-control we are teaching, a preschooler is gradually becoming capable of controlling his actions. But at this point he cannot control his feelings. We can teach him to control the actions which would be the outcome of the feelings ("I'm mad at you; I'd like to hit you!") while still not condemning the feelings themselves.

This does not mean a child is forever allowed to say anything he wants at any time no matter how it may affect someone else. Controlling *how* feelings are expressed is another significant learning experience, one modern psychologists have largely overlooked. They have taken a basic biblical principle of freedom with control ("Be angry but sin not . . .") and have distorted it to mean that it does not matter what you feel, you may express it any way you choose. This is not true. It matters a great deal how we learn to express our emotions. This is one of a parent's key responsibilities in the life of his child.

But the foundation for that control must be a healthy attitude toward feelings themselves. And preschoolers are just not yet in a position to make the distinction between the sort of feelings they can express openly and those they should reserve for a talk with mom or dad. A child of five is ready to begin making distinctions of this kind. But the foundation for the emotional freedom and sensitivity which will lead toward this control must be laid at three and four with an atmosphere of total expression without fear, guilt, or repression. There will be plenty of time later for teaching that there are times and places and situations for expressing deep feelings and others where they are best left unsaid. This cannot, however, be taught to a two- or three-year-old concerning some of the first deep emotions he is dealing with without at the same time inhibiting his spontaneity. (You must remember we are speaking here of the gradual learning of self-control. In the area of discipline and authority, anything does *not* go. Defiance must be met, not simply brushed aside until a child is five.)

Gender Identity

It is during a child's preschool years that he will establish in his own mind his identity as a male or female. This means far more than simply knowing whether he's a boy or a girl. It involves knowing on a deep level what it means to be a man or woman. This comes about primarily by strongly identifying with either mother or dad as the ultimate "man" and "woman." This is a crucial aspect of his overall psychological health. It comes about as little girls imitate their mothers and little boys emulate their fathers. Teachers and other adults play an important role as well.

Hormonal changes are making themselves felt for the first time, too, but most important in a solid gender image is the parents' attitude toward the boy or girl. When you are happy with, and thankful for, your child's gender and convey that to him or her, your child will mature as a normal boy or girl if given adequate models to imitate.

Acquiring a strong masculine image is especially difficult for young boys who are not able to spend large amounts of time with their fathers. Time is always crucial for a child, but during the preschool years this is a unique need young boys have which only their fathers can meet. It will be impossible for them to form strong mental images of a man unless they have opportunities to see one.

Initial Sex Education

In addition to gender identity, a preschooler is beginning to form other basic attitudes toward sex differences and his own sexuality. Many are not aware that children of this age begin to be very curious. Telling your preschooler about sex is a very low-key thing that is hardly more than simply responding to his questions as they come. And the questions will begin as soon as three and along with them elemental (and harmless) "investigations," either alone or in a group of other curious children. The byword for the parent here is "calmness." At this point it is innocent enough. But you should be prepared for it nonetheless with some well-thought-out responses. There are a host of helpful books available to assist you in formulating answers and to guide you. It should be a joyful experience—not an awkward one—to discuss sex with your child.

The Family Romance

Every boy—at some time during this stage—falls in love with

his mother, and every girl falls in love with her father. Both fantasize it to think they will one day grow up to replace the current spouse. Many aspects of this stage are common to older romances. The little boy and girl will adopt techniques designed to win over their "lover" and jealousies will often set in when it becomes obvious that mom or dad is seriously interfering with his plans. A little boy, for instance, wants mother all for himself and resents his father for depriving him of her.

This is not something that can lightly be brushed off as "cute." The feelings run deep. If handled insensitively, deep emotional scars can result. A parent must be sensitive to these feelings in his child and do everything possible to assure him or her of the parent's love. But it must be made clear (though gently) that mama is already married to daddy.

The rivalry between father and son can be hard on them both, as can the tension between mother and daughter. Both parents need to pray their son or daughter will not develop guilt feelings. Down deep a young boy needs his father and loves him, but at the same time he can occasionally grow to temporarily fear and resent him. These conflicting emotions must be handled with great love and tenderness.

Usually by the time a child is six, this stage is passed and once again both mother and father come to represent the ideal whom they strongly identify with. It takes time, however, during the preschool years, for these feelings to subside.

Relationships with Friends

Between three and six, coupled with his learning to move out beyond the security of the home, a child is learning to function in groups of other children. It is a different world than the world at home, with different rules and new demands. This is often where a child first comes to grips with his own strengths and weaknesses. This is where he learns to function socially—to share, to express himself, to participate, to wait, to play in a group. There is joy in it for a child, because independence always feels good. But there are fears and dangers as well, which parents must be listening and watching for. Self-esteem can be quickly cut to shreds by a child's peers, who are often very blunt and cruel in what they say. A parent cannot simply turn his child loose. Environmental control—taking responsibility for the expanding boundaries so that your child will be positively helped (*not* over-protection)—comes into play prominently here.

If a child can make it through his first entry into peer relationships with his selfhood intact, he will have acquired a very healthy sort of emotional toughness to weather future battles for acceptance and bouts with rejection. Relationships with friends *always* hurt. Parents must make sure this hurt is channeled into the child's ultimate good. They must not act simply as a shield which keeps all pain away. An amount of surface pain must be allowed in order to build a child's tough self-reliance, while at the same time a parent absorbs the deep emotional pain that would lead to harmful injury.

Intellectual Growth

During the years from three to six, a child matures from being barely able to talk to a youngster ready for school and capable of reading and writing—a remarkable jump in just three short years. To come this far, and to acquire the basic learning skills necessary to succeed in school through the years, he needs a strong educational foundation.

Many adults mistakenly suppose that intellectual capabilities are innate, something you are born with. But as scientific investigation has consistently shown, this is not true. A child learns to think according to the teaching he receives and the stimuli he encounters in his early years. All environments are rich with learning potential, but a parent must teach his child to focus in on things that will stimulate his mind in thought. As with infants, sensory awareness is the foundation for learning. A child must be encouraged to use his senses—to feel things, to distinguish between smells, to listen for unusual sounds, to appreciate flowers and trees and lawns and ditches, to notice the differences between leaves on different trees, to feel the texture of redwood bark or of an old oak tree of velvet versus silk, to notice the smells of pine needles or the pulp mill or leaves burning, to tell the siren of the ambulance from that of the fire engine, to listen for the sounds of various birds, to touch the wet nose of a cow and to hear the resonant "moo." You teach an awareness of all these things by your interest in them and by pointing them out continually. The most commonplace homes and yards have infinite possibilities. He needs to use his hands, ears, and eyes continuously. This is his foundation for all intellectual growth, for these sensations of the senses somehow imprint themselves onto the brain and generate thought-activity there. The actual sight is only like the pebble thrown into the water; its implications in the brain are like the rings that follow the splash, widening beyond sight.

To integrate this process with a child's dawning creativity, he needs to be able to "make" things with his hands. He therefore needs crayons, scissors, magazines and paste, colored posterboard, a blackboard with colored chalk, scraps of wood and cloth, blocks, dress-up clothes, construction toys, playdough, books, and a bulletin board on which he can hang his creations proudly. All these, along with the firsthand experiences you introduce him to will give him a good feeling for learning and will whet his appetite for more.

If you are talking to your child, he will learn to talk. But he will not automatically acquire other fundamental learning skills. They must be taught. There are three areas where your preschooler needs some groundwork teaching that only you can provide. These are: writing, reading, and mathematics.

Many still hold to the notion that there are harmful side effects to trying to teach a child such intellectual concepts too early, before he reaches school age. But numerous studies show that early teaching of concepts in these areas gives a child a terrific boost, both intellectually and emotionally. Whereas physical skills can come too soon and in the wrong order and can cause problems, the same does not appear to be the case with learning skills. A child who learns to walk too soon without adequate crawling and muscle development will often suffer certain difficulties later. But the child who learns to talk at an early age seems to be nothing but better off for it. This presupposes of course that such early mental development is free of any sort of pressure and is achieved in a balance of the other principles necessary to train a child.

To stimulate your child's capacity to both write and read, books need to occupy a special place in his growth. This means more than simply reading to him before bed. It involves his becoming familiar with your town's library, buying books of his own, and it especially means your reading to him often, allowing *much* interaction with the story and the pictures. This is an excellent way for him to learn to see, hear, touch, and so on in his imagination.

When a child is three-and-a-half or four he can begin to learn to print letters. Begin with the easiest capital letters. It will take a lot of time and it must be fun for him—zero pressure from you. It may take a year just to learn the letters. There's no hurry. You can begin to show him the order to put the letters in to form his name and other simple words. Pursue what he shows an interest in. Don't plan out a rigid structure. All true learning is self-motivated. It cannot be forced upon you.

Wooden or magnetic letters can be a help too. Making books that your child thinks up is great fun for him and a great motivation to learn still more. A book can include pictures or anything he wants you to write down. At first he'll dictate, later he can actually write the book himself. The fact that it's his very own, from start to finish and top to bottom, is something of a confidence-builder on the level of the miraculous for him (that is, if you didn't force it upon him).

Language can be made interesting to a child by developing and arousing his curiosity about the meaning of new words he encounters. Every moment you are with him you should be carrying on a dialogue about the words you see together and their meanings—in books, on boxes, on signs, at the store, and so on. Words are everywhere. Call his attention to them. It will play a part in helping him want to learn to read.

It is a long-held belief that is now being seriously challenged that only a trained schoolteacher should teach a child to read. Studies now show that the key in a child's future reading ability is not the teacher at all, but the mother. Those children whose reading ability is consistently highest in the early grades are those whose mothers stimulate their interest in books, words, reading, and writing; such parents have materials—paper, felt pens, glue, scissors, etc.—around the house to use and actively encourage their children to "create"; they discuss words and their meaning with their children; they teach their children to print; they make books and the library a regular part of the family routine; and they take their children on frequent "field trips" where many sorts of experiences are discussed.

A preschooler who learns the basic elements of reading is

given a great boost toward needed independence when he enters school. He is also given a great amount of confidence; his first year in school can be an enjoyable one rather than one filled with the pressure of *having* to learn to read, or else. In addition, reading is the most significant avenue into the world. The sooner it begins, the more opportunities a child has to avail himself of all there is for him to see and understand. But as in all things, if a child is pressured into learning to read, more harm will be done than good.

Teaching your preschooler basic mathematical skills is best done in the form of "games." Everything you do can be called a game, and it should be. If it's not fun for your child, drop it. Counting is the most basic mathematical skill. This doesn't mean simply memorizing a long string of words which you call "numbers." It means teaching him to really know what "one" and "five" and "eleven" actually *mean*. This is best accomplished by slowly learning to count small objects.

Even before a child can count he can begin to play with Cuisenaire Rods, which will fascinate him. (There is a kit called the Cuisenaire Rods Parents Kit which gives you guidelines for using the rods.) When he is four or five and has learned to count to eight or ten, you can begin to play very simple dice games where you move a "man" the number of squares shown on the dice toward a final goal. (You can make your own games easily. Pleasing a small child is easy and oftentimes a homemade game is even more special to him.)

These three "games" (counting, Cuisenaire Rods, and dice games—all discussed in more detail in chapter 12 of *How to Parent*) will provide your child with a solid mathematical base for entering school. But throughout you must keep in mind how much more difficult mathematical concepts are for him. He is used to words. But numbers and shapes (which you can begin to teach him to draw once he is counting—around four years of age) are more abstract and difficult to grasp.

In teaching preschoolers, never forget their short interest spans. Five minutes may be about it for a single activity. He must enjoy it or he will lose interest and not be motivated to learn from within as readily. Discipline, scolding, pressure, or punishment are absolutely out in all forms of teaching or learning. Mistakes are part of the learning process. Accept them joyfully, and then especially praise the successes. Make it fun and he will learn, and love it.

The poet John Masefield wrote, "The days that make us happy make us wise." Make your child's preschool days both.

14

MIDDLE CHILDHOOD AND EARLY ADOLESCENCE

Six to Sixteen

Middle Childhood

Toward the end of the preschool stage, your child acquired a rather stable equilibrium in his personality. This stability will last roughly until he is eleven. This does not mean the middle childhood years are without their ups and downs. Your child will quite suddenly be thrust into two new worlds which will make very heavy demands on him emotionally: school, and the world of his peers. In both of these new realms he will be evaluated not on the basis of who he *is* as a person, but almost solely on the basis of what he can *do*. In this regard, these two worlds have vastly different values than he has been accustomed to at home. And all three worlds have varying and sometimes conflicting standards for specific behavior. What constitutes "good" behavior at school, with friends, and at home may be entirely different.

These are years, therefore, with an underlying stress attached to them. A child is trying to forge a self-image from three different angles all at once. The positive side of this, of course, is that he is being prepared to live in the midst of the larger society. This is really his first venture out into the world at large.

The preschooler was aware of the world mentally. But he was totally shielded and protected from it in terms of his emotions. He was making tentative overtures outward, but he was still very much bound up in the family unit. But with the advent of first grade, a child is immediately out *there* on his own. He must now find ways to emotionally cope with what must seem an unfathomably huge world of giants and unknowns. This he does in two ways. First, he tries to learn as many skills as he can. This involves his schoolwork (where failure is always noticed) and it involves learning the various skills that give him recognition and acceptance among other children his own age (athletic abilities, being able to compete in various games, etc.). The competence aspect of self-esteem takes over almost entirely when it comes to school and peers. Without feeling he is accepted in these areas, he quickly senses an inferiority to everyone else around him.

Secondly, a first grader learns to cope with his new environments and expectations by gaining a sort of emotional strength from his friends. The psychological dependence on the family is slowly replaced by being accepted in the peer group, which takes on more importance through the next few years. A shared loyalty and support gives a child something to lean on. A child unaccepted by his peers at school is a child who really is alone. A group can be only two people and still provide an emotional comfort.

The intense importance placed on abilities rather than personal worth during childhood points out the urgent need of parents to make sure their child does acquire certain skills. A child need not be a superstar. He need only be average in a wide range of skills. He simply needs to be accepted, not idolized.

Physical skills are very important here—throwing, running, catching, swinging, climbing, etc. Athletic games (of a million different varieties) and activities are the "stuff" childhood is made of. To survive, a child must be capable of performing at least well enough that he does not stand out as uncoordinated or inept. Though a parent may think such skills are unimportant, he must recognize the *extreme* value placed on them by children. And he must do what he can to help his child compete in his world.

Physical abilities are not the only things of importance during this age. This is also the time when many other types of interests begin to surface—collecting, an interest in following organized sports teams, music, reading, hobbies. These middle childhood years, therefore, are vital for building esteem within the child. This is when certain natural inclinations and interests of a child begin to be seen more clearly. And parents must look for these interests and natural "bents" in order to draw them out and further encourage their child. Self-confidence is maximized when a child learns to do well something he himself is deeply interested in. We cannot force an interest onto a child. We can only seek to discover which ones God placed in him and then give the child the opportunity to discover them for himself. An overzealous father who makes his son practice free throws an hour every day when he would rather be rummaging through his coin collection or practicing his trumpet will only make him hate basketball. Certainly he needs some elementary ball-handling skills, but his real esteem will come from his father's interest in those things the child has chosen to pursue.

The child begins to see his family in a different light during this period. He may experience feelings of ambivalence toward his parents and siblings. A child is feeling the need to become increasingly free, yet at the same time he seems to need the security and comfort of the family more than ever. As he is gaining in independence and trying to grow psychologically to the point where he needs you no longer, a child begins to see you in a much more human perspective. He is now realistically aware of your shortcomings and inconsistencies and is not above pointing them out. This, too, is an important part of his growth toward independence, as are the many freedoms he increasingly demands.

Yet throughout the years of middle childhood, children retain a closeness with their parents that is one of life's sweetest love relationships. This is a time for in-depth, one-to-one relationships between each parent and each child. This is the time he most fully needs a model to imitate and an emotional ally in the midst of his struggles. Though he sees you as God no longer, nevertheless your child still holds you in such high esteem that you can greatly influence him through a deepening relationship. He needs you to lead him into meaningful relationships as a model for future ones he will experience with others. Because of this open receptivity to you as a person, the middle childhood years provide ample opportunities for you to correct mistakes you may feel you made when he was much younger. This is an especially important time for you to share deeply in the things he likes to do. For now he genuinely wants you for his friend. You mustn't push yourself upon him, for his independence often requires him to determine how far the relationship is to go. But when he is ready, go as far with it as you can.

Six-Year-Old

Though the years from six through ten are relatively tranquil on the whole, there are yet some major adjustments to be made which tend to keep the emotional pendulum swinging back and forth. Following the equilibrium of five, the six-year-old finds much of his comfortable past breaking up and reacts with characteristic first grade self-centeredness and rebelliousness. He is not so much a rebel as he is simply seeking ways to blow off emotional steam created by the psychological pressure he feels as a result of the major changes that are being forced upon him. Formal schooling is new and demanding and he finds the pressure to conform and succeed difficult to cope with at times. Many of his outwardly obnoxious habits and attitudes are the result of this intrusion of school into his life. He enjoys school; nevertheless it is demanding.

The six-year-old will often seem to behave in ways quite unlike himself. No matter what his temperament he will assume more sanguine characteristics. He will demonstrate confusing and even violent changes in emotion; he will monopolize conversations and always seek to be the center of attention; he has difficulty finishing jobs; he is feisty, energetic, enthusiastic, rambunctious and a braggart, a tease, a dawdler, and a procrastinator. He will often seem to go out of his way to instigate a conflict with his mother and oftentimes a father seems to handle him best.

All these things are the result of his being eased out of the comfortable and secure nest of home and family into the expanding world of school, friends, the neighborhood, and society. They are in a sense his defense mechanisms to cover the uncertainty he feels about having to adjust to the new environments he is being thrust into. The demands he makes, the new fears he feels (often of things like wind and rain and thunder and insects), the physical fatigue that often follows a day at school must all be lovingly viewed in light of the enormous emotional change he is going through of having to "cope." It is a year of expansion for him. He is branching out in many new ways all at once. This has many positive sides as well. He sometimes feels like a young and daring explorer. He is (in spite of its complexities) enjoying every moment of life when his emotions are more positive.

Parents can help him adjust by being patient with his emotional swings and by not placing added expectations of their own upon him. He cannot use any additional frustration of having to perform. He gets enough of that at school. He needs you as someone he can always come back to for comfort and refuge in the process of his exploration of new vistas. Though you must apply no pressure, nevertheless your six-year-old does need occasional help, both with schoolwork and with his physical skills. Success at school and among his peers is one of the bases for esteem throughout childhood. You must not put your own added expectations on him, but you must help in whatever ways you can to see that he achieves the level he wants to achieve. Be available!

The six-year-old begins to place a much higher importance on "the gang" and it provides him with a security in the midst of the pressures of school. He does not yet know how to play well with others, yet somehow knowing they are "around" helps him psychologically. These early relationships, however, like his emotional uncertainties and outbursts, will mature and provide a base on which to build future relationships.

Seven-Year-Old

If the six-year-old is typically a sanguine, the seven-year-old is typically a melancholy. He now slows down and begins to mentally assimilate what he has experienced in his previous year. Life runs more smoothly for him. He is calm, cooperative, rational, and more tactful than he was at six.

It is an inward year for him. He is quietly in the process of trying to sort out the things he has experienced as a six-year-old and the feelings that have been inside him. It is a year of reflection, introspection, with its times of dejection. He needs time to "just sit" without pressure from parents to *do* something. His thinking is work for him. This year is a major step in the direction of his maturity and independence.

This is not to say the seven-year-old is a deadbeat. He still has a fantastic reserve of energy which must find physical outlets to keep his emotional steam from building to the boiling point.. This is an especially important year for a child's relationship with his father. He is getting along better with his mother once again, but he is reaching out in new ways for a deep relationship with dad. The seven-year-old boy needs to talk about "men-things" one-to-one, and a girl is especially responsive to a father who helps her appreciate her femininity.

Two things that surface in this year quite often are fighting (mostly in boys) and an acute perception of fairness. Though usually the desire for fairness in others far exceeds the child's own commitment to be fair, it is nevertheless a time for parents to pay close attention to the justice of their methods. Fighting among young boys is normal and must be taken in stride. Pray for healing of memories when necessary.

The second grade year is usually a good one. But the seven-year-old is sensitive right now. Criticism can cause instant tears while praise will often work wonders. Remain sensitive to his mental search for his own individual niche.

Eight-Year-Old

Eight is an expansive age. The six-year-old was thrust into the world, the seven-year-old withdrew to try to figure it out, and now the eight-year-old is ready to go out to meet the world with gusto. This could be considered the "choleric" year, the year of being on the go, of being active and busy and exuberant about a hundred new things. The eight-year-old is trying out upon the world the personality and self he tried to put together at seven. He is hungry for any kind of new territory. He tries to maintain a self-sufficiency which is up to tackling any new task. Of course, this is often a front, and frustrations still cause him to burst into tears. He remains thoroughly a child. (Crying, by the way, is very natural even for the most well-balanced and happy children until they are twelve. Never criticize them for it.)

Eight is usually the time when boys and girls begin to definitely separate themselves from each other. This, along with an eight-year-old's self-confidence, which is no longer trying to please absolutely everyone, makes eight the time for the emergence of some friends as closer than others. And it is usually the time when the first full-fledged "best friend" comes along. It is a new experience in intimacy beyond the confines of the home and a child and his best friend seem to have a mutual and constant need to be together.

The eight-year-old is branching out in many ways toward maturity and toward interests outside the home and family. Collecting things becomes interesting (coins, stamps, bugs, baseball cards, rocks, postcards—anything); organized groups start around this time (all manner of sporting groups, scouts, etc.); possessions are becoming increasingly important; a love of table games is at a peak; and scary movies and stories are fascinating. Many of these things are attempts to master fears, exercise control over something other than yourself (collections, games, etc.) and participate in society at large.

A child of eight is hard at work entering into the flow of a bigger life. His ways of relaxing (often TV and comic books) might seem trivial to you, but to him they *are* important. He has the same need to occasionally escape that an adult does. His love of possessions makes this a good year for magazine subscriptions, his own books, and furniture in his room. Don't push these things on him but realize his need to find out what ownership is like.

Nine-Year-Old

In many ways it is impossible to tell a nine-year-old from an eight-year-old. He is basically extending himself outward in the same ways, further and in a more mature fashion. He is now much more a self-sufficient, self-motivated individual. Though many of his activities are similiar to those he had at eight, they are now marked with an individuality that is his. He can now be treated much more like an adult and responds well to it. The past year has given him an increased maturity to make more of his own choices. His attention span has greatly increased; therefore, he can carry through more difficult projects to the end. This makes it a good time for him to learn skills and techniques (without having to perform with perfection) from his parents. The nine-year-old boy has a great interest in sports. And it is a good year to introduce a child to musical instruments if he has the urge to learn.

The growing maturity and independence of the nine-year-old cannot make you expect more from him than he is capable of. He is still young and will occasionally revert in behavior several years. Don't ever chide him for this. Expecting a child to be mature sooner than he is able will nearly always impede the process.

Ten-Year-Old

The tenth year brings to middle childhood the same sort of

consummation that five does to the preschool years. The ten-year-old is basically calm and positive, as he has attained both the resources and poise from the past two years to deal with the world in a reasonable way. He has not attained this state by "leaving behind" anything. He now thoroughly enjoys everything life has to offer: his friendships, school, the companionship of his family, games, collections, and outdoor play. Though he is generally outgoing, in some respects this could be considered the "phlegmatic" year because of his pleasant attitude toward most things. He enjoys school and can now begin to handle certain topics on a more grown-up level than before.

This is not to imply that a ten-year-old is without his difficulties. Jealousies and conflicts between brothers and sisters flare up now, as do other momentary outbursts of anger. And he is not the least bit meticulous about his work and room and responsibilities at home.

Ten is the year when girls especially—and to a lesser degree boys—need to be started on the road toward more specific sex education. Most girls to not begin menstruation until they are eleven or older, but now is the time for preparation. The book and cassette tapes *Preparing for Adolescence* by James Dobson (Vision House) should be reviewed by parents and some of the instruction begun at ten. Other books are helpful as well.

During the years of middle childhood a child's self-concept is added to and altered by three different worlds in which he must live and relate: the world of your home, the world of the school, and the world of his peers and close friends. Understanding the specific influences each of these worlds brings to bear upon him, and the corresponding pressures inherent in all of them, will help you discover ways you can help him relate and succeed in all three areas. This "success" is not primarily in the eyes of the world. By success I simply mean that your son or daughter, in a sense, "gets by" with a positive self-image and a healthy attitude toward God, himself, and others. Childhood is so filled with esteem-damaging influences at every turn, your boy or girl requires a certain measure of success just to keep his self-concept afloat.

It is vital you remember that these stages of growth we are looking at are for the majority of normal children. But your son or daughter is *not* "normal children" and never will be. Everything in his life will have its complexities. Everything here must be adapted to your child as he is. When I was nine and ten (supposedly the crowning years of middle childhood), I experienced two positively horrible years in the world of school and my peers there. Yet in another realm I had a relationship with my "best friend" (a church friend rather than a school friend) that I still look back on with longing. And your child too will bring great individuality to these patterns. Don't expect him to be "like the book."

School

The first five years of school represent a huge step emotionally for any child. They greatly increase his need to know that you love and accept him totally on the basis of who he is—because at school just about all that will matter will be what he does. There are a number of things you can do that will help him at school. This does not mean to simply help him get good grades, but to help him experience enough positive successes that he feels good about himself. Remember, what a person can do and accomplish is half of his self-esteem.

1. Find out what your child is being taught in his particular grade. Your memory of your own school days won't be nearly

enough. Your knowledge must be specific enough to do you some good and twenty-five years is enough to fog anyone's memory. In addition, today's elementary school curriculum has changed dramatically. *A Parent's Guide to Children's Education* by Larrick provides a fine overview of various subjects that are covered in elementary school.

2. Make sure your child learns to read. Continue with the preschool-type reading and language activities; provide books, read to him, and keep abreast of any reading problems that come up. If your child is reading, it is a good sign, even if he is simply reading comics. Anything that he is motivated to read on his own will help him read better. It has long been one of the most serious mistakes of English teachers to force "good literature" on children and with it a disdain for reading altogether. If he is interested, subscribe to a children's magazine. However you can do it, help him to love and enjoy the printed page.

3. Help your child grasp basic mathematical concepts. This will mean a commitment on your part, as well, since so much of math is taught differently now. Games of infinite variety continue to provide an enjoyable means for learning some basic ideas. Whatever you do, don't ignore the "new math" and hope it will go away. It won't, and your child needs to get a feel for it to succeed in school.

4. Teach your child how to study. He will never learn this in school, yet so much of his success in school depends upon it. Homework should not usually begin until the fourth or fifth grades and this is the time for some regular study habits. Provide your child with a place to study and a regular time for working on school assignments. (Right after school and after watching TV are the worst times. The best is probably between dinner and TV.) In these early grades such study times must be low-key, no pressure. But it is a good time to gradually work them into your

child's regular, daily routine. This habit will be a great help to him in the coming years.

Once the habit pattern is fixed, you need to teach your child *how* to study; the difference, for example, between reading and studying a certain chapter in his history book. Show him how to pre-read (getting an overview from all the bold print, titles, pictures, maps, and so on). He should look over the questions at the end and think about them in the context of the chapter he has just gone through quickly. Teach him to summarize what he has learned in his own words.

Then (preferably the next day after a chapter has been pre-read) your boy or girl should read the chapter thoroughly, trying to pay close attention to the questions, the main topics, etc. If possible to make this easier for him, buy your own textbooks so he can mark in them.

This sort of study will have to be taught, for the natural way to read is simply to passively work your way through a chapter. This active reading is altogether different and must involve him in the material. Applying pressure is not the way to teach him, but when he does have these study skills, he will enjoy books and study more, will find school less demanding, and will not fear tests. Another good technique for teaching him is to change every title or heading into a question (i.e., change "The Pilgrims Seek Religious Freedom" to "Why Did the Pilgrims Seek Religious Freedom?") and then to find the answer to his question as he reads. Teach him to look for main points (marking them in his book or writing them down) so that in reviewing he need only go back over the major points, not the entire chapter. Teach him to summarize orally.

These skills, along with knowing how to take notes, study for tests, use a library, use a dictionary,* use an encyclopedia, and other study skills will give your child invaluable head starts in

* For definitions with a moral and christian base, I particularly recommend Noah Webster's *First Edition Dictionary* available from Foundation for American Christian Education, 2946 25th Ave., San Francisco, Ca. 94132.

many areas in school.

5. There are two classic reasons for "underachievers." First, parents who exert strong pressure on a child to succeed (usually completely unknowingly) subconsciously give him a faith-picture of failure which then fulfills itself in poor grades and lack of motivation. Secondly, parents can cause failure in a child by not allowing him to let off emotional steam through the years. This can happen in a number of ways: making him repress emotions, not providing sufficient physical outlets for his energy, not taking the time to listen to him. Any of these things can eventually surface in a child whose hidden emotions of anger or aggressiveness or failure find their expression through low grades. They can be a subconscious form of rebellion, an unemotional method of self-expression.

6. Make "good grades" a low priority item. Of course you should praise good grades, but realize how little elementary school grades mean ultimately. Many stories are told of famous men in all walks of life who did poorly in school. Your child's grades mean virtually nothing in terms of his ultimate meaningfulness in life. Pressure from you *of any kind* to succeed will usually backfire at your child's expense.

Friends and Peers–"The Gang"

As a child is leaving the small world of his family to seek a new identity of his own in the larger society, his relationships with his friends act as an emotional buffer and support until he is ready to stand on his own. Among such a group of equals he will learn vital socialization skills he could never learn from you. The rules to which he must conform to be accepted by his peers are independent of you as parents, and of all adults. And learning to function in life without adults is a major step toward independence. When a child is so tied to his parents that he cannot mingle freely with others his own age, he misses out on some very important social learning. Parents have the unenviable task of being responsible for their child's welfare and actions while at the same time backing off to allow this sort of random training to take place.

One of the most important things your child needs from you during this time is that you understand the tremendous psychological importance to him of the secrets, the forts, the rules, the adventures, the shared games and activities, the overnights together, and the hanging around. He needs these things. You can help him function, both at school and among his friends, by helping him with physical skills that will give him status. Girls need these skills as well as boys. They will not get anything like the level of practice and encouragement and personal attention they need from a half an hour of PE daily at school. You also need to give your child the emotional strength to handle teasing and insults. For among children his own age he will certainly receive his fair share. Share his pain and teach him not to allow these things to wound his esteem. You will need to pray about these times together. You can maintain an element of control over the nature of activities your child participates in by encouraging him to be a part of organized clubs—4-H, Cub Scouts, Brownies, YMCA groups, and so on. Knowing from personal experience the tremendous excitement of building a "fort," this is a good age for a father to teach his son to use several basic tools that will allow him to work on such projects with friends.

While maintaining a watchful eye, like the teacher whose students were working independently, allow your child to fully enter into his friendships with others. You cannot exercise total control, but if you are able to steer things, it is of course best that his friends are from Christian homes. The negative and Satanic influences of "the world" (in the spiritual sense) are everywhere and are seeking to devour our children. We must not become so paranoid that we overprotect our children and cause them additional emotional problems. But as Christians we can never forget our heavy responsibility to protect our children spiritually. This certainly means watching over the various influences that press in upon them during their critical childhood years.

Family

That your child is maturing and becoming somewhat independent in no way implies he isn't still highly dependent on you. Throughout his childhood years, his relationship with you will have a regular out-and-back swing to it. He will launch out into the world, then withdraw back into the family once again as a highly dependent child. It is paradoxical, but even as he is in some ways resisting you and trying to cut the emotional cords, he is at the same time strongly identifying with you and modeling his life after yours.

During the middle childhood years, as never before, the attitudes, values, and feelings of a parent are absorbed by a child. During this time of life a child is developing a conscience, he is learning the difference between right and wrong, he is forming positive and lifelong ideas about God's character and what a relationship with Him means. All these things he is largely getting from his parents. And perhaps most importantly, he is slowly coming to grips with a clear image of the sort of adult he himself wants to be.

These years then are the most important for close, one-to-one relationships, especially between fathers and their children. A parent cannot relax in his relation to his child at any age, but the years from six to ten stand out as containing unique opportunities for the expression of the parent-child relationship. Though a parent must recognize his child's need for occasional independence, he must seek every opportunity to build this close companionship with his son or daughter. A child will sometimes put up a rather stoic front, but down inside he can never get enough time alone with dad.

A parent can find ample opportunities to participate with his child in large group activities (i.e., being a camp counselor or a leader in some other organized group). There is no end to the sort of activities you can discover together: going to the store, library, or out for lunch, hiking, swimming, to the beach, a movie, a sporting event, a business trip, a camping trip, fishing, and field trips to dozens of places. And what can compare with simple roughhousing, games of catch, or quiet talks? The more spontaneous the occasion, the deeper the closeness that is felt. Family activities are wonderful for everyone, from camping trips to board games to drive-in movies.

Children between six and ten have some special needs that can only be met at home. They need to be fully accepted for who they are. They especially need praise; they are getting enough negative reinforcement outside the home. They need to be accepted *where* they are—as childish at times (needing your patience and love) and yet as soon-to-be young adults (needing your respect). Allow them to have a voice in the decisions that affect them personally without giving them too much to bear. Above all, they need a very close and intimate relationship with each parent throughout these years. It is this relationship—above all the other influences and factors of this era of childhood—which will lay the foundation and prepare them for the tumultuous period which they are approaching—adolescence.

Preadolescence

To come to any understanding of a child, a parent must grasp the significance of certain key transition phases he must go through. Though the ten-year-old was contented and well-adjusted, it could not last forever. Adolescence is just around the corner, and the teen years are among the more turbulent of life. A child of ten would be ill-prepared to face adolescence. He needs a buffer period in which to ready himself, a transition from childhood into adolescence. This generally occurs during the eleventh and twelfth years.

Sometime during the sixth and seventh grades the biological, psychological, and emotional forces begin to erupt inside a child to prepare him for puberty. He is not yet there, but his body is building up to it through many hormonal and glandular changes. Understanding that much of it is purely physiological is the first important step for a parent. It helps to explain the enormous appetite, the extraordinary energy which seems to drive a child to the point of exhaustion (at which time he needs a great deal of rest); it sheds light on the drastic mood changes and irritability and restlessness.

But in addition to these physical changes, there are other factors at work as well. As with the other transitional stages, one of the purposes of preadolescence is to make a break with the past. It is necessary to loosen and shift around in a preliminary way the earlier balance of childhood. Adolescence will massively break apart this equilibrium so that a higher and more sophisticated level can be attained. And the introductory years of eleven and twelve set the stage for that major overhaul.

One of the most visible qualities of this "breaking apart" process is a questioning and resisting of adult standards, codes, and values. This will not usually erupt into outright rejection until the middle-teen years. But the signs of approaching storm clouds are becoming apparent. What a child is going through (in the long range) is trying to become an adult himself, but to do so he must rebel against that very adulthood in order to prepare himself for it. Until now he has pretty much accepted adult standards without deep questioning. Now for the first time, his mind and emotions are calling many of those standards into question. This is not because he is going to permanently reject them, but simply because such questioning (of everything!) is one of the important steps toward true insight and maturity. When an adult comes face-to-face with his own doubts and questions regarding some aspect of his Christian life, he is usually led (perhaps after much soul-searching) into a much more profound walk with the Lord at that particular point. Doubt and questioning often pave the way for deeper wisdom and maturity.

This is what a preadolescent and adolescent are going through. They are casting off the past in order to discover adulthood for themselves. It is a painful process—far more than a simple mental questioning we adults experience. It is deeply linked to their emotions and their bodily changes. It's no wonder they are often confused and in turmoil.

An additional factor which exerts tremendous pressure on the adolescent is the slowly dawning awareness of the opposite sex. By fourteen or fifteen, of course, this "awareness" has usually become an obsession. But during the preadolescent years this emerging attraction displays itself as disgust and aversion. This is but a defense against something rising up inside that is new and which young boys and girls do not understand—a compelling interest in the opposite sex. For so long, especially among their peers, both boys and girls have ridiculed and completely avoided the opposite sex. To display an interest now would seem like treason. It is therefore *never* something that is admitted and surfaces instead as a boy pulling the hair of a girl he is secretly interested in, and a girl deriding a boy she is thinking about. Naturally, girls precede boys in most of these preadolescent developments, but it is especially apparent when it comes to this opposite sex "attraction."

These three forces then—biological changes, questioning and rejecting the adult norms, and a growing preoccupation with the opposite sex—are the factors underlying much preadolescent behavior. It is helpful for a parent to be aware of them, because behavior at this age is likely to be rather difficult to handle without an explanation. There is a growing resistance to parental standards and authority. To avoid an incorrect assessment of this, a parent must recognize that his child is not so much rejecting his authority as he is the values system of the entire adult society. However, his father and mother represent this "establishment" to him subconsciously. He therefore harasses his parents even though he loves them deeply. It is paradoxical yet it appears to be one of the only ways a child is able to express his fight to become himself.

As part of this subconscious effort to irritate his parents, a preadolescent is obnoxious and self-centered in as many ways as he can apparently devise. But equally a part of much of his behavior are the biological changes his body and emotions are experiencing. He is moody, belligerent, restless, critical, talkative, defiant, distrusting, suspicious, irritable, and independent. He will seek to squirm out from under (or openly come out against) all requirements for responsibility in the family. He will be intolerable of the behavior of younger brothers or sisters. And he has an uncanny knack for choosing his actions so that they attack precisely the point of his parents' psychological make-up that is most annoying and unnerving to them. His "old nature" has been long studying to find those chinks in the parental armor and now the darts begin to fly right through them. By this time he knows you *too* well.

Accompanying his questioning of the adult value system comes a corresponding allegiance to the value system of his colleagues. Oftentimes this "value system" is designed to reflect an exact inversion of what is acceptable to adults. Part of being acceptable with your peers is doing what is unacceptable to parents, teachers, and adults. As a result this is the time when smoking, petty theft, adult magazines, and swearing begin to find their way into the lives of even the most "upstanding" youngsters. Therefore this is an age where it is crucially important that your child have Christian friends and a Christian youth group of some kind to act as his gang and peer group. (Obviously you must have begun much sooner to instill different values than the world's, but at this age the children your child "hangs around with" take on a much greater importance.) Christian children and Christian groups and gangs and cliques will still go through these same emotional and psychological adjustments, but the chances are they will not induce one another into the same sorts of "unacceptable behavior." Your child needs to rebel and express himself. He does not need to become an experienced thief. Understanding is necessary, and great patience and love. But sin cannot be tolerated. You must see that your child has healthy ways in which to rebel and let off emotional steam.

Remember two vital things about this age. Number one, it is painful for a child to cast off what has been an enjoyable childhood. Part of him does not want to rebel against you because he loves and needs you. Therefore, he is often confused deep down about his own actions. So this is a time for flexibility and patience. Secondly, there are *great* personal differences in the way children go through these things. Every eleven-year-old does not become a juvenile delinquent. Some make these changes and adjustments with relative ease. Again, don't expect "normal" behavior from your child, for there is no normal.

Eleven-Year-Old

At eleven a child suddenly exits childhood banging and crashing his way forward. His parents will probably not recognize him. Their once (so recently) pleasant child has become loud, assertive, selfish, and moody. He talks (argues whenever possible) constantly, interrupts, never stops eating, and stiffens at every request made of him. His emotions are sometimes violently up and down. His feelings get hurt, he is often frustrated, and can fly into a rage or a burst of laughter. He is often rude, disagreeable, and grumpy. He is going through a host of profound changes that surface in many aspects of his behavior. The well-established balance he had such a short time ago is being turned upside down.

His thoughts and activities now revolve around his social life. He is in the process of becoming a "youth" rather than a child, but the social life of preadolescents is difficult. Relationships are new at the levels where they are being forged. It takes time to learn to relate as teen-agers rather than as children. There is a great deal of social learning and training going on at this stage. As an eleven-year-old responds in a group of others his age, however awkwardly, he is finding out more about himself. By reacting against others, he is gradually finding his own identity.

His behavior is ordinarily worse at home than it is elsewhere because of the ultimate in authority which parents represent, but this cantankerousness and abrasiveness are results of his trying to assert himself in a positive way. As before, the positive must begin with a negative. So your eleven-year-old will often challenge and confront you, if only to get a response. He is trying out his newly discovered *self* and you have the job of being his guinea pig. He will do anything to get out of chores, and will argue with you on fine, legalistic points very defensively.

It helps to know that this is a temporary stage. In the long run it is not really that important that his room be clean and that he always do his "fair share." This is a time for some flexibility (while at the same time you do not allow him to run roughshod over you). He needs you to understand that his appetite will sometimes suddenly change and that he is often so wired with energy that sleep is impossible while at other times he cannot budge at three in the afternoon. These are often physical things he cannot alter. They just come up upon him and he's stuck with them.

This is a time when it is easy for parents to make the mistake of thinking they are unimportant to their son or daughter. Not true! He is often expressing himself very critically and negatively, but, down deep, part of him is still a child. (Watch his behavior when he is sick. He wants you there every minute.) True, he may reject some of your advances toward intimacy during this time. But he wants you to make them and will certainly respond to your love on a deep level. This is a time for one-to-one activities of closeness. A boy wants to do "man things" with his dad. Though he often may seem to be rejecting everything about you, don't let this fool you. If you have been a good parent, your responses to him now will make him love you more deeply. In a sense he *has* to rebel at the level of his soul, but at the spirit level you will be further cementing the lifelong bond between you all the time.

Twelve-Year-Old

Fortunately, children remain eleven but one year. After a

year of questioning and challenging a child begins to mellow. He relaxes a bit. He is beginning to discover a little of his true self and doesn't feel he must push quite so hard to assert it. There is a sense of tolerance, reason, and humor in a twelve-year-old. He becomes enthusiastic in a more positive and interested (rather than negative) sense. Though chores and responsibilities are still uninteresting to him, he is not so likely to instigate arguments over every small thing. He will not volunteer to work, but will be slightly more cooperative.

His emotions stabilize somewhat but he is still subject to fluctuations in physical energy (mainly because he is so active that he periodically wears himself out). For most twelve-year-olds, this is a time of dramatic change as they leave elementary school and enter junior high. This is a big step and many times actions and emotions that surface may be reactions to the new and strange and insecure world of school.

Twelve can be an age of more overt boy-girl interests (the influence of the junior high system where seventh, eighth, and ninth graders are thrust "together" greatly increases this). Girls especially are maturing rapidly at this time. Menstruation usually begins when a girl is twelve and she needs emotional (and informational) support from both her father and mother.

Boys around twelve begin to become more totally "boys" in their interests, as do girls. Both enjoy mystery and adventure stories. But boys now begin to read about and be interested in hunting, football, motorcycles, and guns, while girls read romances.

For a parent to make it through these two years with as few scars as possible (on himself and his son or daughter) one of the most effective things that can be done is to realize that it will pass. This opens the way for less rigidity. Cracking down on every little thing will usually only make it worse. It is a time when it is very important that a parent save his real authority for what he considers the major issues. If every time an eleven-year-old turns around he is being reprimanded for something, he will quickly loose what motivation he has left to obey. Remember, he is trying subconsciously to annoy you. If you must discipline him for being obnoxious, that is probably your own lack of patience showing through. Try to be mellow yourself and save the showdowns for outright sin and disobedience of major proportions.

Then too it is important (as it is at every age) that you look deeper than the surface behavior. Don't constantly fight your child. Be aware of his attitudes, the pressures he is experiencing, the changes taking place inside him. Be sensitive to the world as he is feeling it. Along with this is your need to respect him as a person who is rapidly growing up. Though it may not look like it, he is ready to assume more responsibility and will respond well when you give it to him.

Parents can be a great help at this age by seeking to provide opportunities for a boy or girl to express what are often "wild" emotions in safe ways. Every child growing into adolescence needs outlets for wildness. If you can provide them with safe ones, so much the better. Sports are good because they release a lot of trapped energy and emotion. Smoking is something nearly every child tries. How much better for a parent to bring this out in the open. My parents introduced us to the subject by having an evening where we all sat around smoking tea leaves in a pipe. A family back-packing adventure or camping trip provides opportunities for demonstrating independence and maturity in a healthy way. Many young people turn to stealing and drugs simply as "something to do." If a parent can see such needs in advance, he can usually keep his child from things that will get him into serious trouble, but it takes a level of special commitment and involvement.

With this, however, is a need to know when to let a child go. Overprotection can have the same negative effects as boredom. This is a stage where parents must walk a fine line. A twelve-year-old needs his parents, but at the same time needs to test his own legs.

Early Adolescence

Of all the stages your child passes through, adolescence is the most confusing, complex, and difficult—for you and him. This is a societal difficulty as much as anything. In our complex culture it takes a great amount of preparation and study to enter into even the most elementary of adult occupations. The transition from childhood into this demanding and skilled adult life is therefore a long one. And vocation is not the only factor by any means. A child needs a wide range of experiences before he is fully ready to step into his mature adult role.

The central task of adolescence is to find out who one is as a separate entity. Coupled with this is the need to acquire complete and total independence by the time one emerges from adolescence. In the early years of adolescence (approximately twelve or thirteen until fifteen and sixteen), a teen-ager is trying to work out his selfhood and independence basically in the framework of his family. But in later adolescence, he is working within the larger framework of society, especially with respect to his vocation.

Many of the ambivalent, conflicting forces that a child has felt within himself all throughout his life come to a head in the adolescent period. It is like there is a war going on inside him which one day is reaching out to grasp every ounce of independence it can get, and the next is withdrawing unsure of itself. It is not easy to break deep ties and often the only way he can find to do so is to openly revolt.

Reaching out to stand alone becomes particularly a frightening matter in the face of the physical changes puberty brings. Most children are not adequately prepared for what to expect (Dobson's book and tapes *Preparing for Adolescence* are helpful here). They almost universally feel ugly, awkward, and self-conscious. Teen-agers who mature according to a different timetable than most of their friends suffer most of all. And with these changes come entirely new sexual urges with which they must cope.

A very important adolescent development (which is usually overlooked because of more glaring issues) is the dramatic strides taken intellectually by a teen-ager. He is able to think in altogether new ways. This is basically a good thing. He is able to think logically concerning more complex matters, he can form abstractions and nonliteral interpretations, and is able to grasp multiple meanings found in words or ideas.

However, there is an aspect of it that deepens his occasional doubts and depressions. That is his newfound ability to probe his own mind—introspection. He is acquiring for the first time his own ideas and beliefs. This is a major breakthrough toward independence, but in the early years of adolescence it only compounds his tendency towards self-doubts.

At the same time these new areas of thought enable him to plan for the future and give him broader perspectives. He is usually filled with a youthful idealism that is quick to condemn what he sees as false values in his parents—but this also gives rise to a dawning concern for spiritual matters and a teen-ager is ripe for a close walk with the Lord. (Often, however, teen-age

Christians must go through a sort of "spiritual adolescence" at some later point in life to re-think their faith on a much more profound level than they had originally accepted it.)

All these developments in the life of a teen-ager are brand new. They are inexperienced in dealing with their impulses and in putting their capabilities into practice. It takes time to learn how to deal with it all. Parents, therefore, must not make the mistake (nearly universal) of expecting their teen-agers to be more mature than they are capable of being. Give them time.

Thirteen-Year-Old

At thirteen most girls have gone through puberty and a good many boys are in the midst of it. It is a year of reflection and introspection as one attempts to grasp what is happening to him and what he is feeling inside. It is a moody, uncommunicative year. A thirteen-year-old is preoccupied with himself and keeps his distance, even from his parents. He is embarking on the period of true rebellion which eleven and twelve paved the way for. On his mind almost as much as wanting to break with the past is a desire to understand himself. And he is worried about himself, afraid that he won't develop properly or that he won't be attractive or will have pimples. Many parents would describe their thirteen-year-olds as "touchy"—emotionally on edge.

A great deal of this inner probing has to do with the physical changes that are taking place and with physical appearance. Both boys and girls spend time in front of the mirror wishing it could tell the future as well as reflect the present.

Thirteen-year-olds, because of their preoccupation with themselves, are sensitive. It is easy to deeply wound their feelings. They try to hide what they really feel as completely as possible. But they have multitudes of feelings and spend a great deal of time musing on them. Their minds are constantly at work. And after a year of trying to find some balance inside, they are ready to emerge at fourteen.

Fourteen-Year-Old

After a year of adjustment to being a teen-ager, his growth spurt, his feelings of inferiority, his sexual urges, his desire for independence, and his new mental awareness, a fourteen-year-old is ready again to step out into the world. He will be more relaxed and easygoing, but of course rebellion is also becoming more open. Since boys are usually a year or two slower to develop than girls, fourteen is many times the awkward age for boys as twelve and thirteen is physically for girls. Because of this time lag, girls of this age are much more interested in older boys than ones their own age.

This is the year when an interest in teen-age "things" begins in earnest—rock music, parties, a genuine attraction to the opposite sex from both directions, dances, motorcycles, and so on. The fourteen-year-old is more self-assured and is more able to let his emotions come out. This, however, often results in outbursts of anger or tears. He is tougher than at thirteen, but is still going through rapid changes.

Fifteen-Year-Old

The outgoing and enthusiastic fourteen-year-old gradually enters a time when he begins to catch a glimpse of the great unknowns on the horizon. Fifteen is a year of transition from the surface "fun" aspects of adolescence to the more serious times ahead. A fifteen-year-old knows adulthood is approaching, and he knows it is a serious business. He begins in earnest to noticeably separate himself from his family. He is now looking for independence in more definitive ways.

And in many ways a fifteen-year-old is ready for it. He is

much more perceptive and serious. He is coming to know himself more deeply. He has the need like he did at thirteen to be alone, but now these times are often mentally productive. He will still be quiet and doubtful, but his complex feelings are showing him many things.

Fifteen is another period lacking in equilibrium, a hard year in school, when if it were not for his friends he would not be able to cope well at all. Ever on his mind is more independence!

Sixteen-Year-Old

Sixteen is another time of balance and stability, in some ways reminiscent of ten. The sixteen-year-old has come through the intense emotional struggles for independence and self-confidence and feels he has achieved them in certain ways. He is now able to relate to his parents and teachers more as equals, no longer feeling threatened by everything they do and say.

Sixteen is a pivotal year. It sums up what has come before and consolidates it in preparation for years of late adolescence which will carry a teen-ager into adulthood. The sixteen-year-old is on the verge of even more sophisticated struggles for growth and freedom, but at this point he is content with how far he has come. Driver licenses and part-time jobs add to the adult status a sixteen-year-old is feeling to a great degree. It is also a focal time educationally. The junior year in high school is usually the point at which some definite decisions must be made regarding the future—college, jobs, trade school, etc. All these factors thrust him into a position of independence, a position he has sought for so long. This is a year that in many ways forms a bridge to the future and sets a teen-ager on course toward it.

These teen-age "sketches" have been very brief, obviously too brief for a thorough understanding. (For more detail I recommend *How to Father,* chapters 11, 12, 13, with the exception of the author's remarks regarding the morality of modern sexual mores.) There are some very specific things we can gather from these principles regarding the most effective way to handle our teen-age sons and daughters.

The teen years are often chaotic for a family. The normal way of explaining this is through teen-age behavior, but this will not provide a thorough enough explanation. It is also necessary to look at a parent's reactions and behavior. Unconsciously, it is very difficult for a parent not to take his teen-ager's rebellion and search for independence personally. The anger a parent feels as a result of his child's disobedience is at least partially due to his own bewilderment at being seemingly rejected after all the things he has done for his son or daughter. When a parent allows hurt feelings to change into angry ones, the stage is set for a battle of nerves throughout adolescence. Normal emotional reactions of teen-agers then become even worse and erupt into endless conflicts where everyone is hurt.

Three things a parent does can keep these turbulent years from getting out of control:

1. Try to understand what your son or daughter is going through. It is a very difficult time for him, with confusing emotions. He needs you to remain strong enough not to give in, even to him. Always view his rebellion as a healthy step toward adulthood, recognizing that his forward progress has much negativity attached to it.

2. Don't take things personally. Recognize that what surfaces may not necessarily be his true feelings toward you.

3. Keep communication open between you and your teen-ager. Let him talk to you about his ups and downs without

lectures, rebuffs, or arguments. When he makes outlandish statements designed to get your goat, don't be swept into a pointless argument. This is a time for maturity on your part.

AFTERWORD

15

YOUR TOTAL RELATIONSHIP WITH YOUR CHILD

Putting Everything Together

We've covered a lot of ground together, from the idealistic precepts in Parts I and II to the nitty-gritty specifics of Parts III and IV. Quite possibly this has seemed more like two separate books to you, or maybe three.

Training a child effectively is a complex job. If we're going to make any use of all these ideas we've discussed, now we are going to have to put all these various aspects of the process together into some sort of useful whole. They do form a unity and they do all tie together. If you leave anything out, you will weaken your effectiveness as a spiritual parent.

The basic principles of child training are found in Part II. Part I tells us how make those principles come alive. You cannot do those things discussed in Part II—discipline, train, teach, lead, instill with self-esteem, prepare—without applying the ideas of Part I.

The latter chapters give us the basis for individualizing those principles. Part III tells us about our own particular child and how to take into consideration his own unique temperament and emotions. Part IV gives us the developmental insight to apply the principles to his particular stage of growth. Parts III and IV color our entire relationship with our child. Without this awareness of him as a unique person who is going through unique things at every age, we will be unable to make specific application in the *now* in which he lives.

A Child's Individual Reflecting Lenses

I look at it in this manner: we are feeding the same principles into every child, but each one has an individual temperament and emotional and spiritual make-up which act as lenses to reflect those principles in certain ways. Then those principles are further reflected as they pass through the particular lenses of the stage of development the child happens to be in at the time. Once a certain principle finally emerges as a specific and concrete action for a particular child on a certain day, the variations are infinite. There is never one "right" way to apply a principle. To know what is right for a certain boy or girl, all the various prisms that make up the total individual must be taken into account.

A certain action, therefore, which might be the perfect response for one child, might be very harmful for another. And individual children will even change as well. No parent can think that knowing the principles will do any good in itself. Coupled with it is knowing your child. You must be keenly aware of his individual lenses of temperament, emotion, development, and so on. Oftentimes additional factors enter the picture to further alter the application. In our family we have a "twin factor" which we are always conscious of as an added "lens" through which the principles must pass. And most families have various relationships between brothers and sisters which work in a similiar manner. No principles can be applied in a vacuum. If we were applying these ideas to laboratory mice or dolphins it might be much simpler. But we are dealing with people, and the variations and implications are infinite.

A Parent's Job

Your responsibility as a parent, then, is to determine which specific response is right for your child in a certain situation. To make that determination, you cannot limit your attention to any certain principle or any certain aspect of your child's personality. Everything contributes to what your child needs from moment to moment. For example, your six-year-old will tend to be brash, noisy, and aggressive; he will therefore need a fairly firm disciplinary hand. But within a year he will have grown more withdrawn, thoughtful, and introspective as he tries to assimilate many things inside his own mind. Then at eight he will once again be expanding outward, as he was at six, but in wider and more mature ways. It will be impossible to discipline a seven-year-old as you do a six-year-old. He will be thoughtful, quiet, and reasonable and you will often find yourself being downright permissive with him. If you tried the same thing when he was six or eight, it could backfire in your face.

At each of these ages, though his basic temperament and emotional balance remain roughly the same, a child's specific ways of expressing himself will change. Certain things in his personality will come to the surface, others will sink below the surface for a while. Your responses must take this into account. Each age will have a unique set of temperamental, emotional and spiritual needs. Your relationship with your child must depend on all these factors.

Take as another example two brothers with different temperaments. One is an outgoing sanguine, the other a withdrawn melancholy. The melancholy is highly self-motivated, a rapid learner with great intelligence, and always gets top grades. He succeeds at everything he tries. The sanguine is the family's "front man." Everyone likes him, he is a natural leader, and popular wherever he goes. But deep inside these brothers cannot help but compare themselves with one another. The sanguine feels inferior to his brother's intelligence and thinks of himself as a failure. He compensates by repressing these feelings, and hides his true emotions by being all the more sparky and seemingly full of life and happiness. The melancholy, on the other hand, subconsciously envies his brother's exuberant personality and popularity with people. He reacts by withdrawing further into himself and compensates with his high level of success.

Both boys have tremendous strengths. Neither has anything to feel inferior about. Their parents must demonstrate this truth to them and must gear their relationships so as to draw those strengths out. All their responses will have to be entirely individual, taking into account the boys' vastly different natures and needs for esteem.

Here, also, is a example from our own experience. When our twins were two-and-a-half, our youngest son was about six months old. They were right in the middle of their "rebel-transition" stage when their younger brother learned to crawl and began to infringe upon their world in more overt ways. Conflicts naturally arose. They would be demanding of Judy's time in the midst of a feeding and would get upset whenever he started chewing on any of their toys.

Our obvious question was, "What do we do? Is this a time to

be firm and simply tell the boys, 'You've got to learn to share and be patient and unselfish'?" We felt cracking down on them like this could lead to an early resentment toward their younger brother. Or, on the other hand, we wondered if we should cater to the twins' wishes seemingly at their brother's expense?

At first glance this appeared to be a situation where a certain form of discipline was called for. Then we remembered the "lens" of development and realized that in about six months two significant things would happen: The older boys would be three and would become much more cooperative, and the younger would be walking and exploring. This made us realize that much of the conflict could be avoided by simply stalling until that time. Our toddler's need for intense activity would come at a time when the older boys would be more emotionally capable of allowing it. By making an issue of it now, we would run the risk of instilling resentments. By waiting, much of that would be avoided. Viewing discipline through the perspective of their stages of growth gave it a more complete meaning.

In addition to not seeing a child's constantly growing and changing needs and methods of expression, a common parental mistake is to interpret most problems through one particular lens. Secular psychologists have tried to discover everything there is to know about child psychology and development, yet modern parents with all this knowledge at their disposal continue to raise children with unmet needs. They have usually taken only one particular aspect of the process into their training. If any problem will come from your reading this book, it will probably be your overstressing one particular principle or method of applying it. How natural it is to read about something new (such as the need for deep emotional wholeness, or the effect of temperament) and begin to interpret everything that comes up in that particular light. Your new insight will have undoubtedly helped you in some ways, but through your neglect of the other areas you will not be able to provide wholeness. Your responses will begin to be faulty because they fail to take enough factors into consideration.

It is vital, for instance, that you manage your children as rebellious and in need of discipline at the same time you are trying to be sensitive to their inner needs. This is extremely difficult to do. Your natural response is to underemphasize the discipline you may feel is necessary in order to compensate for the other factors.

In certain instances this would be a wise judgment. But in other circumstances, it might not be what your child needs. If his will is strongly exerting itself in rebellion, then it must be broken. If you totally love your child and are not afraid to express it, and if you follow the principles of instilling self-esteem and pray for inner healing when necessary, then he will not suffer from your discipline in the long run. You must not sacrifice one need (to learn authority or to gain independence) to deal with another (such as an emotional lack of self-confidence). The emotions will certainly play a role in determining how to discipline and how to guide toward independence, but there can be no "either . . . or" omissions in your application.

As children grow they have constant needs, both positive and negative—areas where they need boundaries and areas where they need to be released to soar. They require many types of training all at once; overbalance is a danger that will try to sneak in every day. Be on constant guard against it. Every part of the process blends and flows together with every other part.

The need is present daily to stand back to assess your behavior and evaluate the changing effects of various prisms which reflect the principles. Evaluation must be in light of God's Word and His guidance and common sense. And the perspective of time is imperative; in just a couple of weeks,

Satan can sometimes dull your awareness and cause you to begin reacting in all the wrong ways. But if you are staying well-practiced in all the principles (Part II) and are constantly applying them in the loving light of your child's uniqueness (Part III) and are aware of his changes (Part IV), then there will be little Satan can permanently accomplish in the lives of your children.

A Prayer

As you begin to apply all these ideas to your specific child and situation, it may help to share with you the general sort of prayer my wife and I pray for our boys. This is not because we are in any sense "experts" or this prayer is an "ideal." This is merely an example to help you begin to form your own. You'll quickly discover methods of application I've never thought of.

It has greatly helped us to deal with our children simply as children during the day, but to pray for healing and so on at night (except when needs arise which obviously need immediate prayer).

This does not mean we become insensitive during the day to everything that could be working on them. We try to recognize the tremendous drain that comes from emotional struggles going on as part of the growing up process. If Paul, at the height of his maturity in the Lord, cried out in confusion, "What I do is not what I want to do . . . the good which I want to do, I fail to do . . . miserable creature that I am, who is there to rescue me out of this body doomed to death?" (Rom. 7:16, 19, 25, NEB) then surely the struggles which often torment our children inside must be enormous. They are sensitive and fragile in many ways and being caught in the crossfire of a spiritual or emotional battle can be a fearful and confusing thing.

At the same time, however, we recognize the need of our

children to learn to submit their wills to our authority. Separating dealing with memories in our nightly prayers from the various aspects of teaching and training we provide throughout the day has been useful. It is a way to isolate the child himself (what we deal with during the day—discipline, training, teaching, etc.) from the influences on him (what we deal with at night—emotional hurts, spiritual warfare, etc.). When we forget there are two distinct things to deal with—the child and the influences on him—we often become confused in our thinking.

When dealing with our child as himself we pretty much apply the principles in Part II as they are. Naturally we consider his temperament and stage of growth. We find we must pretty rigidly keep his growing *self* in our thoughts throughout the day. Then at night in praying for him we try to take all the various outside factors into account, especially trying to implant our specific faith-picture of him into his subconscious and into ourselves, while we ask God to draw it out of him. We don't usually cover all parts of this prayer every night. Sometimes certain things will need a heavier emphasis.

> Lord, we lift up David to you. We thank you for him. Bless his life in every way. Fill us with more love for him and help us to show that love to him in more practical ways.
>
> We ask now that you would be at work in his mind and spirit. Make his subconscious whole and pure. Cleanse his memories of any hurts. Be present in his past, wipe clean any hurts he has suffered that we are unaware of, and in his future to keep any emotional wounds from penetrating his permanent memory. Focus your healing love and power on his hospital stay at the time of his hernia operation, heal his

memory of that time and of the fear and uncertainty it may have caused him. Give him good memories of today. Blot out the negative memory of his spanking this afternoon. Let it help to break his will, but keep his spirit joyful and full of enthusiasm. We pray too that you would quickly heal his cough and runny nose, and keep his ears from becoming infected.

Give us increased sensitivity to his world, his needs, his emotions. Keep us from inflicting any hurts on him. Let us love him practically and meaningfully in every aspect of his life.

Lord, we praise you for your love and goodness. We praise you for your work in David's life. We praise you for our family and we thank you for it.

We thank you, Lord, for David and for the man you are making of him. We bless you for the qualities of concern, love, unselfishness, joy, wisdom, gentleness, and humility you are instilling in him. Focus our attention on his positive qualities of optimism, faithfulness, friendliness, and thoroughness. Open our eyes to see the glorious person he is becoming in you. Completely rid our minds of his negative characteristics. Help us to know him and to be able to deal with him as a boy with needs in certain areas. Show us those needs. But do not let us reflect overly on them. Give us a totally positive and wonderful faith-vision of David. We thank you that this is not just something we have dreamed up, but that David really is in your sight a man of God with these attributes.

Show us daily what David's emotional needs are. Help us to supply them. Implant within him a healthy and positive and realistic picture of himself. Keep him from self-doubts. Give him, at the same time, a humility and a love of others and of you. Impart your Spirit to him deep in his heart.

Finally, Lord, make us the sort of parents David needs every moment. Forgive us of our selfishness. Keep any hurt from coming to him from us. Make us willing to give, to sacrifice, to love. And above all, we ask you to supply the love David needs. You be the bridge between the love he needs and what we in our humanness are able to give him. Be at work in his emotions and in his mind. Let him grow with capabilities and qualities that will give him good feelings about himself. Help him to feel acceptance from us. Keep us from perfectionistic demands on him that will cause him to feel unworthy. Help us daily to draw an understanding and loving line for acceptable behavior. And we especially pray that David will come to know you in a real way.

Now, Lord, protect David throughout this night. Encircle him with your love and fill him with your Spirit. Be at work in his subconscious. Fill it with thoughts of you. Give him good dreams. Keep him from any fear this night. Help him to wake up refreshed and happy and full of life tomorrow. Thank you, Lord.

An Exhortation

I'm in the business of selling Christian books. It's exciting and I love it. One thing I've discovered, though, about people who enjoy reading—myself included—is the tendency to make the reading *itself* sort of a hobby. We often read for the pleasure of doing it, not particularly for what we are going to get out of it personally or spiritually. And that's okay as far as it goes. What could be a more pleasurable way to relax for a mental break than to curl up in front of the fireplace with a George MacDonald novel?

The danger comes when we read a book that is meant to make a difference in our lives, a book of principles, but read it in the same way we read a novel. When it is over we put it away, and that is that. To read a book of this sort in this manner, to agree that the principles are true but not to then set out to apply them, is dangerous. For when we fail to *do* principles we have come to recognize as true, a small part of our sensitivity—our spiritual ears—becomes dulled. Of course it's a different matter if we don't feel a book has spoken accurately about a certain aspect of the Christian walk, but when we read something we do know is true, we *must* do it or else become hardened to God's future work in our lives. Hardness of heart isn't something God arbitrarily puts inside certain people. It's the natural result of ignoring His voice time after time after time. Obedience to the principles is what makes them real and what further tunes our spiritual ears to God's voice.

This is such a book. This is a book of principles. My goal has not been to entertain. Naturally, if you disagree with the things I've said you should probably put the book away and disregard it. But if, on the other hand, you have read this book and know the principles to be valid, then you simply must *do* them. And so must I. That's all there is to it. Don't let this book be mere words to you. If you want it to work, in your family, in the lives of your children, then you must struggle daily to put the principles into action. None of this can be put on "automatic." You *make it work,* every day, by diligently applying the principles.

You will not become a drastically more effective parent overnight, probably not by next week either. Being a good parent is a lifelong affair involving as much your own education and growth as your child's. This is no cause for alarm, for God is able to cover your child in the midst of your mistakes, and from them, you can grow.

And this is the key!

You *can* grow and learn and improve. Over a long period of time you *can* make radical improvements in your home and in your relationship with your child. But it takes a major investment of time and effort, a major commitment involving every one of your priorities in life. By picking and choosing a few ideas here and a few ideas there, from this book and others you read, while you basically continue on about the way you did before, you will never achieve the results God intended you to see in your family. It takes a significant commitment which will never come about half-heartedly.

There are, of course, many ups and downs in this process and many different stages both you and your child will go through. If your children are now eight, ten, and twelve you may wonder after reading all this, "Is it too late for *me*? How do I begin at this late stage?" But it is never too late. This is one of the wondrous things about God's grace, it can enter *any* situation, *any* time, and make changes. Certainly the major influences in a child's life will come early. But there is always time (especially with the Lord's help) for positive influences to have an impact. God is able to work even after your children leave home.

So no matter what your situation, your age, or your past, God is able to work in your family relationships in magnificent ways. You must let Him, of course. And this means *doing* what He has given you the capability to do—loving your child through these principles we have discussed. He will not do this for you—but as you begin, He will see that your sincere efforts pay large dividends in your child's life.

Bibliography

This book reflects much of what I have learned from others. Maybe this is one reason I so strongly urge further reading. This bibliography acknowledges the personal debt I feel to other writers who have given me ideas and have set the wheels of my mind turning. In just about every area of my thinking, I often find that I am a very unoriginal person; I am a composite of the various teachers who have crossed my path. I am deeply grateful to them—and I would now turn you to their works as well.

In a recent book I read dealing with similar subjects, there was a bibliography of nearly 450 entries. I take a slightly more conservative view. I would like to recommend books to you that I consider outstanding. There are *many* others, but these are the essentials as I see it.

Christenson, Larry. *The Christian Family*. Minneapolis: Bethany Fellowship, 1970.

Dobson, James. *Dare to Discipline*. Wheaton: Tyndale House, 1970.

Dobson, James. *Hide or Seek*. Old Tappan, NJ: Revell, 1974.

Dobson, James. *Preparing for Adolescence*. Santa Ana, CA: Vision House Publishers, 1978.

Dobson, James. *The Strongwilled Child*, Wheaton: Tyndale House, 1978.

Dodson, Fitzhugh. *How to Parent*. New York: New American Library (Signet), 1973.

Dodson, Fitzhugh. *How to Father*. New York: New American Library (Signet), 1975.

Hunt, Gladys. *Honey for a Child's Heart*. Kentwood, MI: Zondervan, 1969.

Kelly, Marguerite and Parsons, Elia S. *The Mother's Almanac*. New York: Doubleday, 1975.

LaHaye, Beverly. *How to Develop Your Child's Temperament*. Irvine, CA: Harvest House, 1977.

LaHaye, Tim. *Spirit-Controlled Temperament*. Wheaton: Tyndale House, 1966.

MacDonald, Gordon. *The Effective Father*. Wheaton: Tyndale House, 1977.

MacNutt, Francis. *Healing*. Notre Dame, IN: Ave Maria, 1974.

Narramore, Bruce. *Help! I'm a Parent*. Kentwood, MI: Zondervan, 1975.

Phillips, Mike. *A Christian Family in Action*. Minneapolis: Bethany Fellowship, 1977.

Stapleton, Ruth C. *The Gift of Inner Healing*. Waco, TX: Word Books, 1976.

Welter, Paul. *Family Problems and Predicaments*. Wheaton: Tyndale House, 1977.

Cassette tape sets: from Vision House Publishers, Santa Ana, CA.

Dobson, James. *Preparing for Adolescence.*

Dobson, James. *Self-Esteem for Your Child.*

Other Books by the Same Author

A Christian Family in Action

Growth of a Vision

Does Christianity Make Sense?